The social history of Canada

MICHAEL BLISS, EDITOR

Canada and the Canadian question

GOLDWIN SMITH

WITH AN INTRODUCTION BY CARL BERGER

UNIVERSITY OF TORONTO PRESS

Reprinted 1973

Printed in the United States of America

for University of Toronto Press

Toronto and Buffalo

ISBN (casebound) 0-8020-1821-1

ISBN (paperback) 0-8020-6124-9

LC 70-163837

The original edition of this work appeared in 1891
and was published by the Hunter Rose Co of Toronto

An introduction

BY CARL BERGER

'IT IS A strange transition from the States to Canada,' Friedrich Engels reported in 1888. 'First one imagines that one is in Europe again, and then one thinks one is in a positively retrogressing and decaying country ... in ten years this sleepy Canada will be ripe for annexation.' 'We have come to a period in the history of this country,' Wilfrid Laurier wrote at the same time, 'when premature dissolution seems to be at hand.' The late 1880s was a time of extreme self-doubt and crisis in Canadian national life and there were few sensitive observers who remained indifferent to the contrast between the optimism which accompanied the creation of the new nationality in 1867 and the frustration, depression, and disintegration evident everywhere twenty years later.

The cultural conflict triggered by the execution of Riel and aggravated by the controversies over French-language rights became so bitter that men doubted whether these tensions could be contained within the framework of Confederation. The transcontinental railway and the National Policy of protection had failed to generate sustained prosperity and integrate the regions. From the west came the first organized expression of agrarian protest against eastern domination; in 1886 the Nova Scotia legislature endorsed a resolution favouring secession from Confederation; and Honoré Mercier rode to power in Quebec on a wave of separatist emotion and then proceeded to behave as though he were already the head of an independent state. Thousands of young Canadians left for the United States; one of the familiar figures in the popular novels of the day was the youth who goes to the States, succeeds, and returns to marry the girl he left behind. Both as a solution to the economic depression and as a means to ensure its own political survival, the Liberal party adopted a policy of unrestricted reciprocity with the United States and to some this appeared as another attack upon the very structure of the country. The great debate surrounding the election of 1891 began with the respective merits of commercial policies and was soon translated into a question of national identity.

Canada and the Canadian Question was written in this atmosphere of pessimism and gloom. It was not a dispassionate and disinterested analysis; in fact, the book was intended to support the cause of freer trade with the United States but appeared after the election was over. It was a tract for the times and the argument for a case. The regions of Canada, ran the argument, were isolated from each other and were northern projections of the regions of the United States. To force commerce in an east-west direction in defiance of nature stultified economic development and corrupted political life. British and French Canada had nothing in common; French Canada was in fact a nation and English Canada did not have the digestive power to assimilate it. English Canada itself was being assimilated to the social and cultural life of the United States. Confederation was held together not by the natural bonds of geography, race, language, or commercial interest but by corruption and the vested interests of politicians and protected manufacturers. Canadian nationality was a lost cause and her ultimate fate was an amiable incorporation into the American Republic.

Though this analysis and conclusion were rooted in the circumstance of the time, Smith's book transcended its immediate origins to become one of the most effective and challenging critiques of Canada ever penned. It is an enormously illuminating series of impressions with sparkling insights into Canada's social history, political practice, cultural life, and the ambiguities of her economic growth. It represents the mature reflections of a keen intelligence which had pondered the fundamental questions of Canada's national existence and saw them in terms of the wider movements of opinion in Europe and North America. Smith was not a completely neutral observer of the Canadian scene and what he saw was filtered through a particular point of view and described in terms of his own social and political philosophy. His own outlook, in short, must be established before the value of his observations can be weighed.

Born in England in 1823, the son of a prosperous physician, Smith was educated at Eton and Oxford. He took an early and active interest in political discussion and journalism, knew all the great Victorians, and became one of the major advocates of Manchester liberalism. He was Regius Professor of Modern History at Oxford from 1858 to 1866, taught at Cornell University from 1868 to 1870, and settled in Toronto in 1871. Though he had a considerable reputation as a historian he had little capacity to enter into the minds of men who lived in another age and to see the world in their terms. He treated history as a repository of moral lessons and he carried into the past not only the concerns of the present but also its animosities. He wrote American history to interpret the Republic to English readers, British history for the education of Americans, and

Canadian history to prove that the country had no future. His real talents lay in the field of journalism and political comment; his style was lucid, forceful, and epigrammatic, and the range of his interests was extensive. He wrote with equal ease and self-confidence on English literature and the crisis in religious faith; on the Jewish, woman, and Canadian questions; on social reform, British and American politics, nihilism in Russia, and imperial relations. Smith had an unbounded faith in the independence of thought and freedom of expression and a pronounced distaste for the party-dominated press in Canada. One of his major contributions to Canadian intellectual life was his support for such magazines as the *Canadian Monthly and National Review,* the *Week,* and, of course, his own *Bystander.*

Smith remained a bystander, even an outsider, in Canadian life. He came to Canada at forty-seven when his tastes and convictions were firmly fixed; happily married, he lived in isolation and had few intimate friends. There is a coldness and aloofness about his writing which in part reflects his estrangement from Canadian society. 'No doubt he is inclined to be too high-wrought, severe, and scornful,' wrote Matthew Arnold, 'and whoever has lived in the centre of the life of the old world cannot but find the life of the new ... wanting in many things ... [M]uch of his sense of acerbity comes from his sense of isolation.' Independently wealthy, the style of his life was comfortable if not opulent. His Toronto home – the Grange – had a domestic establishment of nine servants and it reminded his many English visitors of an English country house. Young Vincent Massey, then a student at the university, visited the old man just before his death in 1910 and was especially impressed by Smith's adherence to social ritual, particularly with 'his handing the keys of the wine-cellar to the butler, who was asked to bring up a bottle of sherry.'

Smith was not an original thinker, and one suspects that his pre-eminence in Canada was due as much to the low level of the intellectual landscape around him as to the penetration of his thought. Though the main tenets of his social and political philosophy were derivative he did fuse them into a distinctive and slightly unorthodox creed. Nineteenth-century English liberalism was a revolt against the heavy hand of history and its mission was to break down those restrictions and restraints in economic, social, and political life that had been inherited from the past and sanctioned by tradition. It sought to destroy hereditary and aristocratic privilege and the connection between church and state, to establish laissez faire and free trade in economic life, to extend the franchise to the middle classes, and to end the exclusiveness of empires. It was founded on a belief in the existence of generally beneficent economic laws which governed social behaviour and on the conviction that the sphere of state activity should remain as narrow as possible. Unlike the extreme apologist for laissez faire, Herbert Spencer, who virtually confined the role of the state to protecting the property of men and guarding the virtue of women, Goldwin Smith recognized that government had to function as an organ of the entire community and that it had an obligation to protect those who could not protect themselves. He supported protective legislation for children, public relief for the sick and aged, and was one of the earliest advocates in Ontario of a public welfare system as a replacement for sporadic and capricious private charity. He was ready also to support municipal ownership provided that the government of cities was placed outside politics and given over to expert administrators. But this was the limit to which he would go in modifying the harsher doctrines of an earlier age. His outlook, as Malcolm Ross has noted, was a good example of the 'illiberalism of the liberal mind.' His humanitarianism was outraged by the oppression of the Boers in South Africa and his heart bled for the maltreated elephant in the Toronto zoo, but he categorically rejected suggestions for old age pensions, income tax, minimum wage laws, and limitations on working hours. Though he had welcomed the removal of legal constraints on trade unions he abhorred strikes and resorts to force in industrial relations. In the 1880s and 1890s when Henry George was advocating a single tax and Edward Bellamy was summoning the forces of reform in support of a program of nationalization, Smith was haunted more and more by the spectre of socialism, industrial violence, and the inflammation of class hatreds. His addresses to the working class were only homilies from the age of self-help. His fear of class war and his genuine humanitarianism moved him to endorse minor reforms but he came down heavily on the side of the iron laws of political economy. He was a faithful member of what he called the 'armies of order, property, and civilization.'

For Smith the really creative social agencies were unimpeded individual initiative and work, the family, and religion. 'The family,' he wrote, 'is more important than the State; it is a deeper source of character and happiness ...' It was in the household that character was moulded and proper conceptions of duty and obligation instilled. One of the reasons why Smith opposed compulsory free public education was because he saw it as a means by which the state would usurp the proper function of the family. And one of the many reasons for his sustained opposition to female suffrage and the 'Revolt of Women' generally was his belief that once women could vote and enter the labour market they would 'introduce' conflict into the domestic scene. If 'woman demands equality she will have to resign privilege; she cannot be at once the partner and the competitor of man.' Smith was as much a moralist as anything else and he was fearful of the 'Eclipse of Faith' which was the product of Darwin's discovery of evolution, the application of historical criticism to biblical texts, and the unsettling effects of rapid social and industrial change. Though he was sceptical of formal religious doctrines and articles of creeds, he was never indifferent to moral values and ethics. He personally believed in the essential truths of Christianity and saw religion as the real mortar of society. What he dreaded most of all was that the collapse of religion would drag down society itself. To Smith one of the more encouraging aspects of Canadian society was that this challenge to the whole basis of civilization was so little in evidence.

One of the most curious features of Goldwin Smith's outlook was the degree to which he remained generally faithful to the tenets of mid-Victorian liberalism long after liberalism in England had made its peace with collectivism. Just as he rejected John Stuart Mill's conclusions regarding the equality of the sexes, so too he remained impervious to the argument that liberalism, in order to protect and foster the essentials of its purpose, had to adopt collectivist or semi-socialist techniques. The result was that he gradually found himself a stranger in late Victorian England in the same way he had always been a bystander in Canada. What was regarded by his admirers as a testament to his steadfast attachment to principle might equally be seen as a case of arrested development and blind allegiance to exploded doctrines. But whatever it was, this same tendency was evident also in his attachment to the Little England view of the future of colonies.

In his collection of articles, *The Empire,* published in London, England, in 1863, Smith echoed the liberal indictment of the imperial system. Colonies were economic liabilities and in military terms they were sources of danger not strength. The end of the colonial system and the inauguration of free trade among nations would promote interdependence, reduce rivalries and conflict, and herald the day of lasting peace. He looked forward to the time when the white-settlement colonies – Smith always excluded India and Ireland from these calculations – would become independent nations and he supported the short-lived Canada First movement because he thought its aims identical with his own. Though the institutional and economic bonds of empire would disappear Smith believed that the tenacious and powerful ties of language, law, tradition, and political ideals would remain. 'The ties of blood, of language, of historical association, and of general sympathy, which bind the British portion of the Canadian people to England,' he wrote in 1878, 'are not dependent on the political connection, nor is it likely that they would be at all weakened by its severence.' The British Empire, as an empire, would vanish, and in its place would appear a galaxy of free nations within an English-speaking community. The United States belonged to that community and was separated from it only by a historical accident and the memory of past quarrels. That the rupture of 1776 be healed, and that the 'moral federation of the whole English-speaking race' be cemented, was Smith's deepest and most abiding hope. His strongest argument for the dissolution of Canada was that her 'reunion' with the United States would further this noble cause.

The other side of Smith's faith in the superiority of Anglo-Saxon civilization and the unity of the English-speaking peoples was an extremely critical and unsympathetic view of those lesser breeds who stood outside the pale of this civilization. Like many others in his time Smith was obsessed by racial questions and thought in terms of racial categories. At various times the Irish, Jews, French Canadians, Negroes, and southern European immigrants became objects of his dread. For all his invocations to the brotherhood of man his Anglo-Saxonry had a harsh, bitter side. Of the North American Indian, he wrote: 'The race, everyone says, is doomed ... Little will be lost by humanity.' Toward the Jews as a people he was consistently hostile. Commenting on anti-Semitic outbreaks in Europe in 1883 he noted: 'The main root of the evil in Hungary now is, as it has been everywhere and in all times, the position of the Jews as an intrusive and parasitic race, subsisting upon the labour of other races by usury, and at the same time maintaining towards the Gentiles, on whom they prey, an exclusive and unsocial bearing, which adds to the bitterness of the extortion.' The immigrants from southern and southeastern Europe in the United States, he contended, were not only primarily responsible for outbreaks of industrial violence in the 1880s and 1890s, but the foreign element which was untrained to self-government posed a threat to the Anglo-Saxon leadership of the Republic. Not the least of the advantages of continental union would be that the British Canadians would strengthen the forces of stability within the United States and thereby offset the influence of the immigrants. It is not surprising that Smith, like Lord Durham before him, hoped for the destruction of French-Canadian culture and nationality by the onward sweep of Anglo-Saxon civilization. He genuinely admired the simplicity, courteousness, and domesticity of French-Canadian society and came to appreciate Quebec as a bulwark against imperial consolidation, but in his treatment of its history he followed the path of the American historian Francis Parkman, whose anti-Catholic prejudices he shared. Royal control, monopoly, and regulation had stifled development in the Old Régime; the aim of the missionaries was to create a kind of northern Paraguay. The conquest was a blessing, but it was followed by the extension of liberties which the French used to protect an outmoded and unprogressive society. Because he thought of racial unity as an indispensable basis of nationality, envisaged French Canada as an obstacle to Canadian unity, and despaired of the assimilative capacities of English Canada, he saw the only solution to the French-Canadian question as obliteration by the superior resources of the United States.

Closely related to his sublime faith in the progressive power of Anglo-Saxon civilization was Smith's recurrent emphasis upon the social gulf that separated America from the old world. England was the home of aristocracy, privilege, hierarchy, militarism, monarchy. America had no feudal past and was the living embodiment of liberal democracy, social equality, and liberty of conscience. For him the United States represented the almost ideal society and everything the English liberals were striving to attain. A strong supporter of the North in the American civil war, he told a Boston audience in 1864 that 'An English Liberal comes here not only to watch the unfolding of your destiny, but to read his own ... the present civil war is a vast episode in the ... irrepressible conflict between Aristocracy and Democracy.' 'The more one sees of society in the New World,' he explained in 1878, 'the more convinced one is that its structure essentially differs from that of society in the Old World, and that the feudal element has been eliminated completely, and forever ...' This dichotomy between the 'democratic hemisphere' and the feudal legacy of the old world runs through everything he wrote, and it was the chief premise upon which he based his impressions of English-Canadian society. The basis of society in English Canada was identical to that of the United States. It rested on an independent land-owning class of farmers, its spirit was thoroughly democratic and equalitarian, and this spirit suffused all institutions and habits. Nothing aroused Smith's horror more than what he saw as attempts to intrude old world and alien institutions into the hemisphere of democracy and he was particularly forceful in denouncing the office of governor general, the 'mock monarchy' at Rideau Hall, and the conferring of titles on Canadians.

Though this notion of social democracy assumed a central place in Smith's conception of the unity of the North American continent, by 1891 he was also aware, sometimes uncomfortably so, of the disturbing and unlovely features of democracy. Far from being an uncritical apologist for democratic politics, he was repelled by excessive partisanship and corruption and was sceptical of the virtues of the universal franchise. Democracy, to him, was vitiated by a lack of deference and respect for authority; it was rough, crude, and turbulent, bordering on an anarchic individualism. What he missed in North American political life was the presence of a leisure class which devoted itself to public life and the service of the country. In Canada there was no such class. 'It has very few men of wealth and leisure, still fewer of those who, having inherited wealth, are at liberty from their youth, if they possess the sense of duty or the ambition, to devote themselves to politics.' As a consequence political leadership passed to 'an inferior class of men' who pandered to the mob and maintained power through bribery and 'government appropriations.' What Smith hankered for was the leadership of a cultivated élite of patricians not unlike the English aristocracy. By stressing these deficiences in Canadian political life, Smith neatly turned the tables on those Canadian nationalists who insisted that their institutions were British and therefore more stable and ordered than the republicanism of their neighbours. In fact he came to the conclusion that the checks upon the popular will in the American constitution and the reservoir of public-spirited citizens in the United States made that country less vulnerable to factious democracy than Canada.

Canadian farmers had a special place in his affections not only because they constituted the basis of a society which he admired but also because they were most receptive to the idea of freer trade with the United States. The 'great industry of Ontario is farming,' he wrote, and he described the rush of population to the cities with no enthusiasm. Nor did he have any enthusiasm for the industrialism which the protectionist policy was calculated to call into being. The charge was regularly made that freer trade with the United States would simply turn Canadians into hewers of wood and drawers of water. To which Smith replied: 'It is not obvious why the producer of raw materials should be deemed so much beneath the factory hand; perhaps looking to the effect of manufacturers on national character in England we might think that a nation would be wise in contenting itself with so much factory life as nature had allotted to it.' Smith clearly envisaged the Canadian economy as naturally subsidiary to that of the United States. As he put it in 1902: 'Not only are the countries conterminous and interlocked, but their population, the bulk of it at least, is identical, while in their products they are complements of each other; Canada supplying timber, minerals, and water-power, the United States manufacturing on a large scale.' This was in keeping with his idea of the natural division of labour: it was also expressive of his preference for the kind of society that such an economy would sustain. His main charge against the national policy of protection – which he had once supported – was that it defied nature and aggravated sectionalism. But beneath this indictment ran the feeling that protection had artificially created a protected class of manufacturers and a potentially revolutionary class of workers. Smith was no romantic opponent of industrialism, but his worry about the social consequences of industry and his denunciation of the plutocrats in the later 1890s suggests that he unhappily came to recognize that the society of the new world had begun to resemble that of Europe in its social problems and class tensions.

The word which best conveys Smith's total impression of Canada is the word 'artificial.' The really vital factors determining her development were the unity of the English-speaking people, the geographical, economic, and social unity of the continent, and the free and uninhibited play of economic forces. These were the 'primary' forces, the 'fiat of nature.' Canada was an artificial, merely 'political expression,' in the sense that she represented a defiance, based on tenuous sentiments, of these powerful primary factors. In Smith's mind, the attempt to create a separate nation through railways and tariffs seemed as illegitimate as attempts by the state to extensively regulate economic activity. And from this tension between the 'natural' and the 'artificial' arose all those Canadian problems which were so obvious in the late 1880s and which Smith diagnosed with such verve and delight.

The conventional criticisms of Smith's book were originally stated at the time of its publication and have been repeated ever since. It was noted that his writing style was a true mirror of his processes of thought and that his epigrammatic approach led to exaggeration and misrepresentation. This was an impression gained by non-Canadian readers of his other books as well as a judgment made by exasperated nationalists. 'He writes as if he were irritated, with an air of belligerency and a readiness to attack,' Woodrow Wilson commented on Smith's history of the United States; 'I must say that I am affected by this volume of Mr. Goldwin Smith's very much as Walter Bagehot was affected by Mr. Canning. "He was a man of elegant gifts, of easy fluency, capable of embellishing anything, with a nice wit, gliding swiftly over the most delicate topics; passing from topic to topic like a *raconteur* of the dinner table, touching easily on them all, letting them go as easily; confusing you as to whether he knows nothing, or knows everything." ' Essentially the same thing was said, much less gracefully, of *Canada and the Canadian Question.* Smith's major blind spot was his incapacity to penetrate into the sentiments and emotions which underlay the sense of Canadian nationality. In a perceptive review of Smith's book, George M. Grant, principal of Queen's University, rejected his insistence on geographical determinism and the intractability of the French-English division, and corrected many errors of fact. But Grant's essential objection was grounded upon a nationalist emotion and a conservative conception of nationality as the product of slow, organic evolution. He did not deny that commercial union would be profitable; what he denied was that profitability should be the main standard used to determine the future of the nation. Men, and nations, were more than the playthings of natural forces; both were free, within limits, to make their own history. Every 'nation must be ready to pay a price, must be willing to transcend difficulties in order to realize itself, to maintain its independence, to secure for itself a distinctive future.' Smith could not appreciate Grant's nationalism which was grounded on the belief that Canada would find her place in the world as a major force within the British Empire. He could not because of an ideological rigidity which precluded him from coming to terms with those forces which were changing international relations in the later nineteenth century, and also because of a deliberate conviction that emotions and sentiment were negligible factors in human affairs in the long run.

These criticisms qualify Smith's observations and set them into perspective, but they do not deny them. His book is supremely important in Canadian nationalist thought because he asked the question which all Canadian nationalists have since tried to answer: what positive values does the country embody and represent that justifies her existence?

FURTHER READING

The best studies of Smith's thought, to which this introduction is much indebted, are Elisabeth Wallace, *Goldwin Smith: Victorian Liberal* (Toronto, 1957); F. H. Underhill, 'Goldwin Smith,' in his *In Search of Canadian Liberalism* (Toronto, 1960), 85-103; and Malcolm Ross, 'Goldwin Smith,' in *Our Living Tradition: Seven Canadians,* ed. Claude T. Bissell (Toronto, 1957), 29-47. The historical background of the crisis of the late 1880s is described in Peter Waite, *Canada, 1874-1896: Arduous Destiny* (Toronto, 1971), chapter 11; and the intellectual context of the debate over the national future is discussed in F. H. Underhill, *The Image of Canada* (Toronto, 1964), chapter 3, and in C. Berger, *The Sense of Power: Studies in the Ideas of Canadian Imperialism, 1867-1914* (Toronto, 1970). G. M. Grant's review of Smith's book is in the *Week*, VIII, 1 and 15 May 1891 and reprinted in part in C. Berger, ed., *Imperialism and Nationalism, 1884-1914: A Conflict in Canadian Thought* (Toronto, 1970). Another cogent critique from the imperialist position of Smith's views on the Canadian future is G. R. Parkin, *Imperial Federation: The Problem of National Unity* (London, 1892), especially chapter 7. Smith's other works which deal in large part with social issues are *The Bystander,* Jan.-Oct. 1883, *Essays on the Question of the Day* (Toronto, 1893), *Guesses at the Riddle of Existence and Other Essays on Kindred Topics* (Toronto, 1897), and *Commonwealth or Empire* (New York, 1902).

Canada and the Canadian question

GOLDWIN SMITH

Contents

The appendices in the original have been omitted from this edition.

Chapter 1

The subject

The natural *v.* the political map /
The Provinces of the Dominion and their economical relation /
The question propounded

WHOEVER WISHES to know what Canada is, and to understand the Canadian question, should begin by turning from the political to the natural map. The political map displays a vast and unbroken area of territory, extending from the boundary of the United States up to the North Pole, and equalling or surpassing the United States in magnitude. The physical map displays four separate projections of the cultivable and habitable part of the Continent into arctic waste. The four vary greatly in size, and one of them is very large. They are, beginning from the east, the Maritime Provinces – Nova Scotia, New Brunswick, and Prince Edward Island; Old Canada, comprising the present Provinces of Quebec and Ontario; the newly-opened region of the North-West, comprising the Province of Manitoba and the districts of Alberta, Athabasca, Assiniboia, and Saskatchewan; and British Columbia. The habitable and cultivable parts of these blocks of territory are not contiguous, but are divided from each other by great barriers of nature, wide and irreclaimable wildernesses or manifold chains of mountains. The Maritime Provinces are divided from Old Canada by the wilderness of many hundred miles through which the Intercolonial Railway runs, hardly taking up a passenger or a bale of freight by the way. Old Canada is divided from Manitoba and the North-West by the great freshwater sea of Lake Superior, and a wide wilderness on either side of it. Manitoba and the North-West again are divided from British Columbia by a triple range of mountains, the Rockies, the Selkirks, and the Golden or Coast range. Each of the blocks, on the other hand, is closely connected by nature, physically and economically, with that portion of the habitable and cultivable continent to the south of it which it immediately adjoins, and in which are its natural markets – the Maritime Provinces, with Maine and the New England States; Old Canada, with New York and with Pennsylvania, from which she draws her coal; Manitoba and the North-West, with Minnesota and Dakota, which share with her the Great Prairie; British Columbia, with the States of the Union on the Pacific. Between the divisions of the Dominion there is hardly any natural trade, and but little even of forced trade has been called into existence under a stringent system of protection. The Canadian cities are all on or near the southern edge of the Dominion; the natural cities at least, for Ottawa, the political capital, is artificial. The principal ports of the Dominion in winter, and its ports largely throughout the year, are in the United

States, trade coming through in bond. Between the two provinces of Old Canada, though there is no physical barrier, there is an ethnological barrier of the strongest kind, one being British, the other thoroughly French, while the antagonism of race is intensified by that of religion. Such is the real Canada. Whether the four blocks of territory constituting the Dominion can for ever be kept by political agencies united among themselves and separate from their Continent, of which geographically, economically, and with the exception of Quebec ethnologically, they are parts, is the Canadian question.

Where the subject is so complex and so disjointed, to devise a satisfactory arrangement is not easy. Writers and readers of the history of the Dominion too well know how wanting it is in unity. For the special purpose of this work, which is neither elaborate description nor detailed history, but the presentation of a case and of a problem, it seemed best first, briefly to delineate the Provinces, which are the factors of the case, then to sketch their political history, leading up to Confederation, then to give an account of the Confederation itself, with its political sequel, up to the present time, and finally to propound the problem. The general reader, if any one answering to that description ever takes up this work, may skip the chapter on the Federal polity, the subject of which to the reader specially interested in Colonial institutions will probably seem the most important of all. To impart anything like liveliness to a discussion of the British North America Act one must have the touch of Voltaire.

The writer knows too well that he is on highly controversial ground. All he can say is that the subject is clearly and practically before the public mind; that he has done his best to take his readers to the heart of it by setting the whole case before them; that his opinions have not been hastily formed; that they have not, so far as he is aware, been biassed by personal motives of any kind; and that he does not think that the honour or the true interest of his native country can for a moment be absent from his breast.

Chapter 2

The French province

Canada proper a French colony / Dominion of the Papacy and the Church in Quebec / The French peasantry and their lot / Rapid increase of their numbers / Their occupations / Hold of the Church upon them / Wealth of the Church / The Jesuit and his relation to education / The *Parti Rouge* / The Guibord affair / Recent change in the character of the Church / Attitude of the Church towards the State, and towards the British and Protestant population / Ecclesiastical pretensions and nationalist aspirations / The Quebec Premier the champion of both / He apostrophises the Tricolor / Relations between the British and French race in the Province / Extrusion of the British / Protestant strongholds / Exodus of French Canadians to New England / The Irish at Montreal

With regard to this and the following chapter, the writer owes acknowledgment to *Picturesque Canada,* edited by Principal Grant, D.D., and also to the article by Dr. Prosper Bender, on the French Canadian Peasantry, in the *Magazine of American History,* August, 1890.

THE ELDEST first. Canada proper was a French colony. To the *habitans,* as the Quebec peasantry are called, it is a French colony still; for they know no Canadians but those of their own race. French enterprise it was that first looked down from the high-pooped barque, in which,.without chart or quadrant, it had braved the wide and wild Atlantic, upon the St. Lawrence, then running between forests full of bears, moose, and beavers, and roamed by a few human wolves in the shape of Red Indians. The true Canada is the river explored by Jacques Cartier, with its shores, its affluents, and the country of which it is the outlet. A royal river it is, bearing on its broad breast of waters Atlantic steamers a thousand miles from its mouth, and running between high banks, while its rival, the Mississippi, spreads over vast flats of mud; its weak point being that the frost of Canadian winter binds it half the year in chains which invention has been tasked in vain to loose. Quebec and Montreal are the only historic cities of the Dominion, and Quebec alone retains its historic aspect. Even in Quebec there are in the way of buildings but scanty remnants of the Bourbon days. But the citadel, the prize of battle between the races, the key and throne of empire, stills crowns the rock which stands a majestic warder at the portal of the Upper St. Lawrence; and the city with its narrow, steep, and crooked streets, crouching close under its guardian fortress, recalls an age of military force and fear in contrast to the cities of the New World, with their broad and straight streets spreading out freely in the security of industrial peace.

Quebec is a surviving offset of the France of the Bourbons, cut off by conquest from the mother country and her revolutions. Its character has been perpetuated by isolation like the form of an antediluvian animal preserved in Siberian ice. Just now the ice is in appearance freezing harder than ever, though there are ominous crackings and rumblings which to the listening ear seem to portend dissolution, and do certainly portend critical change. The Bourbon monarchy is gone, and very faintly is its image replaced in the heart of the French Canadian by that of the alien monarchy of Great Britain. The aristocracy is gone, since the seigniories instituted by Louis XIV – poor counterparts of Old World seigniories even while they existed – have been bought up and abolished, though a slight influence is retained by a few old families. The power of the notary rests on a foundation of adamant which no conquest or revolution can overthrow. But it and all other powers, political or social, are small compared with that of the priest. Quebec is a theocracy. While Rome has been losing her hold on Old France and on all the European nations, she has retained, nay tightened, it here. The people are the sheep of the priest. He is their political as well as their spiritual chief and nominates the politician, who serves the interest of the Church at Quebec or at Ottawa. The faith of the peasantry is medieval. It is in Quebec alone on the Western Continent that miracles are still performed. The shrine of Ste. Anne de Beaupré is thronged with pilgrims and thickly hung with votive offerings, though her cures are confined to ailments of a certain class, chiefly nervous, and she has not restored a limb or healed anybody of cancer. A bishop writing to the people of his diocese about his visit to Rome assumes that they receive as undoubted truth the legend of the three fountains marking the three boundings of St. Paul's head after it had been cut off, and that of St. Zeno and his 10,203 companions in martyrdom. Not only have the clergy been the spiritual guides and masters of the French Canadian, they have been the preservers and champions of his nationality, and they have thus combined the influence of the tribune with that of the priest.

The *habitant* is a French peasant of the Bourbon day. The "Angelus" would be his picture, only that in the "Angelus" the devotion of the man seems less thorough than that of the woman, whereas the *habitant* and his wife are alike devout. He is simple, ignorant, submissive, credulous, unprogressive, but kindly, courteous, and probably, as his wants are few, not unhappy. If, in short, there is an Arcadia anywhere, in his village most likely it is to be found. He tills in the most primitive manner his paternal lot, reduced by subdivision, executed lengthways, to a riband-like strip, with, if possible, a water-front; the river having been the only highway of an unprosperous colony when the lots were first laid out. His food is home-raised, and includes a good deal of peasoup, which affords jokes to the mockers. His raiment is homespun, and beneath his roof the hum of the spinning-wheel is still heard. His wife is the robust and active partner of his toil. Their cabin, though very humble, is clean. Such decorations as it has are religious. The Church services are to the pair the poetry and pageantry of life. If either reads anything it is the prayer-book. There are, however, *Chansons Populaires,* though probably more read by the cultivated than by the people, and there is a folk-lore brought apparently from Old France, perhaps from the France before Christianity.[1] The domestic affections among the *habitans* are strong; that grand source of happiness at least is theirs; and two or more branches of the same family are found living in harmony under the same roof. The *habitant* is not cultivated or aspiring, but his life is above that of the troglodyte of *La Terre.*

Close observers think that they can still trace the race characters of the two districts of Old France from which the French Canadians came, and distinguish the Breton Celt from the more solid and shrewder Norman; but the general characteristics prevail. It is denied that the language is a *patois*, such as a Parisian could not understand, though there are in it old Breton and Norman words and phrases. English words and phrases have also intruded, but these French patriotism is now trying to weed out.

The French Canadians breed apace. To them, as to the Irish, the Church preaches early marriage and speedy re-marriage in the interest of morality, and to multiply the number of the faithful, perhaps also with an eye to fees. From a return just laid before the Quebec Legislature it appears that for the grant of a hundred acres of land bestowed as a reward upon families boasting twelve or more children, there are 1009 claimants. One family numbers twenty-three; a family of twenty-six has been known. There is no saying what bound there would be to the extension of the French if they did not prefer pills made of paper with a likeness of the Virgin to vaccination as a preventive of smallpox. As it is, they are overflowing in multitudes into New England, and threaten, in conjunction with the Irish, who are also settling there in great numbers, to supplant the Puritan in his old abode. They are also displacing the English in Eastern Ontario, and making the politicians of the province feel their power. The digestive forces of Canada have been too weak to assimilate the French element even politically as those of the great mass of American Englishry have assimilated, sufficiently at least for the purposes of political union, the French population of Louisiana. Instead of being assimilated, the French Canadians assimilate, and Scotch regiments disbanded among them have become French in

1 See an interesting article by Mr. Edward Farrer, a distinguished Canadian journalist, in the *Atlantic Monthly* for April, 1882.

language, in religion, and in everything but name and face. The factories of New England welcome the French not only on account of the cheapness of their labour, but because they are tractable, amenable to factory discipline, and not addicted to industrial war.

Farming is not the only pursuit of the French Canadians in their own country. With it they combine one of a more stirring kind. They furnish a large proportion of the lumbermen. The forest wealth of Canada is immense, though it is now, unfortunately, being fast reduced not only by the axe, but by forest fires, which the carelessness of trappers or tramps kindles, and which are terrible in their destructive range, while governments, their thoughts engrossed by the party conflict, have left the forests to take care of themselves.[1] For lumbering winter, when the snow makes slides, is the season, so that the French peasant may combine it with the cultivation of his little farm. Picturesque writers dwell with rapture on the romance of life in the lumber shanty, the forest ringing with the axe, the glories of the winter landscape by sunlight and by moonlight, the healthiness of the work, the vigour and skill which it calls forth, and the joviality of the gangs, touching with poetry even "the huge pan of fat pork fried and floating in gravy."[2] In the dangerous work of guiding the logs down the stream, above all, great nerve as well as agility is displayed. The lumber shanty is also a school of temperance, for in it no liquor is allowed. Nor does religion fail to say her mass there, or to unpack her bale of ecclesiastical wares.

The land east of Quebec city is poor; even with the help of the lumber trade subsistence is rapidly outrun by population, and if there were not this ready outflow into the adjoining states of the American Union, Quebec would be a second Ireland, and an analogy would be presented which might be useful in teaching Irish reformers to deal with the fundamental problem of congestion rather than try to feed a heedless and thriftless people with statutory

1 In Ontario a forest-ranger has now been appointed, in the person of Mr. Phipps, who had done good service in calling attention to the subject.

2 See *Picturesque Canada*, vol. i, "Lumbering," where a complete and very interesting description of the trade and all that relates to it will be found.

parliaments. But the priest looks on emigration with an evil eye; it takes away his flock, and those who return, as not a few do when they have earned some money in the New England factory, are apt to bring back with them the mental habits of a free commonwealth. Schemes of "repatriation" have been formed, but of course in vain, and desperate attempts are being made to turn the current of emigration northwards to Lake St. John. Shipment to the French settlement in Manitoba is another device of the same policy; but the star of French colonisation in Manitoba is waning low. This is one quarter from which danger threatens the Church's "ancient and solitary reign." Another is the railway, which, by bringing the peasant and his wife within the attraction of the city with its luxuries and vanities, corrupts the rural simplicity and contentment approved with good reason by the Church. Hence fulminations of clerical wrath against social corruption which would prove the Church's system a failure if they were taken literally and without allowance for the fervour of the pulpit.

While the people are poor the Church is, for such a country, immensely rich. Not Versailles or the Pyramids bespoke the power of the king more clearly than the great Church and the monastery rising above the cabins bespeak the power of the priest. Exactly how great the wealth of the Church in Quebec is cannot be told; no politician dares to move for a return. A hundred millions of dollars (£20,000,000 stg.) would probably be a low estimate of her realised property, while her income is reckoned at ten millions. Bishop Laval acquired from the Government the seigniories of the Petit Nation, the Island of Jesus, and Beaupré, the last of which, beginning a few miles below Quebec, runs along the St. Lawrence for sixteen leagues, with a depth of six leagues measured from the river.[1] Favours have more recently been obtained from obsequious governments, while all legal facilities are given by legislatures not less obsequious. The Church has, by law transmitted from the Bourbon days and recognised at the Conquest, the right of taking from all members of her own communion tithe (though the amount of the impost has been reduced to a twenty-sixth) and money for building and

1 Parkman's *Old Régime in Canada,* p. 164.

repairing churches.[1] Masses for souls are everywhere a source of revenue to her. She is always investing with profit. Besetting the people from the cradle to the grave with her friars and her nuns, she daily gathers in money, of which none ever leaves her coffers, even for taxes, since she asserts her sacred immunity from taxation. Lotteries, in spite of their affinity to gambling, are sanctioned to add to the holy fund. To add to the holy fund priests do not disdain to peddle ecclesiastical amulets and trinkets.[2] Nor does Ste. Anne de Beaupré perform her cures for nothing. Meantime the mayor of St. Jean Baptiste, a village annexed to Montreal, states that of the seventy-five hundred people of that village, six thousand are too poor to protect themselves against smallpox, and the city must come to their assistance, while *Le Canadien* of Quebec calls upon the governments of the Dominion and the Province to provide work for the people of the counties below Quebec whose crops are a failure,

1 The tithe was by law only of cereals. The *habitant* took to growing peas to evade the impost; but the Church followed him up and he gave way. Of late he has taken to growing hay, but the Church again follows him up, and this time her exaction is the more severe because a heavy tax has been imposed on hay by the United States. In cities, the Church has begun to impose a poll tax on those who do not pay tithes. The curé generally succeeds in collecting by ecclesiastical authority, though resort is sometimes had to the Parish Commissioners' Courts. A district magistrate at Sherbrooke, not long ago, condemned a *habitant* to pay $4 (two years' tax of $2 per annum) imposed by the Bishop of St. Hyacinthe. The magistrate, who is a lawyer of thirty years' standing, based his decision partly on the decree of the bishop and partly on the fact that defendant's family had the spiritual services of the curé, for which he awarded a *quantum meruit.* The case is reported in the *Revue Legale*, a law report edited by a judge of the Superior Court of Montreal, without any question of its soundness. In the Province there has also been a long struggle against paying tithes to the movable missionaries. But the Superior Court has also sustained this impost, though the old French edict declares that settled curés alone had the right to collect tithes.

2 See for this the article "Romanism in Canada" in the *Presbyterian Review*, New York, July, 1886.

warning them that unless the Matane Railway be pushed on to give the people bread there will be an exodus which will be ruinous to the Dominion. The treasury of the Province is empty, and her financiers are fain to levy political tribute on the Confederation or to raid by taxation of financial companies on the strongbox of the commercial Protestants at Montreal. The Reformation was perhaps to a greater extent than is commonly supposed a movement of economical self-preservation on the part of communities whose land and wealth were being absorbed by the Church.

The champions of the Church say that for all that she takes she gives full value in the shape of morality and charity. Her charity, if it means the control of charitable institutions, is not unconnected with her finance. It is probably on financial grounds, in part, that she is at this moment struggling to keep the lunatic asylums in her hands. But she has made the people in her way moral, as well as in her way religious. Her rule is almost Genevan in its austerity; balls and low dresses are denounced as well as Opera Bouffe. The relations of the sexes are watched with a jealous eye. Probably the most favourable specimen of the Roman Catholic system anywhere to be found is in Quebec, where, be it remembered, the Church has been under British rule, linked to a British province, tempered in her action by British influences, and stimulated by Protestant emulation. Nevertheless, looking to the condition of the people on the one hand, and the vast array of churches, convents, and rectories on the other, we are reminded of Edmond About's saying about the peasantry of the Romagna, who were backward and unprosperous though they had fourteen thousand monks preaching to them the gospel of labour.

What the mind of the Church is respecting popular education we know from the history of countries such as Southern Italy, Spain, the Roman Catholic provinces of Austria, and the Spanish colonies in South America, where she has had it all her own way. The Jesuit boasts of his services to education in Canada and elsewhere: he has no doubt cultivated the art to great perfection after his kind; but the objects of his attention as an educator have been youths destined for the priesthood, or sons of the rich and powerful whom it was his aim to draw into his net, and to whom he imparts a set of showy and superficial accomplishments serving mainly to allay the thirst for truth. In Quebec the Church has it not all her own way. She is exposed to the rivalry and criticism of a body of Protestants on the spot, and of a still larger body in the Dominion. She has therefore taken up popular education, but she has taken it up without zeal and given it an ecclesiastical turn. The days may have gone by when by a Statute of the Province of Quebec school trustees were authorised by law to sign with a mark; but illiteracy still prevails. The mayor of a town cannot always write. Mr. Arthur Buies, a French Canadian journalist of eminence, cites a witness who, having held a high official position, and lived in a rural district for fifty years, deposes that among the men between twenty and forty not one in twenty can read, and not one in fifty can write; that they will tell you that they have been at school but have forgotten all they learned; and that what the "all" was you will be able to guess when you know that the teachers were mostly young girls taken from the convents with a salary of from 200 to 400 francs a year, and chosen because their priests were unable to pay the convent tuition fees.[1] This account seems to be borne out by the inquiries of the Massachusetts School Inspector among the French Canadian immigrants in Massachusetts, though these are likely to be not among the least active-minded or intelligent of the community from which they come. In fact education for the masses is probably little more than preparation for the first communion. The series of school books in use in the Province is highly ecclesiastical and very poor.

The school history is a characteristic work.[2] It scarcely mentions British Canada, treats the British as alien intruders, exults in French victories over them, imputes to them insidious designs of crushing French nationality, and glorifies the priesthood for having preserved it from their attacks. Lord Durham, the author of the hated union with British Canada, is accused of having scattered money broadcast for that object, and Sir John Colborne is charged with ravaging the country at the head of seven or eight thousand men when the rebellion was over and order had been restored. The Conquest, the pupil is taught to believe, was followed by eighty years of persecution, of religious intolerance, and of despotism, during which

1 Arthur Buies, *La Lanterne*, Montreal, 1884, p. 113.

2 Abrégé d'Histoire du Canada a l'usage des Jeunes Etudiants de la Province de Québec, par F. X. Toussaint, Professeur à l'Ecole Normale-Laval. Approuvé par le Conseil de l'Instruction Publique, Montreal, 1886.

England was following, with regard to Canada, the sinister policy which she had pursued with regard to Ireland. This is a primer sanctioned by the Council of Public Instruction in a province styled British. There is at present no ill-feeling among the French Canadians against Great Britain. British rule has been too mild to provoke hatred. British Royalty when it visits Quebec is perfectly well received. But Great Britain is a foreign country to the French Canadian.

There is in Quebec a circle of French literary men containing some names of eminence; but it is hardly more connected with the Church and her people than was the literary circle of the eighteenth century with the Church and her people in France. It draws its intellectual aliment from Paris, where some of its members are well known, and M. Frechette, the poet of French Canada, has won a crown. Probably it is itself better known at Paris than in Quebec.

In this Paradise of Faith there is a serpent called the *Parti Rouge*, though it is not Dynamitard or Atheist, but merely Liberal, or at most free-thinking, and opposed to clerical domination. It had at Montreal a literary society called the *Institut Canadien*. This society, for taking heterodox literature, was excommunicated as a body by the Church. Guibord, one of its members, died under the ban, and the Church refused to let him be buried in the Catholic cemetery where he had owned a lot. The Provincial courts upheld the sentence of the Church. But the Privy Council on appeal, after debating the question, as Carlyle says, with the iron gravity of Roman augurs, decided that men must, according to the Canon Law, be excommunicated individually, not in the lump; consequently that Guibord had not lost his right to burial in the cemetery. The Church showed fight, the militia were under orders, a huge block of granite was prepared to protect the grave from desecration, a collision seemed to be impending, when the Bishop of Montreal cut the knot by proclaiming that in whatever spot the excommunicate might be laid that spot would thereby be cut off from the rest of the ground and deconsecrated; so that in the rest of the ground the faithful might sleep uncontaminated and in peace.

Till lately, however, the Church of Quebec remained a true daughter of the Church of monarchical France, and kept her Gallican tradition, giving Caesar his due, and living at peace with the civil power. But at length the same change has passed over her which has passed over the Roman Catholic Churches of Europe, since, having lost the allegiance of the national governments, they have been compelled to throw themselves for support on their spiritual centre, and to exalt without limit the authority of the Pope. Ultramontanism has come, and in its van the Jesuit bearing with him the Encyclical and Syllabus, his own work. Having, besides his surpassing skill in intrigue, the ecclesiastical influences of the time in his favour, he captures the Episcopate, fills the Church with his spirit, extends his empire on all sides. The Sulpician order, Gallican in sentiment, whose great seminary rises over Montreal, after a bitter struggle goes down before him, and resigns to him in part the cure of the wealthy city. Against the University, the last fortress of Gallicanism or Liberal Catholicism, his batteries have opened. From his own pulpit, or through the lips of bishops who speak as he prompts, he denounces Gallicanism as a pestilent error, brands Liberal Catholicism, the Catholicism of Montalembert and Lacordaire, as insidious poison, reasserts in the language of the Encyclical the medieval claims of the Papacy to domination over conscience and over the civil power, scornfully repels the idea that the priest is to confine himself to the sacristy, claims for him the right of interference in elections, the censorship of literature and of the public press. Against Protestantism and its pretended rights he proclaims open war; it has no rights, he says; it is merely a triumphant imposture; no religion has any right, or ought to be treated by the State as having any, but that of Rome. Rome is the rightful sovereign of all consciences; and will again, when she can, assert her authority by the same means as before. War is declared against religious liberty, progress, and the organic principles of modern civilisation. On such a course the ship of the French Church of Quebec is now steering, with the Jesuit at the helm. If she holds on, a collision can hardly fail to ensue. It has been said very truly that the Jesuit always fails. This world would be strangely ordered if he did not. His wisdom has never been equal to his craft. When by craft he had got James II into his hands, he, by want of wisdom, hurried the king along the road to ruin. He may do the same with the Nationalist party and politicians of Quebec. In the history of the Order, as often as the marvellous labours of the sons of Loyola *in majorem Dei gloriam* seemed on the point of being crowned with success there has come an *afflavit Deus et dissipati sunt*. But though the Jesuit has always failed, his failures have been tremendously costly to humanity.

The ascendency of Ultramontanism has been aided by the change which has taken place in the position of the clergy. They used to hold their cures, under an ordinance of Louis XIV, by a fixed tenure, like the freehold of an English rector. But they have now been put generally on the footing of missionaries, removable at the pleasure of the bishop. The old-fashioned curé, a man something like the English rector of the old school, quiet and sociable, is passing away, and his place is being taken by a personage of a more stirring spirit, and better suited to be the minister of Ultramontane ambition.

With this advance of ecclesiastical pretensions comes a sympathetic growth of nationalist aspiration. The dream of a French nation on this continent has long been hovering before the minds of French Canadians, though it is hard to say how far the idea has ever assumed a distinct shape or formed a definite motive of action. The Abbé Gingras in a pamphlet some years ago, after glorifying the Dark Ages, justifying the Inquisition, and reviving the claims of Innocent III, set forth what he deemed the necessary policy of French Canadian statesmen towards the Dominion, describing it as one of conciliation, more or less elastic, with the creation of a papal and French nationality always in view as its covert aim. But now the twin movement has taken a more pronounced form. M. Honoré Mercier has risen to lead Ultramontanism and Nationalism at once, and has been raised by their joint forces to the Premiership of the Province, while the old Conservative or Bleu party, which corresponded to the Gallican party in the Church, has suffered a complete overthrow. M. Mercier proclaims himself the devout liegeman of the Pope, wears a papal decoration on his breast, seeks the papal blessing before going into an election contest, champions all ecclesiastical claims, restores to the Jesuits their estates, and boasts to a great Roman Catholic assemblage at Baltimore that he has thereby redressed the wrong done by George III. At the same time he avows his Nationalism in language that makes British ears tingle. At the unveiling of a joint memorial to Breboeuf, the Jesuit martyr, and Jacques Cartier, the French discoverer, he bids the Red and Blue party of Quebec blend their ensigns in the Tricolor. He celebrates his political victory in a hall profusely decorated with French flags, while only one Dominion flag is to be seen. "Gentlemen," he says, pointing to the Tricolor, "this flag you know; it is the national flag. The government which you have you know; it is the national government. The party which I have before me I know. This flag, this government, and this party are to-night honoured by the National Club. It is a national triumph which we celebrate to-night, and not national merely in name but national in tendencies, aspirations, and sentiments." The French Canadian nation telegraphs its salutations to the Pope, and the Pope telegraphs back his benediction to the French Canadian nation. On a day in September 1887 the French flag was hoisted above the British flag on the Parliament House of Quebec in honour of the French frigate *La Minerve.* This was afterwards said to have been an accident. It was an accident full of omen.

Between Old France and the New France of the priests a gulf was set by the Atheist Revolution. There seems to have been some change of feeling in the minds of the Quebec clergy when Napoleon restored the Church, and when afterwards the old régime came back with the Bourbons. But since 1830 Liberalism, with the interlude of the Empire, has reigned again in Old France and repelled clerical sympathy. The Liberals of Quebec cultivate their connection with the mother country, who begins on her part to meet their advances and to show renewed interest in her great colony. But the moral sovereign of Quebec is the Pope, and the outcome of this movement, if it bears fruit at all, will be a French and Papal nation. The hearts of the French Canadians were, however, deeply moved by the spectacle of the Franco-German War. "If any one," said Sir George Cartier at that time, "would know to-day how far we are Frenchmen, I answer: 'Go into the towns, go into the country, accost the humblest among us and relate to him the events of that gigantic struggle which has fixed the attention of the world; announce to him that France is conquered; then place your hand upon his breast, and tell me what can make his heart beat if it be not love for his country.' "

Lord Durham, coming immediately after what was called a rebellion, but was really rather a war between the two races in Lower Canada, describes not only the estrangement of the races but their mutual bitterness as extreme. The bitterness has in great measure passed away; the estrangement remains. There is hardly any intermarriage; marriages of Roman Catholics with Protestants are in fact interdicted by the Church of Rome. There is hardly any social intercourse either of young or old. Lord Durham said that the two races meet in the jury-box only for the utter subversion of justice. In any political case, or any case in which an appeal can be made to the sentiment of race, they meet only for the subversion of justice still: at least a disagreement of the jury is sure to result. The politicians have to act with British colleagues, with whom they must also associate. They have to speak English, because while French as well as English is recognised in the Parliament at Ottawa a member speaking French only cannot produce much effect; and some of them, Mr. Laurier and Mr. Chapleau for example, are among the very best English speakers. But constant intercourse is confined to the leaders; the British and French members generally, even at Ottawa, live much apart.

As the French population in Quebec increases, the British population decreases; it is likely in time to be thrust out altogether from the whole of the Province except a quarter of Montreal. In the city of Quebec there are now, it is believed, not more than six or seven thousand British remaining, and, as the shipbuilding trade has fled from its former seat, the British element being bound up with commerce, it is likely that the decline will go on. The eastern townships on the south of the St. Lawrence were once entirely British, and were under English law while the rest of the Province was under the Custom of Paris; but that district is now rapidly passing into French hands. The Bishop has the power of creating an ecclesiastical parish which by subtle links draws after it the civil and the municipal parish. The British farmer is harassed by an increase of his assessment as well as by social influences adverse to his peace and comfort. He becomes ready to sell out, and the Church advances money to the Frenchmen for the purchase at an easy rate, which she can do with profit to herself, because in the Frenchman's hands the farm becomes subject to tithe and Church repairs. One Protestant church after another is closed and in one parish after another French is proclaimed as the only language in which the records are to be kept. The commerce and wealth of Montreal are still in British hands, the reactionary ecclesiasticism of the French being little propitious to commercial pursuits. But commercial Montreal in French Quebec is becoming an outpost of an alien territory;

proposals have been made for transferring it from Quebec to Ontario, close to the border of which it lies. Under the present jurisdiction it runs no small risk of being despoiled by the needy financiers of a separate race, as would Belfast if the taxing power in Ireland were committed to Roman Catholic and Celtic hands. Meanwhile the British traders of Montreal think of little but their trade, or of their pleasure, and make no head against the progress of the foe. In truth to make head something like a martyr spirit is required, for the Church can punish in his trade or profession the man who dares to show himself her enemy. Free and bold voices are heard, but they are few, and the ears to which they speak are for the most part closed against anything which, by disturbing quiet, might interfere with the interests of trade.

The less Ultramontane element of the Roman Catholic Church still holds its ground in the Laval University at Quebec, to which Liberals resort, and which has hitherto held Jesuit ascendency at bay. Protestantism has its flourishing place of high education in McGill University, at Montreal, while the Church of England has a small University at Lennoxville. Amongst the strongest bulwarks of Protestantism in the Province is the Presbyterian College at Montreal.

There are French Protestants in the Province to the number, it is said, of about 10,000. These are by origin converts from Roman Catholicism, and may be regarded with interest, as a recurrence of the tendency which gave birth to the Huguenots, but seemed to have been thoroughly crushed out of existence between Ultramontanism on the one hand and Voltaire on the other. They have produced, in the person of Mr. Joly, who was for a short time Provincial Premier, the most thoroughly upright and the most universally respected among the public men of the Province.

The point at which the empire of the Church in Quebec and the Jesuit's ideal polity are most threatened, is the junction with the American Republic, produced by the overflow already noticed, of the French population into the north-eastern States of the Union. This exodus the Church, while she deplores and dreads it, is constantly augmenting, both by her encouragement of early marriages and by her own absorption of wealth. She may send her priests with the exiles and try to extend her reign of childlike submission and uninquiring faith over Massachusetts; but in this she will not succeed. Nor will she be able to prevent the connection between the French from being the conduit of American ideas fatal to faith and tithes. Among the Roman Catholics of Quebec itself there are sectional divisions which may some day lead to rupture, while the intellectual tendencies of the age being what they are, the *Parti Rouge* is not likely to decrease. There are those who suspect that even M. Mercier himself is less narrow in his convictions than from his public professions and actions has appeared. At this moment he is said to be braving Ultramontane ire by transferring the lunatic asylums from religious to secular keeping. But it is in the quarter of the exodus that we may look with most assurance for the beginning of the end.

In the meantime, however, the French Canadians in Vermont, New Hampshire, and Massachusetts, remain French Canadians. They form settlements by themselves. They cling to their language and their religion. They remain in close communication with those whom they have left behind, and population circulates between the two divisions. Thus New France now stretches across the Line into the United States, one section of her being on the British side of the Line, the other section, the proportion of which already amounts to two-sevenths, and is always increasing, on the other side. Let those who dream of a war between Canada and the United States ponder this fact, and remember that they would have to call upon one part of New France to take arms in a British quarrel against the other part.

At Montreal there is a large settlement of Irish, who show their gregarious tendency by dwelling together in a quarter of the city called Griffintown. In the relations of the Irish to the French Catholics difference of race sharpened by industrial competition seems to predominate over identity of religion, to the advantage of the British Protestants, whom the combined force would overwhelm.

Chapter 3

The British provinces

Ontario the core of the Confederation / Its chief industries / Structure of society and social sentiment / Effects of democracy in the household and on juvenile character / City life / The public school system / The Churches / Nationalities and national societies / Canadian respect for law / Public justice and the bench / Social life / The climate / Pastimes / Commerce and industry / Trade organisations / Social problems / City government / Literature, Art, and Science / Journalism / Emigration and native feeling towards the emigrant / Migration of Canadians to the United States / Practical fusion of the two nations / The Maritime Provinces, Nova Scotia, New Brunswick, and Prince Edward Island / Manitoba and the North-West / British Columbia

ONTARIO, formerly Upper Canada, and better designated as British Canada, was the nucleus and is the core of the Confederation. It will be seen on the map, running out between Lake Ontario and Lake Erie on one side, and Lake Huron and the Georgian Bay on the other, Windsor on its extreme point being almost a suburb of Detroit, though separated from that city by the Detroit river. That great tongue of land is its garden, but it has also fruitful fields along the Upper St. Lawrence. It reaches far back into a wilder and more arctic country, rich however in timber, and still richer in minerals. The minerals would yield great wealth if only the treasure-house in which an evil policy keeps them locked could be opened by the key of free-trade. "Rich by nature, poor by policy," might be written over Canada's door. Rich she would be if she were allowed to embrace her destiny and be a part of her own continent; poor, comparatively at least, she is in striving to remain a part of Europe. At present the great industry of Ontario is farming. It is so still, in spite of the desperate efforts of protectionist legislators to force her to become a manufacturing country without coal. The farmers are usually freeholders, but leaseholders are growing more common. Not a few of the farms are mortgaged, as are a good many of the farms in the United States. Let this be noted by those who fancy that to make a happy commonwealth they have only to do away with landlords and divide the land among small proprietors. The mortgagee is a landlord who never resides, never helps the tenant, never reduces the rent. Much of the money, however, borrowed in Ontario has been spent in clearing or improving farms in a new country, and has proved an excellent investment to the borrower. The farms are generally from one to two hundred acres. The Canadian farmer works with his own hands, unlike the British farmer on a large farm who rides about and watches his men work. If he has not sons to help him he hires a labourer, who gets good wages, and lives with the farmer and his family, thus having a rise in life; for in England the farmer is now usually too much a gentleman, and his wife is far too much a lady, to live with the labourer. The system in Canada, however, has of late been changing, and labourers' cottages are beginning to be built. The labour-saving machines which are among the wonderful products of American invention, and of which the self-binder is the paragon, save the farmer much hire of men.

Canada flatters herself that she is ahead of England in their use. Nowhere probably on this continent is the farming high; the land having hitherto been abundant, the farmer has preferred to work out his farm and move on. Thus the yield in some districts has decreased; it is said also that the crops have suffered by the clearing of the land, which exposes them to the cold winds. In a new country there is a general tendency to lavishness and waste; trees have been recklessly cut down, and replanting has been neglected. Hitherto the chief products have been wheat and barley; but a deluge of grain is now pouring down from the North-West, while the M'Kinley Act, if it stands, will shut out the barley from the American market; and the Canadian farmer is turning his thoughts to cattle, which in this climate are free from disease. The aspect of the farm-houses and farms in Ontario will show even the passing traveller that agriculture has prospered, though just now it is depressed and the value of farm property has gone down. The Canadian farmer, however, to earn his living out of the land has to work hard and to bargain hard. Perhaps to the English gentleman who turns farmer in Canada the second is almost as unfamiliar as the first. The season of the Canadian farmer's hardest work is the short and hot summer by which his crops are brought rapidly on. In the winter he carries his grain to market in his sleigh over the good roads which the snow then makes for him, looks after his cattle, or gets his implements into order, and has more time for rest and social enjoyment. His diet is not so good as it ought to be; partly because he cannot bear to keep for himself anything that his farm produces if it will fetch a good price; partly because his cookery is vile. So say those who know him best. Fried pork, bread ill-baked, heavy pies, coarse and strong green tea, account for the advertisements of pills which everywhere meet the eye, and perhaps in part for the increase of lunacy. From liquor, however, the Canadian farmer abstains. He has become temperate without coercive law, and for him prohibition is an impertinence. He is altogether a moral man and a good citizen, honest, albeit close, as indeed he needs to be, in his dealings. He supports his minister and his schoolmaster, though both perhaps on a rather slender pittance. Such is the basis of society in British Canada. Apparently it is sound. The agrarian revolutionist, at all events, has little chance of disturbing a community of substantial freeholders, each of them tilling the land which his father or his not very remote ancestor won, not from a subjugated race with the Norman sword, but from the wilderness with the axe and the plough. Where the basis of society is sound, we can afford to think and speak freely about the rest.

In British Canada, as in the United States, we see that the world gets on without the squire or any part of the manorial system. In Canada, as in the United States, the rich live in cities; they have no country houses; they go in summer to watering-places on the Gulf of the St. Lawrence, or more commonly in the United States, to Europe, or to the cottages which stud the shores and islets of the Muskoka Lakes. Not that the total absence of the manorial system does not make itself felt in American civilisation. Wealth, at all events, is the worse for having no rural duties.

A yeoman proprietor of one or two hundred acres, let the agrarian reformers of England observe, is not a peasant proprietor or of kin to the peasant characters of Zola. Let them observe also that America has been organised for the system from the beginning. In England to introduce peasant proprietorship you would have to pull down all the farm buildings and build anew for the small holdings. In France you had only to burn the chateaux.

In this fundamental respect of yeoman proprietorship, without a landed gentry, the structure of society in British Canada is identical with its structure in the United States. It is identical in all fundamental respects. Canadian sentiment may be free from the revolutionary tinge and the tendency to indiscriminate sympathy with rebellion unhappily contracted by American sentiment in the contest with George III; but it is not less thoroughly democratic. In everything the pleasure and convenience of the masses are consulted. In politics everybody bows the knee to the people. Where there is wealth there will be social distinctions, and opulence even at Toronto sometimes ventures to put a cockade in the coachman's hat. Titled visitors who come either to Canada or to the United States have too much reason to know that the worship of rank is personal, and can survive under any social system. But aristocracy is a hateful word to the Canadian as well as to the American ear. It is politically a word wherewith to conjure backwards. Any exhibition of the tendency would be fatal to an aspirant. If a citizen has a pedigree, real or factitious, he must be content to feed his eyes on it as it hangs on his own wall.

Wealth everywhere is power, and everywhere to a certain extent commands social position. This is the case in Toronto and the other cities of British Canada. But wealth in Toronto society has not everything quite its own way. There is a circle, as there is a circle even at New York, which it does not entirely command. Nor does a young man forfeit his social position by taking to any reputable calling. In that respect we have decidedly improved on the sentiment of the Old World.

One sign of the pervading democratic sentiment is the servant difficulty, about which a continual wail from the mistresses of households fills the social air. The inexperience of masters and mistresses who have themselves risen from the ranks, the dulness of small households which makes servants restless, and the rate of wages in other employments, may in part be the causes of this; but the main cause probably is the democratic dislike of service. Rarely, if ever, will you see a native American servant, and in Canada the domestics are chiefly immigrants. The work in the factory may be much harder, and the treatment less kind than in the household; generally they are; but the hours of work over, the girl calls no one mistress, and she can do what she likes in the evenings and on Sundays. In the household the democratic scorn of service is unpleasantly apt to display itself by mutiny. Ladies complain that the parts of mistress and servant are reversed, and that it is the servant that requires a character of the mistress. People begin to wonder how the relation is to be kept up, and they talk of flats, hotels, and restaurants, a recourse to which would be very injurious to domestic life and affection. It has been suggested that the children of families may have again, as they did in former days, to help in the housework. They would probably like anything which gave vent to their bodily energies almost as well as play. Dishonesty on the other hand among domestics appears to be rare, and a Canadian servant is less punctilious than an English servant in mixing different kinds of work. Another unattractive manifestation of the democratic spirit is the behaviour, in cities at least, of the lower class of Canadian boys, of which even the most silver-tongued of governors-general could not bring himself to speak with praise. Neither the schoolmaster nor anybody else dares effectually to correct the young citizens. Something may perhaps be due to the extensive and increasing employment, from economical motives, of women as teachers. There are those at least who think that this practice is not favourable to subordination or to the cultivation of some manly points of character; while others contend that the gentler influence is the stronger. The question as to the effect likely to be produced on the character of a nation by the substitution of the schoolmistress for the schoolmaster is at all events worthy of consideration. Apart however from any special cause, no one can be surprised at hearing that in a new and crude democracy there is a want of respect for authority, and of courage in exercising it, which makes itself felt throughout the social frame, and on which the young rowdy soon learns to presume. No wonder juvenile crime is on the increase.

It was to be expected that in the democratic hemisphere fustian would at first be inclined to take its revenge on broadcloth for the predominance of broadcloth in the Old World. Roughnesses of this kind, with the servant difficulty and the boy anarchy, are the joltings in the car of human progress on its road to the glorious era of perfect order and civilisation, combined with perfect equality, which the generation after next will see. Meantime the general texture and habits of society are not easily changed. The social ways of man, his social distinctions and his social courtesies, are still much the same in British Canada and the United States that they are in Old England.

A city in British Canada differs in no respect from an American city of the second class. It is laid out in straight streets crossing each other at right angles, with trams for the street car – the family chariot of democracy, which by carrying the working man easily to and from his work enables him to live in the suburbs, where he gets a better house and better air. Nor does city life in Canada differ from that in the United States. It is equally commercial, and though the scale is smaller than that of Wall Street the strain is almost as great. People are glad to escape to the freshness of something like primitive life on a Muskoka islet, or even to get more entirely rid of civilisation and its cares by "camping out" on a lake side. Of late there has been in Canada as elsewhere a great rush of population to the cities. Toronto has grown with astonishing rapidity at the expense of the smaller towns and villages, and fortunes have been made by speculations in real estate. The cause of this is believed to be partly education, which certainly breeds a distate for farm work. Another cause is the railway, which brings the people to the cities first to shop or see exhibitions, and, when they have thus tasted of city pleasures and shows, to live. The passion for amusement and excitement grows in Canada as fast as elsewhere. Railways, moreover, have killed or reduced some country employments, such as those of carriers and innkeepers. This tendency to city life is universal, and it may be said that what is universal is not likely to be evil. But the people cannot afford to be so well housed in the city as they are in the village; their children grow up in worse air, physical and moral; and though they have more of crowd and bustle they have really less of social life, because in the village they all know each other, while in the city they do not know their next-door neighbour. In the cities the people will be brought under political influences different from those of the country, and a change of political character, with corresponding consequences to the commonwealth, can hardly fail to ensue.

The learned professions, and not only the learned professions but all the callings above manual labour, such as those of clerks and of assistants in stores, are almost as much overstocked in Canada as they are in the United States. An advertisement for a secretary at £140 a year brings seventy-two applications. Let young Englishmen who think of emigrating note this. There has been many a sad case of disappointment. We have had educated gentlemen, when they had spent what they brought with them reduced to manual labour, happy if they could get that.

The Public School system in Canada is much the same as in the United States, and as in the United States is regarded as the sheet-anchor of democracy. The primary schools are free; at the High Schools a small fee as a rule is paid.[1] At Toronto University there are no fees for University lectures, but the youth during his course has to board himself, so that except to the people of the University town the education cannot be said to be free. If it were we should be in danger of having a population of penniless and socialistic graduates. As it is there are more than graduates enough. In the city of Toronto in one year $600,000 were levied for Public Schools, including the expenditure on sites, buildings, and repairs, besides the sum expended on High Schools and Separate Schools,

1 The trustees have the option of remitting the fee, and this is commonly done as a reward for proficiency in the public school.

amounting to nearly $100,000 more. Grumblers then began to challenge the principle of the system, and to ask why the man who has one child or none should be called upon for the schooling of the man who has six, when three-fourths probably of the people who use the schools are able to pay for themselves. The answer is that with a popular suffrage ignorance is dangerous to the commonwealth. Unluckily there is reason to believe that of the class likely to be dangerous a good many escape the operation of the system. It appeared from a recent report of the Minister of Education that 25 per cent of the children are not in school at all, while of those on the register the attendance was not more than half the roll. The attendance is higher in cities than it is in the country, where the weather in the winter season is a serious obstacle; but in the cities and towns it is only about 60 per cent. Attendance is legally compulsory, but the law is a dead letter; nor is the well-to-do artisan anxious to have the ragged waif in the school at his child's side. In the New England of early days, the first and classical seat of the system, the Common School would answer strictly to its name. It would be really common to a group of families, all of whom might take a personal interest in it. This would be a different thing from a great State machine maintained by taxing the whole community for the benefit of a certain portion of it, taking education entirely out of the hands of parents and extinguishing, as it must, the sense of parental duty in that respect. In American commonwealths, however, the system of free education, expedient or inexpedient, just or unjust, is a fixture. But British statesmen had better inquire before they take the leap. Some people it seems propose to give not only free education but free breakfasts. Bribery in the old days of corruption was petty; now it is being raised in scale and dignity by demagogues who bribe whole classes out of the public funds. When it is understood that instead of working and saving you may vote yourself the earnings and savings of other people, industry will lose some of its charm.

The Public Schools, saving the Separate Schools for Roman Catholics, are secular. To satisfy the religious feelings of the people some passages of Scripture of an undogmatic character are read without comment. This in strictness is a deviation from the secular principle: thoroughgoing secularists object, and there has been a good deal of controversy on the subject. The practice is defended on the ground that the moral code of the community is a necessary part of education, and that the ethics of the gospel, apart from anything dogmatic, are still the moral code of the community. Clergymen are by law allowed access at certain hours, but this privilege is not used. The organ of religious education is the Sunday School. Of these there are said to be in Ontario nearly 4000, more than half of the number being Methodists, with 40,000 unpaid teachers. The Sunday School is made attractive by entertainments, picnics, and excursions.

The New World has produced no important novelty in religion. Universalism, the only new sect of importance, is but Methodism with Eternal Punishment left out. Upon that doctrine in almost all the Churches, as well of Canada as of the United States, the humanitarianism of democracy has acted as a solvent. Perhaps the Presbyterian Church should be excepted. At least a very eminent preacher of that church in Toronto, who had breathed a doubt some years ago, was compelled to explain, after a debate in Knox Church which recalled the debates of the primitive councils. The two Presbyterian Churches had just united, but their distinctive characters were still visible, like those of two streams which have run together yet not perfectly commingled, and the men of the Free Kirk exceeded those of the Old Kirk in orthodox rigour. Freedom from an Establishment begets tolerance as well as equality: the co-operation of the ministers, of all Protestant Churches at least, in good works is almost enforced by public opinion; dogmatic differences are softened or forgotten, and among the masses of the laity practically disappear. There is even talk of Christian union. Old-standing organisations, with the interests attached to them, are in the way; but economy may in time enforce, if not union, some arrangement which, by a friendly division of the spiritual field, shall enable a village, which neither knows nor cares anything about dogma, to feed one pastor instead of starving three. Of the Protestant Churches in Ontario the largest and the most spreading is Methodism, strong in its combination of a powerful clergy with a democratic participation of all members in church work; strong also in its retention of the circuit system, which saves it from the troubles bred in other voluntary churches by the restlessness of congregations which grow weary of hearing the same preacher. The Presbyterian Church is that of the Scotch, here, as everywhere, a thrifty, wise, and powerful clan. The Baptists also maintain their ground by their austere and scriptural purity, though the great principle of which they were the first champions and martyrs, separation of the Church from the State, is no longer in so much need of champions or in any need of martyrs. Amidst the growing indifference about dogma, the question between infant and adult baptism would not in itself be enough to support a church. The Anglican Church in Canada, as in England, may almost be said to be two churches – one Protestant, the other neo-Catholic – under the same roof. The two live in uneasy union, and hard is the part of their bishop. They are held together by a body of laity unspeculative and attached to the Prayer-book. Neo-Catholicism gains ground fast among the clergy; even a college founded by Low Churchmen to stem the movement finds itself turning out High Churchmen. The Mass, the Confessional, the monastic system, Protestants say, are creeping in. Still the English of the wealthier class, whatever their opinions, generally adhere to their old Church: so do the English of the poorest class, who are unused to paying for their religion, and among whom the Anglican clergy are very active. All the Protestant Churches, even that of the Baptists, have relaxed their Puritanism of form and become aesthetic: church architecture, music, flowers, have generally been introduced. The metropolitan church of the Methodists at Toronto is a Cathedral. There is a tendency also in preaching to become lively, perhaps sensational. The most crowded church on Sunday evenings in Toronto is one in which the preacher handles the topics of the day with the freedom of the platform, and amidst frequent applause and laughter. The Church of Rome, of course, stands apart with the Encyclical and Syllabus in her hand waiting till the time for putting them in execution shall arrive. In Ontario she is mainly the church of the Irish, the race which is now nearly her last hope. She does not appear to gain by conversion. She must be gaining, however, in wealth, for her churches and convents continue to rise. Her prelates affect hierarchical state, go about in the insignia of their order, and claim a social rank as princes or nobles of a Universal Church, which the other clergies are now inclined to challenge. In Ontario she has succeeded in obtaining for herself Separate Schools supported by the State. Upon this question also issue is about to be joined. Apart from ecclesiastical pretensions, and the desire to make the child a churchman first and a citizen afterwards, there seems to be no justification for the privilege.

Roman Catholic children attend public schools in the districts where their sect is not numerous enough to claim a division of the rates without the slightest prejudice to their religion. There is no feeling whatever against Roman Catholicism apart from the feeling against priestly domination or aggression, while in politics the Church is only too strong. A Protestant holding high offices has been seen on his knee before a Cardinal. Orangeism itself in Canada is political, not religious: it still carries in its processions the effigy of William of Orange; but it is a bulwark not of Protestantism, but of a Tory Government; and it goes to the poll and eats at the same party-table with the Roman Catholic, and even with the Ultramontane. North America has had no Torquemada or Alexander Borgia, and has not been the scene of priestly persecution or of papal crime.

In the streets of Toronto the drum of the Salvation Army is still heard. Other revivals have for the most part quickly passed away, but this endures. So far at all events it has in it the genuine spirit of Christianity that it points the road to excellence and happiness not through the reform of others, much less through dynamite, blood, and havoc, but through self-reform.

Wherever books find their way criticism and scepticism must now go with them. There is in Toronto an Agnostic circle, active-minded and militant. What is at work in minds beyond that circle nobody can tell. But there is no falling off in the outward signs of religion. Churches are built as fast as the city grows; their costliness as well as their number increases, and they are wonderfully well filled. Sunday is pretty strictly kept, though there is an agitation for Sunday street cars and the strong Sabbatarians have failed to put down Sunday boats. With regard to the whole of the American continent this appearance not only of undiminished but of increased life in the Churches while free inquiry is making inroads, of which those who read cannot help being conscious, on old beliefs, is an enigma which the result alone can solve. Revision of creeds is in the air, and it is probable that among the laity of all the Protestant Churches there has been formed a sort of Christian Theism in which many, without formulating it, repose. The tide of scepticism does not beat so fiercely against Free Churches as against an Establishment. To suppose that all the religion is hollow or mere custom would be absurd. We must conclude that people in general still find comfort in worship. Nor can it be doubted that belief in God and in conscience as the voice of God is still the general foundation of Canadian morality.

With the British are mingled in Ontario a large number of Irish, who, as in the United States and everywhere else, cling to the cities, follow the priest to the third generation, band together, do a great deal of the political as well as of the liquor trade, and cherish a hatred of England not so bitter, at least not so violent in its manifestations, as that which is cherished by their race in the United States. There are also Scotch-Irish, whose ways are those of the Scotch. There is a settlement of Germans in Waterloo County who remain German, and make excellent farmers and citizens, though they would vote against the prohibition of lager. Gaelic is still spoken in Highland settlements. There is a French settlement in Essex county, beside the Detroit river, a relic of the era of old French fur-trading and adventure. Before the fall of slavery Canada was the asylum of the fugitive slave, as was made known to the world by the famous case of Anderson the slave who had killed a man in escaping from bondage, and whose extradition when demanded was refused, or at least evaded, by the Canadian Courts, the Home Government showing its resolution to support Canada in upholding the right of asylum. Hence there are in Canada a number of negroes, of whom some have done well, in spite of the obstacles of race and climate, and one has attained wealth by an invention. There are scatterings of other races, the last arrival being the Italian with his grinding organ and, we hope, without his knife. The increase of wealth and speculation has not failed to attract the Jew, who brings with him his tribal exclusiveness, his tribal code, his tribal ways in trade. If there is a feeling against him here it is not religious, for on the American continent, while open irreligion still gives offence, each man is free in every respect to choose his own religion.

In the Eastern part of the Province, a non-British element of a more ominous kind appears. The French population of Quebec is overflowing that district and has already in two or three counties almost supplanted the British. It introduces its own ecclesiastical system, and imports its own language into the public schools. Opposition has been aroused, and the advance of the French language in the schools has been for the moment checked, but it is difficult to get party politicians to act with vigour against an invader who has the power of turning several elections. The French press on compactly, acting as a unit in their own interest; and it is not likely that the limit of their extension in Ontario has yet been reached.

Nationalities are not so easily ground down in a small community as they are when thrown into the hopper of the mighty American mill. National societies, or societies which partake of the nationalist character, such as the St. George's Society, the Sons of England, the St. Andrew's Society, the Catholic Celtic League, and the Orange Order, are strong, and their strength gives umbrage to those who see in it a detraction from loyalty to the commonwealth. The passion for association is powerful over the whole continent and gives birth, besides the National Societies, the Orange Order, and the Freemasons, to Knights of Pythias, Good Templars, Oddfellows, Knights of the Maccabees, Foresters, Royal Black Knights of Ireland, and other brotherhoods, benevolent and social. High-sounding titles of office and resplendent regalia probably form part of the attraction. On a wide continent, however, without ancient centres or bonds of union, a man would feel almost like a grain in a vast heap of shifting sand if he did not attach himself to some brotherhood. Some of the brotherhoods march through the streets in military array and go through drill. In industrial communities there is a paradoxical union of love of military show and glory with dislike of standing armies and of military service. The Americans have elected four or five soldiers to the Presidency, besides nominating others as candidates, while England has had only two military Prime Ministers, Stanhope, who did not owe his position to achievements in war, and the Duke of Wellington, who was a great European diplomatist and the real head of his political party. The reception of the Canadian Volunteers when they returned from Fish Creek, Cut Knife, and Batoche, eclipsed the reception of the British army when it returned from the Alma and Inkerman.

The respect for law which prevails in all States of the Union on which slavery has not left its taint, and which is the salt of American democracy, prevails not less among British Canadians. It extends to the judges, who, as a body, have well deserved the confidence of the people. When a master of the press who had trampled at his pleasure on the characters and feelings of his fellow-citizens in general assailed a judge whose decision had offended him, he was made at once to feel that opinion was against him and he slunk away. Some time ago a little clan of local desperadoes was lawlessly slain by some of the people whom its outrages had provoked, and the local jury refused to convict the slayers. This is about the only case of the kind, and though deplorable in itself and generally deplored, it was like some of the cases of lynching in the United States, in part a proof not so much of lawlessness as of the general respect for law. Where no rural police is needed, and none consequently is maintained, when brigandage does appear there is no way of dealing with it except through the Vigilance Committee. Justice in all Canadian courts keeps her gown though not her wig, while in the United States the gown is worn by the Judges of the Supreme Court only. The American or Canadian citizen does not need to be impressed so much as the British peasant; but everybody needs to be impressed, and the Canadian custom is the better. Canadian judges are underpaid. One eminent advocate, after taking a seat on the Bench, found his income so much reduced that he returned to the Bar. It is needless to say that this is false economy, and that there can be no expedition of business without a presiding judge of sufficient eminence thoroughly to control his Court. Democracy, though lavish in general expenditure, which it does not count, is niggardly in salaries, which each man compares with his own earnings. Canada, like the United States, has discarded the Old World distinction between barrister and solicitor. Both sorts of work are taken by the same firm. The system of firms saves a barrister at all events from the sadness of waiting year after year in solitary chambers for briefs which do not come.

Canada flatters herself that in her Courts, as in those of England, criminal justice is more prompt and sure than it is in the United States, where such are the chicaneries, the delays, and the weakness of opinion that to get a murderer hanged is very difficult, however certain his guilt may be. It must be owned, however, that in the recent Birchall case we had a display of sensationalism which showed how faint is the boundary which divides our society from the society of the United States.

Toronto is said to be English, and likes to have that reputation. Of the leaders of society some are English by birth, and all of them keep up the connection by going a good deal to England. This habit grows with the shortening of the passage and the cheapness of the sojourn; not with the best results to Canada, for unless the chiefs of society everywhere will remain at their posts and do their duty, the edifice cannot stand. Canadian boys and youths are sometimes sent to the public schools and universities of England, but seldom, it is believed, with good results. What the boy or youth gains by superior teaching he is likely to lose by estrangement from the social and industrial element in which his life is to be spent, and by contracting tastes suitable rather to the mansions of the British gentry than to Canadian homes. English fashion perhaps presses rather heavily on us. We are apt to outvie London in the heaviness of our dinners and the formality with which they are exchanged, and the once pleasant afternoon tea has become a social battue. Mrs. Grundy has too much power. The easy sociability, however, which delights and refreshes is everywhere with difficulty attained. The man who said that others might make the laws of a nation if they would let him make its ballads ought to have bargained also for the making of the games. English games and sports are the fashion in Canada, as indeed they are among the young men of wealth in the United States. Cricket is kept up in face of great difficulties, for in a commercial community men cannot afford to give two days to a game, while Canadian summer scorches the turf, and there are few school playing-fields and no village greens. Baseball, which is the game of the continent, is played in two hours, and requires no turf. Lacrosse is called the Canadian game, but it is Indian in its origin, and some think that to Indians it belongs. Football is also much played, and under the regular English rule, everything being kicked except the ball. In Toronto the red coat of the English fox-hunter is seen, though it is not to be supposed that foxes can be preserved among democratic hen roosts or freely chased over democratic farms. At Montreal, under the theocracy, you may see a real fox chased over fences as stiff as an English fox-hunter could desire. The Turf, the gambling table of England, has its minor counterpart in her colony. Yachting and rowing are popular, and Toronto has produced the first oarsman of the world: unhappily these also have brought betting in their train. The Scotchman keeps up his Scotch love of curling and of golf. Imitations are generally unsuccessful, and it was not likely that an imitation of the British sporting man or anything British would be an exception to the rule. But Anglomania, whatever it may be worth either to the imitators or to the imitated, is as strong among the same class in the United States as it is in Canada. It angers the loyal Republican and draws from him bitter jests. Nor can the rich men of Toronto be fonder of tracing their pedigrees to England than are the rich men of the United States.

A winter of five months or more, during which cattle must be housed, the thermometer falling sometimes to fifteen or twenty below zero; a vast thaw; a joyous rush into bud and leaf, unlike the slow step of English spring; a summer which, after two or three weeks, turns the country from green to brown, ripens the best of apples, in favoured spots peaches, and brings the humming bird; a clear bright autumn – such is Ontario's year. The great lakes temper the extremes in their neighbourhood while they cloud the winter brightness. The stillness of Canadian winter has departed with the sheltering forests. After winter has set in there is generally a recurrence of the warm weather, with a golden haze in the air, which fancy styles Indian summer. Canadians do not wish to have Canada regarded as a winter country, nor do they quite like to see pictures of the toboggan or snow-slide, the snow-shoe, and the ice-boat sent to England as the symbols of their life. It is true, however, that the winter is long, and that a good deal of the pastime is connected with it. To suit the climate a Canadian house ought to be simple in form, so as to be easily warmed, with broad eaves to shed the snow, and a deep veranda as a summer room; and what is suitable is also fair to the eye. But servile imitation produces gables, mansard roofs, and towers, just as fashion clothes Canadian women in Parisian dresses. Canadians are often told by those who wish to flatter them that as a northern race they must have some great destiny before them. But stove heat is not less enervating than the heat of the sun. The Northern tribes which conquered the Roman Empire had no stoves, and they had undergone the most rigorous process of natural selection, both by exposure to frost and by tribal war.

Considering that of all the banks of British Canada not one in the last twenty years has failed to pay its depositors in full, and that only of one have the notes been at a discount, and this only for a few hours, it may safely be said that Canadian commerce is sound. Englishmen who have speculated have lost; especially if their concern was owned on one side of the Atlantic and managed on the other. But those who have invested in known banks or companies have, it is believed, seldom had reason to complain. The banks everywhere, as the great organs of the commercial system, have enemies in the Socialists, who would wreck and plunder them if they could. Governments also everywhere are haunted by the fancy that, because it is their duty to stamp the coin, they have a right to the profits of the money trade, and they are sometimes inclined to legislate accordingly. But their inclination has been hitherto kept within bounds.

Canadian industry can hardly be said to present any special feature, saving that, owing to the severity of the winter, there is more or less of a close season in out-of-door trades, which, with high wages during the rest of the year, must always be trying to industrial character. Industrial questions, trade unionism, its aims and methods, its conflict with capital and free labour, the upheaval of the labour world by strikes, are the same in Canada as in the United States and England. Canada is, in fact, included in the American organisation of the Knights of Labour, which has thus in a way industrially annexed her. Toronto has her anti-poverty society, for the nationalisation of land. She has Socialism more or less pronounced. She has her Socialistic journalists instilling class hatred into the heart of the working man, inciting the "toiler" to an attack on the "spoiler," and blowing the trumpet of industrial war. The storm may be less violent in the bay than on the wide ocean, but it is part of the universal storm.

Toronto was startled at hearing that four per cent of her people had been receiving some kind of relief. Not a few of the recipients probably were new-comers or wanderers, and few were actual paupers. But these cities have lived fast, and the cares and problems of maturity are already upon them. Still they recoil from the idea of a poor law, and indeed from any regular form of public relief. There is a notion that public relief pauperises. The sentiment is to be respected, but that which really pauperises is relief unwisely given, as private charity is too apt to be. What, after all, is free education but a vast system of public relief, though received for the most part by those who are not in need?

City government in Canada presents the same problems which it presents in the United States, and is likely soon to present on the grandest scale in London, now endowed with representative administration. These elective governments of cities are survivals from the Middle Ages, when each city was a little commonwealth in itself, when its rulers were concerned chiefly with the guardianship of franchises and the regulation of trade, when there was little thought of anything sanitary or scientific, when every man was his own policeman, and when, moreover, the city was a social unit, and the chief men lived in the heart of it, took the lead, and were mayors and aldermen. A city is now merely a densely peopled district in special need of scientific administration. Its social unity is gone, and the chief men live in suburban mansions and are above taking part in municipal affairs, while nobody knows the citizens of his street. Combination for the purpose of selecting aldermen is out of the question, and you come by a fell necessity under the rule of the ward politician, which means maladministration, waste, neglect of public health, and too often jobbery and corruption. New York with its Tammany is the climax to which city government of this kind tends. Toronto has no Tammany, and has had no Tweed. But her debt is heavy, and she is just now much exercised by the problem of administration. Even if there is nothing worse, the ephemeral character of a government annually elected, and with the minds of its members always set on re-election, would preclude foresight and system. Spasmodic attempts at reform are made, but their effect dies away. No one looks for a radical change. A board of commissioners, which some propose, would no doubt be a vast improvement; but it would be very difficult to get the people to part to that extent with their power, though they would be amply repaid in assurance of health and comfort, while the power after all really resides not in the people, as they fancy, but in those who manage the elections. Something, however, is being done in the way of a devolution of the aldermanic power on skilled health officers and engineers. Economy there can hardly be where the money and the power of voting it away are in different hands. There is one city on the continent with the administration of which now everybody, at least everybody who has anything to lose, seems to speak with confidence and satisfaction: this is Washington, which as a Federal district is administered by three commissioners appointed by the President of the United States. Washington has a heavy debt, but this was contracted some time ago. The counties are governed by elective councils, with reeves, which have not very much to do or to spend. Against these no complaint is heard. Of provincial legislation and politics there will be something to be said presently in connection with those of the Dominion.

Canada is a political expression. This must be borne in mind when we speak of Canadian Literature. The writer in Ontario has no field beyond his own Province and Montreal. Between him and the Maritime Provinces is interposed French Quebec. Manitoba is far off and thinly peopled. To expect a national literature is therefore unfair. A literature there is fully as large and as high in quality as could be reasonably looked for, and of a character thoroughly healthy. Perhaps a kind critic might say that it still retains something of the old English sobriety of style, and is comparatively free from the straining for effect which is the bane of the best literature of the United States. The area is not large enough to support a magazine, though the attempt has more than once been made. It is hardly large enough to support a literary paper. Ontario reads the magazines of the United States, especially the illustrated magazines in which New York leads the world. Canada has been at a disadvantage alongside of the United States in falling under British copyright law, and also in having her booksellers cut off by the tariff from their natural centre of distribution at New York. To fill an order at once a double duty must be paid. Let it be remembered also that it is difficult for the sapling of Colonial literature to grow beneath the mighty shadow of the parent tree. It is not so long since the United States were without writers of mark. Even now have they produced a great poet?

To make a centre of Art is still harder than to make a literary centre, because art requires models. There can barely be said to be an art centre in the United States. For art, people are likely long to go to Europe. Of millionaires Canada has not many, and such as there are can hardly be expected to give high prices for pictures and statues where they have no connoisseurs to advise them. Ontario, however, has produced a school of landscape painters the merit of which has been recognised in England. For subjects the painter has to go to the Rocky Mountains, the more poetic Selkirks, the magnificent coast-scenery of British Columbia, the towering cliffs of the Saguenay, or the shores and shipping of Nova Scotia and New Brunswick. Ontario has pleasant spots, but little of actual beauty or of grandeur, if we except Thunder Bay, with some other points on the shore of Lake Superior, and the unpaintable Niagara.[1] In a new country there can be few historic or picturesque buildings, so that the painter's landscape must lack historic or human interest. Nor can there be anything like the finished loveliness of England. The gorgeous hues of Canadian autumn and the glories of Canadian sunset are nearly all, and these often reproduced will tire. That the love of beauty and the desire to possess objects of beauty are not wanting, the stranger may learn by a glance at the display in the Toronto stores or at the house architecture of the new streets, which, whether the style be the best or not, unquestionably aspires to beauty and does not always miss its aim. The rows of trees planted along all the streets and the trim little lawns are proof of taste and refinement which cannot fail to please.

Science, as well as literature and art, has its centres in old countries. But from these, unlike literature and art, it can be imported by the student. Medical science is imported into Canada, as is believed, in full perfection. Canadian surgery performs the most difficult operations with success. The traveller who is borne safely on the Canadian Pacific Railroad along the gorges and over the chasms of the Rocky Mountains will acknowledge the skill and daring of the Canadian engineer as he will acknowledge in all details of the service the excellence of Canadian railway administration. In the International Bridge at Buffalo is seen another Canadian achievement. Ontario is a network of railways; probably she has more miles of them in proportion to her population than any other district in the world; and if they pay no dividends on their stock the British capitalist who has been the chief investor may have the satisfaction of thinking how much he has done to promote the material civilisation of a great colony. In the use of agricultural machinery the Province, it has already been said, believes herself to have outrun the mother country. The dearness of labour here, as in

1 Perhaps some of the most picturesque scenery in Ontario is to be found in the Dundas Valley, on the Grand River, and among the Blue Mountains west of Collingwood. Fine is the view from Queenston Heights, looking down the Niagara River to Lake Ontario. The lake scenery in the Muskoka District, and in the region around Peterboro, is also attractive; so is the river scenery at the outlet of Lake Ontario, among the Thousand Islands of the St. Lawrence.

the United States, has stimulated the invention or adoption of its substitutes. The streets of Toronto are a maze of wires, telegraphic and telephonic, and the chief thoroughfares are lit with the electric light. Every office, almost every house, of any pretensions, has its telephone, and converses not only with the rest of the city but with places fifty miles off. In what some people are still pleased to call Canadian wilds life is almost vexed with improvements.

Journalism labours under the same disadvantage as literature in respect to the smallness of the area. With less than two millions of people, with an attainable circulation for any one paper of hardly more than twenty-five thousand, and considering the expense of telegraphic intelligence, how can a provincial press be maintained on a metropolitan scale? In fact, journalism, so far as the morning papers are concerned, has a hard life. It bears up however, and Toronto reads at breakfast time the debates in the British House of Commons of the evening before, looks on as well as the Londoner at all that is going on in the world, and shares in full measure the unification of humanity by the electric wire. The Canadian Press is, in the main, American not English in its character. It aims at the lightness, smartness, and crispness of New York journalism rather than at the solidity of the London *Times*. There is an interchange of writers with New York. Enterprise in the collection of gossip and scandal is now a feature of the press in all countries and everywhere bears the same relation to taste and truth.

Canada, when the value of the connection is under discussion, is always set down as a place where an Englishman can find a home. A sudden change has come over the attitude of the occupants of the American continent on the subject of Emigration. Till lately the portals were opened wide and all the destitute of the earth were bidden to come in. It was the boast of America that she was the asylum of nations. Now the door is half shut, and there are a good many who, if they could, would shut it altogether. Malthus has his day again. The world has grown afraid of being over-peopled. Moreover, the Trade Unions want to close the labour market. They have forced the Canadian Government to give up assisting emigration, and they watch with a jealous eye anything like assistance to emigration on the other side of the water. There is, however, still a demand in Canada for farm labourers, and the labourer if he is steady and industrious will do well and earn wages which in a few years will enable him to own a farm. There is a demand also for domestic servants, if they come prepared to be useful, and not with the notion that a colony is a place of high wages and no work. For teachers or clerks, it has already been said, there is absolutely no room unless they have been engaged beforehand. The Trade Unions declare that there is no room for mechanics and take every one by the throat who says that a good mechanic may still do well. Setting the cost of living against the higher rate of wages, it is doubtful whether a British mechanic improves his lot by coming to Canada. House rent is high, clothes are dear, and a great deal of fuel is required. The difference in the cost of fuel would soon equal the difference between the price of a ticket to Canada and a ticket to New Zealand. One cannot help wondering that a poor man who works out of doors and who does not dream of repeating the exploits of Attila and Clovis should choose a country where the winter is severe.

The notion that an Englishman enjoys a preference in Canada is pleasant, but not well founded. He is rather apt to be an object of jealousy. Anything like favour shown to him gives umbrage. The appointment of three English Professors in Toronto University roused a feeling which lingered long. From the political abuse of England which constantly offends an Englishman in the American Press, and which is largely a homage paid to Irish sentiment, the Canadian Press of course is free; but social allusions may be sometimes seen not of a friendly kind. If the writers are Irish or Socialists, still the allusions appear. The jealousy is, perhaps, a legacy of the times when most of the high places and good things were in the hands of emigrants from the Imperial country.[1] At all events, it has been with truth said that in any candidature no nationality is so weak as the English. In the United States, on the contrary, while there is a traditional prejudice against England, against the individual Englishman there is none. He is perfectly welcome to any

1 A trace of this feeling lingers in a passage embodied in Osgood's *Handbook of the Maritime Provinces.* "The Nova Scotians have not hitherto sought to qualify themselves by culture and study for public honours and preferments because they knew that all the offices in the province would be filled by British carpet-baggers." It is not here only that the term "carpet-bagger" has been seen.

employment or appointment that he can get. However, an Englishman intending to emigrate had better turn his thought first to Australia and New Zealand where there is no prejudice either against him or his country, and the Irish are not so strong. These remarks have reference, of course, only to the emigrant who goes to a colony to push his fortunes in competition with the natives, not to him who goes to live on his own patrimony or the farm which he has bought, seeking nothing beyond. Nor does what has been said apply to Manitoba, and the recent settlements of the North-West. There all alike are newcomers, and no one has to encounter any jealousy or prejudice whatever.

Lord Durham said in his famous Report on Canada: "There is one consideration in particular which has occurred to every observant traveller in these our colonies, and is a subject of loud complaint within the colonies. I allude to the striking contrast which is presented between the American and the British sides of the frontier line, in respect to every sign of productive industry, increasing wealth, and progressive civilisation. By describing one side, and reversing the picture, the other would be also described." That this was so in Lord Durham's day was not the fault of Canadian hands, brains, or hearts. It is not the fault of Canadian hands, brains, or hearts if the contrast, though softened, still exists and is noticed by the stranger who passes from the southern to the northern shore of Lake Ontario and the St. Lawrence, as he compares Windsor, Hamilton, London, Kingston, and even Toronto, with Detroit, Buffalo, Rochester, and Oswego. The cause is the exclusion of Canada from the commercial pale of her continent, and the result would be the same if an equal portion of England were cut off from the rest. The standard of living and of material civilisation is necessarily higher in the wealthier country. Let the traveller make due allowance for this if he misses an air of homelike comfort in a Canadian house or if he does not find luxury in a Canadian country inn.

It has been said that the want of duties, such as country life provides for the rich in England, is felt in Canada; though it is of course not felt nearly so much in a country where millionaires are rare as it is in the United States, where they abound in every great city. Politics unhappily are repulsive, and a man born to independence is not inclined to put his neck under the galling yoke of party;

otherwise the public service would be the natural occupation of the rich. They might still take part in social effort; they might help to keep the press in good hands; they might even exercise a political influence outside party, and corrective of its spirit. As it is, the heirs of wealth on the American continent are too often men of pleasure, spending half their time and money in London or Paris, while as their wealth excites envy they are a dangerous class. But men who have no duty laid upon them will seldom make duties for themselves, and in this sense at least the Gospel is still true, which says that it is easier for a camel to go through a needle's eye than for a rich man to enter into the Kingdom of Heaven.

From British as well as from French Canada there is a constant flow of emigration to the richer country, and the great centres of employment. Dakota and the other new States of the American West are full of Canadian farmers; the great American cities are full of Canadian clerks and men of business, who usually make for themselves a good name. It is said that in Chicago there are 25,000. Hundreds of thousands of Canadians have relatives in the United States. Canadians in great numbers – it is believed as many as 40,000 – enlisted in the American army during the civil war. There is a Lodge of the Grand Army at Ottawa. A young Canadian thinks no more of going to push his fortune in New York or Chicago than a young Scotchman thinks of going to Manchester or London. The same is the case in the higher callings as in the lower: clergymen, those of the Church of England as well as those of other churches, freely accept calls to the other side of the Line. So do professors, teachers, and journalists. The Canadian churches are in full communion with their American sisters, and send delegates to each other's Assemblies. Cadets educated at a Military College to command the Canadian army against the Americans, have gone to practise as Civil Engineers in the United States. The Benevolent and National Societies have branches on both sides of the Line, and hold conventions in common. Even the Orange Order has now its lodges in the United States, where the name of President is substituted in the oath for that of the Queen. American labour organisations, as we have seen, extend to Canada. The American Science Association met the other day at Toronto. All the reforming and philanthropic movements, such as the Temperance movement, the Women's

Rights' movement, and the Labour movements, with their conventions, are continental. Intermarriages between Canadians and Americans are numerous, so numerous as scarcely to be remarked. Americans are the chief owners of Canadian mines, and large owners of Canadian timber limits. The railway system of the continent is one. The winter ports of Canada are those of the United States. Canadian banks trade largely in the American market, and some have branches there. There is almost a currency union, American bank-bills commonly passing at par in Ontario, while those of remote Canadian Provinces pass at par only by special arrangement. American gold passes at par, while silver coin is taken at a small discount: in Winnipeg even the American nickel is part of the common currency. The Dominion bank-bills, though payable in gold, are but half convertible, because what the Canadian banks want is not British but American gold. Canadians go to the American watering-places, while Americans pass the summer on Canadian lakes. Canadians take American periodicals, to which Canadian writers often contribute. They resort for special purchases to New York stores, or even those of the Border cities. Sports are international; so are the Base Ball organisations; and the Toronto "Nine" is recruited in the States. All the New-World phrases and habits are the same on both sides of the Line. The two sections of the English-speaking race on the American continent, in short, are in a state of economic, intellectual, and social fusion, daily becoming more complete. Saving the special connection of a limited circle with the Old Country, Ontario is an American State of the Northern type, cut off from its sisters by a customs line, under a separate government and flag.

The Maritime Provinces, – Nova Scotia, New Brunswick, and Prince Edward Island, – cover, at least the first two of them cover, the area of the old French Acadie, which, submerged by the tide of conquest, shows itself only in the ruined fortifications of Louisbourg, once the Acadian Gibraltar, in remains of the same kind at Annapolis, and in a relic of the French population. The name, with the lying legend of British cruelty connected with it, has been embalmed not in amber, but in barley-sugar, by the writer of

Evangeline.[1] The Maritime Provinces – the cultivable and habitable parts of them at least – lie a thousand miles away from Ontario, with the French Province between. But they are, like Ontario, British colonies, and in the main identical with it in all social and political respects. Allowance has only to be made, in the cases of Nova Scotia and New Brunswick, for less of farming and more of mining, of shipping, and, in proportion, of lumbering. Prince Edward Island is a farming community with rich lands, almost cut off from the mainland in winter, insular in character, keeping in the ancient paths, and well satisfied with itself. Nova Scotia has a source of wealth specially her own, in her rich mines of bituminous coal. She is also a great fruit-growing country, and Burke would not have called her "a hard-featured brat," at least he would have confined his epithet to her Atlantic front, if he had been eating Annapolis apples. Halifax and St. John are the two winter ports of the Dominion. The harbour of St. John, the tide being here strong, is always open; the magnificent basin of Halifax is very seldom closed. To society at Halifax the presence of the garrison and the squadron lend a military and naval hue.

The newly-opened region of the North-West is as far from Ontario as Italy is from England, while it forms an integral part of the great prairie region to which belong Minnesota and Dakota. It now embraces the province of Manitoba and the districts of Alberta, Athabasca, Assiniboia, and Saskatchewan, carved out of the North-West, and administered as Territories on a system borrowed from the American Constitution. The North-West was the vast hunting-ground of the Hudson's Bay Company, and the field of a singular and noble service, the members of which passed a great part of their lives in lonely arctic posts far away from civilisation and human intercourse, save with wild Indians, getting one mail from England in the year, yet losing nothing of their character as highly

1 Lieut.-Governor Sir Adams Archibald, Mr. Parkman, and Dr. Kingsford have completely disposed of this fiction, and shown that the deportation of the Acadians was a measure of necessity, to which recourse was had only when forbearance was exhausted. The blame really rests on the vile and murderous intrigues of the priest Le Loutre. The commander of the troops, Winslow, was an American.

civilised men. The Company was one of that great group formed in the early days of commercial adventure, most of which outlived their usefulness and have now quitted the scene, but without the support of which, in an age when the globe was unexplored, when international law was hardly known, when piracy and brigandage were rife, when on barbarous shores the trader could look only to his fellow-trader for protection, commerce would scarcely have ventured to put off into the unknown. That the Company should try to keep its hunting-ground intact and bar out settlement from it, by representing it as unfit for cultivation, was no more than might have been expected. The region is a series of vast steppes. It is a sensation not to be forgotten which you experience as, standing upon the platform of the railway car on the road from St. Paul, you shoot out upon that oceanic expanse of prairie, purple with evening, while an electric light perhaps shines on the horizon like a star of advancing civilisation. What is the extent of the fertile land in the North-West, and how great are the capabilities of the region is hardly yet known, but it is known that they are vast. The balance wavered at first between the fertility of the soil on one hand, and the rigour of the climate on the other. The discovery of abundant fuel was required to turn the scale, and coal in abundance, though not of the first quality, has been found. The wheat is the very best, the root crops and vegetables are superb. The enemies of the farmer are the late and early frosts. The grasshopper, another old enemy, has hardly appeared in force since the settlement. Just before harvest time the weather is no commonplace topic, and a deep anxiety broods over the land. More than once the hope of a rich harvest has been blighted. It is idle to deny that the summer is short. But the yield is so abundant that fat years make up for lean years. Experience will teach its lessons, and already the farmer is learning not to trust too much to wheat-growing, but to mix with it the keeping of cattle, which, notwithstanding the cold, are said to do well. The prairie grass turns to a natural hay, which furnishes winter food. In summer nothing can be balmier or more life-giving than the prairie air, nothing more charming than the prairie gay with flowers. In winter the glass falls sometimes to forty below zero, or even lower, but the people tell you that the cold is not felt because it is dry; perhaps also because all the settlers there being young, their blood is warm. If they do not want the thread of aged lives to be cut by the winter's shears they will have to build solid houses, for which happily, in Manitoba at least, they have good building stone and brick. Not to feel the cold in a wooden shanty, with the snow driving through its chinks in forty below zero, blood must be warm indeed. Emigrants should not go to the North-West without the means of providing themselves with good houses, warm clothes, and fuel. This region, however, does not, like Minnesota, lie in the zone of blizzards. It might have been thought that on the prairie, where agricultural machines have full swing, in a climate where close dwelling has advantages, material and social, large farming would, if anywhere, have succeeded, while its success might have been the inauguration of a new industrial and social system. But on the Bell Farm it was tried in the ablest hands, and did not pay. It seems that nothing will make farming pay but the sweat of the owner's brow and the closeness of the owner's fist. Winnipeg shows by the mixture of rough shanties with buildings of a better class and some of the highest class, that she rose but yesterday out of the prairie. She has only just recovered from the demoralisation of commerce by "the boom," a wild burst of gambling in real estate which raged at her birth and drew to her a loose population. But as the centre of distribution, of government, of law, of education, and above all of railways, she can hardly fail to thrive. If Manitoba and the rest of the region fill up slowly, the fault lies, as will hereafter appear, not in anything that nature has failed to do, but in things which man has done. In situation Brandon is superior to Winnipeg. The dead level of the prairie line is broken, and there is a general cheerfulness in the landscape which cradles the thriving young town. The journey seems long over a steppe monotonous as the sea, and with a horizon equally level, to Calgary, where you find yourself in the ranch country, undulating and park-like, with the range of the Rockies full in view.

The immigration has been of a motley sort, and not all of the kind which forms the best material for a new community. The Mennonites work very hard, are thrifty, and will no doubt give up their exclusiveness and become citizens in time, since military service, conscientious dislike of which was the ground of their isolation, has no existence in their new home. The Icelanders, used to such a climate, do well. The Skye crofters have hardly been farmers; they are children of a mild though damp climate; and it was not to be expected that their settlements would look more prosperous than they do. It is lucky that the idea of importing Irish and planting them in shanties over a large district was given up. The Irish are not farmers; they are spade husbandmen, who have hardly handled a plough and have never seen a machine. Nor are they pioneers. Their hearts would have sunk in the solitude, and they would have gone off to their kinsmen in the United States. Young Englishmen as a class have not done well; they have energy and pluck, but not steady industry, self-denial, or the habit of saving. The jesters of the North-West call "remittances from home" the Englishman's harvest. Of a good many the Mounted Police is the last haven. What the North-West needs is the floating population of the continent, farmers to the manner born. To send East-Londoners, who have hardly seen a plough, to the climate and the life of the North-West, is cruel kindness, and so it has proved.

If the North-West fills up, Old Canada will be dwarfed, and, supposing Confederation to endure, the centre of power will shift westward, though the loss by Ottawa of all control over the North-West is perhaps the more likely result.

British Columbia again is separated from the North-West by a triple range of mountains, the Rockies, the Selkirks, the Golden or Coast range, in traversing which the Pacific Railway proclaims the glory of Canadian science. This Province is the Pacific slope of the mountain range, clothed with pine of the noblest size, though not deemed equal in quality to that of Nova Scotia, but hardly within reach of the lumberman except on the lower fringe. Her flora is Pacific, so completely does she belong to that side of the world. Of unwooded land British Columbia has not much, while clearing, where the timber is so heavy, would be too costly; but she has coal at Nanaimo, she has plenty of salmon for canning, and she is understood to be very rich in minerals. There is a project for opening her mineral wealth by a railway carried through the mountain region in concert with the American government. Her climate is warm compared with that of other provinces in the same latitude, and she has an open though damp and raw winter. The vegetation is tropical, not in variety, but in luxuriance. Nothing can be more impressive than a ride in the forest, through the vast and silent arcade of pines and cedars, so gigantic that they almost shut out the sky. The coast scenery, with views of the American Snow mountains, is superb, though one might wish that the "Olympian Range" had a less pedantic name.[1] Vancouver is the leading port of British Columbian commerce. She hopes to have a great Asiatic trade and become a mighty city. Land is accordingly held in that city at fabulous prices, which those will pay who share the gorgeous dream. Victoria sleeps in beauty over her little pile of earnings from the gold-washings and from the trade of early days. Her cottage villas with their rose gardens have an English look, and she prides herself on being English in character and spirit. As she is on an island where the railway cannot reach her there seems to be not much chance of her reawakening to any active commercial life. The most lively thing about her at present is the Chinese Colony, where we come into contact with the advance guard of that countless host which, bar it out with laws and poll-taxes on immigration as you will, hunger driving it on and capital craving for its cheap labour, can hardly be arrested in its march, and may some day possess the coast of the Pacific.

It is in the North-West and in British Columbia that the Red Indian is now chiefly to be seen; for among those on the Eastern Reserves there is little of the pure blood. The race, every one says, is doomed. It has fallen into the gulf between the hunter state and that of the husbandman. Whisky has contributed to its ruin. The sudden disappearance of the buffalo, which is the most surprising event in natural history, has deprived the hunter of subsistence. Little will be lost by humanity. The Red Indian has the wonderful powers of enduring hunger and fatigue which the hunter's life engenders; he has the keenness of sense indispensable in tracking game: he seems to have no other gift. Ethnologists may find it instructive to study a race without a history and without a future; but the race will certainly not be a factor in New World civilisation. Musical Indian names of places and rivers, Indian relics in museums, Indian phrases, such as "going on the warpath" and "burying the hatchet" – these and nothing more apparently will remain of the aboriginal man in North America. His blood is not on the head of the British Government, which has always treated him with humanity and justice.

1 Canadian and American mountains have often names too prosaic. Peaks, instead of being called, like Swiss peaks, the Storm peak, the Silver peak, the Peak of Thunder, the Maiden, are called after railway directors and politicians.

Chapter 4

French Canada before the conquest

Jacques Cartier, the discoverer / Champlain, the founder of Quebec / Coming of the Jesuits / Their missions, heroic exploits, and relations with the Indian tribes / Ursuline convents and hospitals / Aims of the Jesuits / Their rule / Moral decadence of the Order / Foundation of Montreal / The Sulpicians and their relations to the Jesuits / Failure of Quebec as a colony / Epoch of Louis XIV / Royal administration extended to the colony / Colbert's commercial system and the Intendant Talon / The fur trade / Bushranging / Passion for exploration, and feats of discoverers / Abuses under Louis XV / The parish clergy / Moral state of the colony / Contrast between the French and English colonists / The Conquest

The principal sources of this and the following historical sketch, besides the *Relations des Jesuites* and Le Clercq's *L'Éstablissement de la Foi,* are Mr. Parkman's narratives, and the histories of Garneau, Christie, Miles, MacMullen, and Kingsford, with Cavendish's Debates in the British House of Commons, in 1774.

JACQUES CARTIER, though venerated as the founder of the French Colony, was only the discoverer of the St. Lawrence (1535). He made trial of the climate by wintering at Quebec, where he lost many of his crew by cold, hunger, and scurvy, and he opened relations with the Indians in a rather sinister way by kidnapping a chief with three of his tribe. But he formed no permanent settlement: Roberval, his contemporary and successor in the enterprise, totally failed. The real founder of Canada did not appear on the scene until seventy years after. This was Samuel de Champlain (1603-35), one of that striking group of characters to which the sixteenth century gave birth, and which combined the force, hardihood, and romance of feudalism with the larger views and higher objects of the Reformation era. The man would have been a crusader in the thirteenth century who in the sixteenth was a maritime adventurer and the founder of a colony. Champlain, though it does not appear that he ever was of the Reformed faith, and though he ultimately became connected with the Jesuits, had fought for Henry IV, and must therefore have belonged to the more liberal and patriotic party of Roman Catholics. At this time there was beginning to be an exodus of Huguenots to New France, like that of the persecuted Puritans to New England, which came a few years afterwards. Henry IV seems to have encouraged the movement, seeing perhaps how the tide was running in France and guessing what was in store, when his protection should have been withdrawn, for the party to which he had belonged. Had New France been colonised by Huguenots, bringing with them the energy, the industry, the intelligence, and the love of freedom which marked them in their own country, New England would have had a formidable rival, and to the French, not to the English race and tongue the American continent might now belong. French writers look back with a wistful eye to the glory that might have been. As it was, Quebec, with France herself and everything belonging to her, fell into the hands of the Catholic Reaction, and of its incarnation and apostle the Jesuit. The Jesuit of course devoutly excluded the Huguenot, carefully searching vessels lest they should have brought over any one tainted with the pestilence of heresy. Not only did he exclude the Huguenot, but as far as possible he excluded the Jansenist. By this he did the Colony incomparably more harm than he ever, by his boasted activity as a civiliser and educator, did it good. In fact, during the early stages of its history, while it remained under Jesuit domination, it was not a colony at all. It was a Jesuit mission grafted on a station of the fur trade.

The Jesuit missionaries, who came to the settlement in 1625, did for the glory of God and of their Order things which have found in our own day a brilliant and sympathetic chronicler. Our accounts of their exploits are derived from "Relations," written by themselves and published in France, for the purpose of exalting the name of the Order, exciting sympathy with it, and opening the purses of the devout, all of which purposes, not excepting the last, they effectually served. Nor is it possible to put unreserved confidence in the narratives of men the most sensible of whom lived in an atmosphere of miracle, divine and diabolical, saw demons aiming darts at them, received supernatural warnings, and beheld fiery crosses traversing the sky. Yet there can be no doubt that Jesuitism had in New France its heroes and its martyrs. It had martyrs who, with a fortitude which nothing but sincere enthusiasm could have sustained, braved the perils and hardships of the wilderness, endured the worse horrors of life in the Indian hut, and underwent without flinching at the hands of the Iroquois tortures equal physically at least to those which their European brethren were inflicting, or causing to be inflicted, on heretics in the dungeons of the Inquisition. These were at all events victories of the higher over the lower man. It was certain that the Order would draw into it at first some pure enthusiasts; and it was likely that these would wish to go, and would by the policy of the Order be sent, rather to the missionary field than to that of European propagandism and intrigue. Jesuitism is redeemed by its missionary element impersonated in Xavier and Breboeuf. It was their own version of Christianity of course that the Sons of Loyola taught. Perhaps it was a Christianity in some respects not uncongenial to the Indian. "You burn your enemies," said a Jesuit to an Algonquin chief, "and God does the same." In the pictures of lost souls tormented by demons which were presented to them, the Indian might see his own practices ascribed to the Supreme Being. An Indian woman whom the Fathers were trying to convert, refused to be sent to Heaven when they had told her that her dead children were in Hell. Nor can their philosophic eulogist forbear smiling at the frivolity, not to say fetichism, of some of their religious ideas and practices. The missionaries are always looking out with peculiar eagerness for dying children whom, by baptism, in the furtive administration of which rather equivocal stratagems are sometimes employed, they send, as they think, straight from Hell to Paradise. Their thaumaturgy might justify the Indian in calling them, as he did, the French medicine men.

In spite of all the self-devotion of the Fathers and all their heroism, their missions came almost to naught. They had the misfortune to be confronted by the Iroquois, of all Red Indians and of all savages the most valiant, the most politic, and the most fiendish. Champlain, by allying himself with the Huron enemies of the Iroquois, rashly stirred the terrible swarm. By the Iroquois the Hurons, among whom the Jesuits had planted their missionaries and made converts, were overthrown, and in 1649 utterly destroyed. To a Huron it naturally appeared hard that this should be the reward of allegiance to the true God; nor does it seem impossible that by the change the convert may have lost something of the warlike character necessary to save him in the ruthless struggle for existence. A few of the Iroquois themselves were afterwards converted, and the descendants of such converts, under the name of the Caughnawagas, steer the tourist down the Lachine rapids to Montreal. Mr. Parkman gives the Jesuit credit for having by contact softened the manners of the Indians generally; but this seems hardly consistent with his own statements that the Fathers connived at the torture of prisoners by their Indian converts, and that when the Jesuits had become, as in course of time they did, more political than missionary, the converts were launched in scalping parties against the colonists of New England.

The palm of religious heroism must be shared by the Jesuits with the Ursulines. The "Relations" of the Jesuits had fired the hearts of devout women in France with the same missionary enthusiasm, mingled, as the historian fails not to see, with a yearning for personal distinction. These women performed miracles as hospital nurses and as angels of charity in the struggling and suffering settlements, while they were props of a system under which the Colony could hardly be anything but a hospital and an almshouse. A hospital was founded at Montreal, to afford a theatre for the religious activity of these ladies, before there was any need of one, and when the money and the labour were sorely required for other purposes by a settlement feebly struggling for existence. Marie de l'Incarnation seems to have rivalled St. Catherine or St. Theresa in the intensity of her self-devotion, in her erotic transports, and in all that is most characteristic of a female saint. Jeanne le Ber, another saint, was the Simeon Stylites of her sex: she shut herself up for twenty years in a cell behind the altar, rarely speaking, and inflicting on herself incredible mortifications. This might be seraphic, but it was not a practical model for the settler's wife.

If the heroic efforts of the Jesuit as missionary were baffled by adverse circumstances, as the organiser of a colony he failed through the inherent and fatal falsity of his ideal. His object, as he avowed, was to make Quebec a Northern Paraguay, in other words, a community of human sheep absolutely devoted and submissive to their ecclesiastical shepherd. But human sheep are not colonial pioneers. Nor was the ascetic view of the world or the palm held out to self-torturing saintship likely to stimulate the agricultural or commercial effort necessary to place a colony on a sound material basis. The Puritans of New England, it has been justly observed, however austere and however narrow might be their religion, believed in a Giver of material as well as spiritual blessings, and in the material as well as in the spiritual sphere laboured with all their might to carry into effect the Divine intention. To make a Paraguay, moreover, it was necessary that the temporal and spiritual powers should be united in the hands of the priest. To bring this about was in New France, as everywhere else, the Jesuit's constant aim. With the help of devout Governors he to a great extent succeeded, and the result was that petitions were sent to France praying "that an end might be put to the Gehenna produced by the union of the temporal with the spiritual power." The moral code under Jesuit rule was Genevan in its rigour as well as ultra-ecclesiastical in its formality. For breach of its ordinances men were whipped like dogs. It was enforced, as was complained at the time, not only by the confessional, but by a system of espionage which made the Jesuit master of all family secrets and tyrant of all households. To the Jesuit his Canadian realm seemed a spiritual Paradise and the Gate of Heaven, albeit the blessed souls in it lived in constant peril of famine and of the tomahawk. But it seemed by no means a Paradise to some untamed spirits, whose energy as pioneers, though unhallowed, the Colony perhaps could ill afford to lose. These fled from it to the free life of the forest, and became as bushrangers the perpetual scandal of the Government. A genuine and great service was done by the priests in opposing the brandy trade, which was playing havoc among the Indians, and we need not regard the insinuation of a governor with whom they had quarrelled, that they wished themselves to engross the profits of the trade. It is probable, however, that before its fall, the Order had become not only political but commercial in Quebec, as it had in Europe, where the scandalous bankruptcy of one of its commercial houses was among the immediate causes of its suppression. One of the governors at least reports that it was getting the fur trade into its hands. It shared the inevitable fate of all the Orders, which, beginning with a seraphic ideal and a renunciation of all worldly goods, fell from their unattainable aim into corporate ambition, pursuit of inordinate wealth, and a corruption which, contrasted with their professions, brought on them hatred, contempt, and at last the whirlwind of destruction.

Quebec, the Paradise of the Jesuits, had a competitior and an object of jealousy in Montreal, founded in 1642 by Maisonneuve, whose figure belongs to the same group as that of Champlain, though he was more of a religious devotee. Montreal was under the influence of the Sulpicians, a branch of whose Order, the Recollets, had preceded the Jesuits in the Canadian Mission. Quebec accused Montreal of Jansenism and received with a slight sneer of incredulity Montreal miracles, even when they were so little trying to a child-like faith as that of the man's head which talked after being severed from the body. Sulpicianism, on the other hand, spoke with delicate irony of the Jesuit Relations, and insinuated a comparison between them and the tales of the East Indian traveller who made a valiant soldier, when he had fired away his last bullet, load his musket with his own teeth. After the lapse of two centuries and a half this battle between Jesuit and Sulpician, Ultramontane and Gallican, has been renewed.

As an agricultural or commercial settlement New France remained a failure, its only trade being the fur trade, while the Iroquois incessantly prowled around it like wolves and picked off the tillers of the fields who worked with the loaded arquebuse by their sides. The Home Government generally had its hands full of home troubles and distractions, while such aid as was sent from private sources was sent not to the colony but to the mission.

Richelieu, when engaged in reorganising the monarchy on the centralising principle, did not fail to turn his thoughts to the colony. He reformed the Constitution of the Commercial Company, which was in fact its only government other than the priesthood, and sent it soldiers, though in numbers wholly inadequate to its defence. But then came the troubles of the Fronde. When these were past, and over the wreck of feudal independence rose in all its might and glory the administrative despotism of Louis XIV, a dead-lift effort was made to inspire life, after the autocratic fashion, into the colony, and make it the starting-point of a French and Catholic empire which, extinguishing the English and Dutch colonies, should embrace the whole of the continent. The regiment of Carignan-Salières was sent out in 1665 and repressed the Iroquois, while a not less potent agency in the salvation of the Settlement was the advent, as governor, of Frontenac, the Clive of Quebec. By the side of the plumed governor, who, like the governors of provinces in France represented the feudal aristocracy surviving in its state and in its military character under the king, though shorn of its political and military power, came in less showy costume the Royal Intendant, to whom in all administrative matters the power had been transferred. The Intendant Talon was a colonial Colbert – able, active, and upright like his chief; and, like his chief, he did all that could be done under the radically false system of monopoly and protectionism to animate and foster trade. To recruit the population, which between asceticism and the Iroquois was at a very low ebb, large consignments of young women were shipped out by despotic fiat from France, and marriage was encouraged in the same style by means of premiums on offspring and penalties on celibacy. Feudalism, such as it was in France since its teeth had been drawn by the Monarchy – feudalism, that is not political or military but only manorial – was imported into the colony as the land system of the French realm; and a number of seigniories were carved out under which the settlers held their lands as *censitaires*, like the copyholders under an English manor, though with the feudal forms of investiture instead of entry on the court roll. The militia was kept in the hands of a king's officer, and the criminal jurisdiction of the seignior was very small. Some of the feudal incidents, such as the obligation to use the lord's mill and oven, must have been almost a dead letter; but there was an oppressive fee to the lords on sales. So much of democracy there was on the American soil even under Bourbon rule that the peasant would brook no name that savoured of villeinage, but styled himself the *habitant*. The colony was also endowed with a *noblesse* formed out of rather sorry materials, such as the disbanded officers of the Carignan regiment and plebeian settlers whose vanity led them to buy social rank. The result, as plainly appears and might have been surely foreseen, was not a genuine aristocracy, but a false caste of insolence, idleness, and vagabondage, though the genius of the New World so far asserted itself that the colonial gentleman, unlike the gentleman of the mother country, was permitted without loss of rank to engage in trade.

In New as in Old France the despotism was absolute. The Supreme Council which was instituted at this time (1663), and ousted the Commercial Company from all political power, was only another name for the rule of the Royal Governor, of the Intendant, and in matters ecclesiastical of the Bishop. The Intendant by his decrees regulated not only the police but commercial and civil life. Of the local self-government, which formed the soul and the hope of New England, not a germ was allowed to appear. One Governor conceived the idea of providing the colony with a miniature counterpart of the States-General; but he was at once given to understand that the Court, far from wishing to extend the venerable institution to the colonies, was disposed to regard it as obsolete at home. It is needless to say that no organ or expression of public opinion was allowed. The colony was of course under the French criminal law, with its arbitrary imprisonment and judicial torture.

Louis XIV, albeit devout, and more devout than ever when he had fallen under the influence of the Maintenon, still meant to be King of the Church as well as of the State. He had not even shrunk, when his royal dignity was in question, from bullying the Pope. Relations were somewhat strained between the representatives of the Royal power and the head of the Church, Bishop Laval. This prelate, whose name is still great in French Canada and is borne by the Laval University, was the paragon of asceticism in his day. He lay on a bed full of vermin; he ate tainted meat; the wonder is that he escaped canonisation. He was a fast ally of the Jesuits, and a champion of the doctrines which they then preached and are now again preaching on the same field respecting the supremacy and infallibility of the Pope, the independence and liberty of the Church, and the duty of the

State to submit to the Church in case of any conflict between them.[1] Laval, who particularly prided himself on his humility, had frequent disputes with the Governors about precedence, in which the Governors showed more spirit than is shown by politicians when threatened with ecclesiastical displeasure at the present day. They said to the churchman in effect, like their precursor Poutrincourt, "It is your business to obey me on earth and to guide me to heaven." A curb, and a strong curb, was legally imposed on the Episcopal power and ambition by the Royal ordinance, which decreed that the tenure of the *curés* should be fixed, as in France, and that they should be no longer removable at the Bishop's will.

It is needless to say that Monopoly and Protectionism failed to give new life to industry and commerce. Decrees forbidding merchants to trade with the Indians, forbidding them to sell goods at retail except in August, September, and October, forbidding trade anywhere above Quebec, forbidding the sale of clothing or domestic articles ready-made, forbidding trade with the New England Colonies, that is with the natural market, forbidding any one to go there without a passport – decrees giving a monopolist company power to make domiciliary visits for the discovery and destruction of foreign goods, ordering that vessels engaged in foreign commerce should be treated as pirates, and that every one found with an article of foreign manufacture in his possession should be fined[2] – with other like ordinances, produced the same sort of results which similar policy, pursued by men less excusable in error than Colbert and Talon, is now producing in the same field. Nor could exclusion from the natural market be compensated in those days any more than in these by the creation of a forced market in the West Indies or elsewhere. An attempt of the beneficent King to speed the plough by the introduction of negro slavery had no better success, being baffled at once by the climate. The colony made nothing and produced nothing except beaver skins, to be exported to France in payment for the supplies of all kinds which it drew thence. It was consequently bankrupt, coin fled from it, giving place to bad paper, and at last to card money. Even the trade in beaver skins was so

1 See Parkman's *Old Régime in Canada*, p. 166, where the Jesuit Father Braun is cited.

2 Parkman's *Old Régime*, p. 290.

bedevilled by monopoly and government regulation that at one time the company destroyed three-fourths of the stock on their hands to avert a glut. In the fur trade, however, was such life as the colony had apart from the activity of the clergy. Into this were drawn all those who preferred the freedom of the forest to the paternal despotism of the Intendant and the priest. A strange and wild life it was. The bushrangers (*coureurs des bois*) threw off civilisation, lived with the Indians, intermarried with them, learned Indian habits, became more than half Indians themselves, and sometimes were made chiefs of Indian tribes. They took to warpaint and feathers. They took even to scalping, and were in consequence treated by Wolfe as out of the laws of war. They regarded themselves, however, as gentlemen, and it is said that some of the best families in Quebec are descended from this stock.

Closely connected with the spirit of this roving life was the adventurous passion for discovery, which reached its climax in the marvellous exploration of the Mississippi by La Salle. As explorers the French were not less superior to the staid and plodding New Englander than they were inferior to him in industry, commerce, and the qualities requisite for building up a commonwealth. To the Jesuit missionaries, too, is due the credit of wonderful exploration, notably on the Upper Lakes. It was natural also that in the magnificence of their schemes, military and territorial, the French should have the pre-eminence. With no other basis than a settlement of a few thousands of people on the St. Lawrence they aspired to the extension of their Empire by a chain of military posts westward to the Mississippi and down its whole course to New Orleans. In their vaulting ambition the men of New France were true Frenchmen.

Supposing a despotic administration to be inspired by probity and beneficence, its eye cannot see nor can its arm reach across the Atlantic. Colbert meant very well to the colony, and even his King meant well. But after Louis XIV and Colbert came Louis XV and the Regency, Pompadour and Dubois. Then began in the unhappy dependency a reign of unbridled corruption and abuse. Peculation and extortion to an enormous extent were carried on by a gang of officials, at the head of which was the Intendant Bigot, whose chateau near Quebec was a sort of outpost of the Parc aux Cerfs. It is astonishing that, vexed as they were with imposts, pillaged as they were by scoundrels in office, and harassed as they were by compulsory service in the militia and on public works, the peasants of Quebec should have remained true as they did to their King and to France. Pompadour was not so hostile as Maintenon to Huguenots, and would not have opposed their settling in New France. But the Huguenot was now extinct; in his place had come Voltaire.

The historian bespeaks our sympathy and admiration, not only for the missionary, but for the parish priest, who went about through the sparse settlements of a wild peasantry, along the inhospitable shore, performing Mass, baptising, confessing, and preaching, in defiance of great hardship and no small peril. These men, no doubt, after the downfall of asceticism, kept alive such religion and such morality as there was. But of morality there seems in the closing days of the colony to have been as little as there was of industry or trade. The soldiery, the bushrangers, the fur trade and its roystering fairs, the association with the Indians, the habits and examples of Pompadourian Intendants, appear by their united agencies of corruption to have morally ruined the Northern Paraguay. Of education there had never been any except that which the Jesuits gave to the boys destined for the priesthood, or to the sons of the few people of quality. French gaiety remained; so, we are told, did the polish of French manners, and the Colonists, we are also told, spoke French well.

The French colonist, however, if he was backward in the arts of peace was not to be despised in war. This he showed in the long conflict with the English colonies and their mother country which fills the closing period of this history. The very absence of industrial and commercial pursuits preserved the military character. The bushranger was the best of bushfighters and could act in perfect unison with his savage comrade the Red Indian. The New Englanders, though they came of the Ironside blood and had the making of the best soldiers in them, were not soldiers, but traders and mechanics. Wolfe speaks very disparagingly of his Colonial Rangers. The first capture of Louisbourg by a Colonial army supported only by a British fleet was a stroke of luck, due to the mutinous state of the garrison and the weakness of the Commandant. Moreover the English colonies were divided in their councils: they had with the independence and self-reliance the stiff-neckedness of republicans, and the weakness in joint action which it entails. It was very hard to bring each colony to take its part in any common enterprise or furnish its contingent to any common force. The French, on the other hand, were united under the absolute command of the Royal Governor, who could call them all to arms and dispose of everything they had for the King's service. Nor were the French nobles, by whom the governorship was held, ill-fitted for the military part of their work. Frontenac especially was a man of great genius for war as well as of iron character; he left a name dreaded by the English Colonists and renowned in Canadian history, though sullied by his murderous employment of the savage; not that anybody abstained from the use of this vile auxiliary, whose subsequent introduction into the revolutionary war by the British was not the horrible innovation which rhetoric painted it, though assuredly it was a crime as well as a blunder. Superior as they were in population and in wealth, the English colonies might have been lost had they not been united, as far as they were capable of union, and supported by their mother country. As soon as her arm, after a long and desperate struggle, had laid low their formidable rival and assured their safety, she was made to feel what had been their real tie to her.

The conquest of Quebec is familiar to all; and has been narrated by Mr. Parkman in the two most charming volumes, perhaps, even of his charming series. If he fails in anything, perhaps it is in not perfectly painting the character of Wolfe, one of the most interesting, if not one of the most important or dazzling, figures in military history. Near the famous battle-field on which the steadiness of the British soldier, reserving his fire for the decisive volley while his comrades were falling fast around him, determined that to his race, not to the French, should belong the New World and its hopes, stands the monument raised by the victor to the joint memory of Wolfe and Montcalm. The warlike aristocracy of France and the military duty of England could not have encountered each other in more typical forms. Voltaire, more philosopher and philanthropist than patriot, celebrated by a feast the transfer of New France from the realm of despotism to that of freedom. Mr. Parkman says: "A happier calamity never befell a people than the conquest of Canada by the British arms."

Chapter 5

French Canada after the conquest (1759)

What was to be done with Quebec? / The question settled by the American Revolution / Military rule / British concessions to the conquered people preserve their allegiance during the American invasion / The Quebec Act / Incoming of royalist refugees from the American colonies, and formation of an oligarchy of conquest / With the French Revolution comes a resettlement of Quebec / Policy of Pitt / Attempt to separate the races by dividing the colony into a French and a British Province / Failure of that attempt / Political conflict between the two races in Lower Canada under the Parliamentary Constitution / Want of information and of decision on the part of the Home Government / British rule an improvement on French rule / War of 1812 / The French Canadians again faithful to Great Britain / Renewal of civil strife after the war / Ineffectual mission of Lord Gosford / Rebellion breaks out and is suppressed / End of the Constitution / Military opinion as to the value of Canada as a dependency

QUEBEC HAD been won. What was to be done with it? The highest wisdom said, "Add it to the New England Colonies by which it will soon be assimilated, and leave the whole independent, content with the Empire of British civilisation over the New World, and with the moral supremacy which the mother country, provided the filial tie remains unbroken, is sure to retain." Cromwell had meditated giving the Colonies Jamaica. But such a policy was beyond the ken of the statesmen of that day, and few even among the calmest observers had any conception of it. We must remember, moreover, that in times before Adam Smith a distant dependency seemed to everybody to have real value inasmuch as the Imperial country monopolised its trade. Still the question remained whether Quebec should be left French and governed as a conquest or made English. That question was settled by the American Revolution, which compelled the Imperial Government to court the French of Quebec and respect their nationality. That a revolt of the American colonies would follow when the curb of French rivalry had been removed was surmised by clear-sighted men at the time, albeit it would be hard to accuse England of blindness, because she failed to foresee that the requital of her supreme effort on behalf of her American colonists would be their secession. Mr. Samuel Adams and the rest of the Boston counterparts of Wilkes and Horne Tooke, who fomented the quarrel till it became revolution and civil war, should have had a little patience and waited till Quebec had been not only conquered but made English. To make her English as she then was would not have been hard. Her French inhabitants of the upper class, had, for the most part, quitted her after the conquest and sailed with their property for France. There remained only 70,000 peasants, to whom their language was not so dear as it was to a member of the Institute, who knew not the difference between codes so long as they got justice, and among whom, harsh and abrupt change being avoided, the British tongue and law might have been gradually and painlessly introduced.

While the war lasted, and for a short time afterwards, the government was military, and the ultimate policy of the British Government with regard to the conquered Province was in suspense. That the government should at first be military was inevitable, and French writers who speak of this with indignation must remember what was the conduct of the House of Bourbon or of the French

Republic to countries overrun by their armies. They should remember the plan which was sanctioned by Louis XIV for the treatment of New York in case it should be conquered, and according to which Protestantism would have been uprooted, all property confiscated, the inhabitants generally deported, and those who remained put to convict labour on the fortifications.

The Americans called upon the Canadians to join them in their revolt. But the Canadians had already begun to taste the fruits of the Conquest. They had been released from the vexations of constant military service and allowed to till their farms. Their religion had been respected to a greater extent even than was required by the terms of the Treaty of Cession. Not only were the parish clergy left in possession of their tithes, but the religious orders also, saving the anti-national Jesuits, had been left in possession of their estates. Bourbon despotism and corruption had departed. Instead of arbitrary tribunals, trial by jury had been introduced, though the *habitant* at first hardly understood the boon, while the Seignior thought it a derogation from his ragged dignity to be judged by shopkeepers and peasants. The Puritans, or rather ex-Puritans of New England, had made the retention of Roman Catholicism in Quebec one of the counts in their indictment of the British Government. In an address to the British people they spoke of the religion of the Canadians as one "that had drenched Great Britain in blood and disseminated impiety, bigotry, persecution, murder, and rebellion through every part of the world." Afterwards, calling the French Canadians to freedom, they treated the religious question in a different strain. "We are too well-acquainted," they said, "with the liberality of sentiment distinguishing your nation to imagine that difference of religion will prejudice you against a hearty amity with us. You know that the transcendent nature of freedom elevates the minds of those who unite in the cause above all such low-minded infirmities. The Swiss Cantons furnish a memorable proof of this truth; their union is composed of Catholic and Protestant States, living in the utmost concord and peace with each other; and they are thereby enabled, ever since they bravely vindicated their freedom, to defy and defeat every tyrant that has invaded them." The Quebec clergy, however, did not forget the former and as they probably thought more sincere manifesto. Their weight was cast into the other scale, and their chief, the Bishop of Quebec, exhorted his people to be true to British allegiance and repel the American invaders. To the blandishments of Franklin and his coadjutors the priests replied that Great Britain had kept her faith, preserved to the French people their laws and customs, shielded their religion, left the monasteries their estates, and even ordered the military authorities to pay honour to Catholic processions.[1] Nor did the Seigniors like the look of revolution. The peasantry were slow to move, rejoicing to have got back to their homesteads and thinking that it was not their quarrel; the city of Quebec narrowly escaped capture by the Americans under Arnold and Montgomery; but the behaviour of the invaders helped to stir up the people against them, and the Province was saved. The Governor, Sir Guy Carleton, was a man worthy to command. Had he been in the place of the torpid Howe, the heavy Clinton, or the light Burgoyne, there might have been a different tale to tell.

The danger, however, had determined the policy of the British Government and led to the practical abandonment, as it proved for ever, of the thought of Anglicising Quebec. The settlement embodied in the Quebec Act, framed by Lord North's government, not only secured to the French people the free exercise of their religion and to the priesthood its revenues, but established the French civil law and French procedure without juries. It put an end to the military dictatorship by giving the Province a governing Council which was to be partly composed of Catholics; an Elective Assembly could not have been safely given to people recently conquered, nor did the French themselves demand it; they had been accustomed only to obey, and were satisfied if their rulers were just. The Quebec Act was opposed as anti-British by Chatham almost with his last breath. It was opposed also by Burke, but not on the ground of hostility to the Roman Catholic religion. "There is," said Burke, "but one healing, Catholic principle of toleration which ought to find favour in this House. It is wanted not only in our colonies, but here. The thirsty earth of our own country is gasping and gaping and crying out for that healing shower from heaven. The noble lord has told you of the right of those people by the Treaty; but I consider the right of conquest so little and the right of human nature so much that the former has very little consideration with me. I look upon

1 Garneau's *History of Canada*, Bell's edition, vol. ii, p. 148.

the people of Canada as coming by the dispensation of God under the British government. I would have us govern it in the same manner as the all-wise disposition of Providence would govern it. We know He suffers the sun to shine upon the righteous and the unrighteous; and we ought to suffer all classes without distinction to enjoy equally the right of worshipping God according to the light He has been pleased to give them." The earth of England unhappily was to gasp and gape for the healing shower for another half-century. Burke's view as to the treatment of the conquered was noble, but it would have extinguished conquest altogether. Yet Burke himself was no enemy to aggrandisement by war.

By this time, however, it was not only with the French, or with the difficulty which their nationality presented, that the British Government had to deal. After the Conquest a number of British adventurers, for the most part it seems not of a high class, had settled in the Province and had at once got its commerce – for which the French peasants had no turn – into their hands. Presently came a crowd of American Royalists, driven into exile by the Revolution, and full at once of extreme British feeling and of wounded pride. These men aspired to being an oligarchy of conquest. At the same time they thought that they ought to carry the British Constitution, with all the liberties and privileges which it gave them, on the soles of their feet. Both as a limit to their ascendency, and as a curtailment of their British freedom, the Quebec Act was hateful to them, and they laboured vehemently, with all the engines which they could command at home, for its repeal. So far they succeeded that *Habeas Corpus* was restored. The troubles which lasted till 1841 had now begun.

In 1791 came, with the progress of the French Revolution, another crisis of opinion in England, and in connection with it a resettlement of Quebec. The political date of the discussion is marked by the quarrel between Burke and Fox. Pitt now laid his hand to the work. His plan for putting an end to the strife between the conquering and the conquered race was separation. He divided Canada into two provinces – Lower Canada for the French and Upper Canada for the British, many of whom had fled to those wilds from the United States after the revolutionary war. This policy was approved by Burke. "For us to attempt," said Burke, "to amalgamate two populations composed of races of men diverse in language, laws, and habitudes, is a complete absurdity. Let the proposed constitution be founded on man's nature, the only solid basis for an enduring government." Pitt was scarcely acting in harmony with this oracle when he bestowed on the French as well as on the British Province an exact counterpart, or what was supposed to be an exact counterpart, of the British Constitution. Each Province was to have, besides the Governor who represented the Crown, a legislative council nominated by the Crown to represent the House of Lords, and an Assembly elected by the people to represent the House of Commons. The Governor was furnished with an Executive Council, the counterpart of the Privy Council, at least as the Privy Council was in the days when it really advised the sovereign, not of the modern Cabinet. Of the extension of the Cabinet system to a dependency nobody then dreamed. It was assumed that the Crown would govern through its representative, and shape its own policy with the aid of ministers chosen by itself, much as it had in Tudor England, though with a general regard for the wants and wishes of the people signified through their representatives in an Assembly. The whole British polity, civil and ecclesiastical, was to be reproduced. Provision was made for an aristocracy by empowering the Crown to annex hereditary seats in the Upper House to titles of nobility. Provision was also made for a Church Establishment by setting apart an eighth, or, as the Church construed the Act, a seventh, of the Crown lands as Clergy Reserves. The genius of the New World repelled from the outset the attempt to introduce aristocracy made by Pitt, as it had, though not so decisively, repelled the similar attempt made by Louis XIV. The attempt to introduce a Church Establishment took more effect, and was destined to be the cause of much trouble. The Test Act being declared not to extend to Canada, both Houses of the Legislature and all the offices were thrown open to Roman Catholics. Pitt thus carried what it might have been hoped would prove the first instalment of Catholic Emancipation. Prejudice against the Roman Catholic Church had yielded, even in the breasts of British Tories, to the hatred of the common enemy, the Atheist Revolution, while to aristocracy the French signiories became more congenial than ever. In the British Province British law, both civil and criminal, was established; in the French Province was established the criminal law of England with the civil law of France, based on the custom of Paris. By giving up

Lower Canada to the French and to French law, the Act of 1791 finally decided that French nationality should be preserved, and that British civilisation should not take its place. Thenceforth England brooded like a misguided mother-bird upon an egg from which, by a painful and dangerous process, she was to hatch a French Canadian nation. New France would soon have been cut off from her mother country by the Revolution and the war which followed. From the rest of the continent she was cut off by race, language, and religion. She would in all probability have come to naught had she not been placed under the ægis of conquerors powerful enough to protect her nationality and constrained to protect it by their fears.

Pitt's policy missed its mark. The two races were not separated by the division of the Province. The British still clung to the trade of Quebec, which their commercial energy had begun to develop, and still struggled to maintain their political ascendency over the conquered race. Their strongholds were in the Executive, in the Legislative Council appointed by the Crown, and in Downing Street, to which they had almost exclusive access. The stronghold of French patriotism was the elective Assembly, in which the French soon had a large majority. The French did not at first care for free institutions, nor were they fit for them: an autocratic governor ruling them justly, sympathetically, and economically, would have suited them much better than any parliament. Neither their priesthood nor their seigniors liked anything of a republican cast. But they grasped the votes which Imperial legislation had put into their hands as weapons to be used for the protection of their nationality and for the overthrow of the oligarchy of Conquest. The situation was much the same that it would have been in Ireland had the Catholic Celts been admitted to Parliament and formed a majority of the popular House, while the House of Lords, the Castle, and the influence of the Imperial Government had remained in the hands of a Protestant minority. Had the demand of the French for an elective Upper House been conceded, the British minority would, as Lord John Russell said at the time, have been left absolutely at the mercy of the French. Patriot leaders soon appeared, and oratory could not fail in a community of Frenchmen. The English had brought with them the Press. To combat British journalism French journalism soon started into life, and, among the French who could read, became an organ of perpetual agitation. The battle-fields were the control of the revenue and the civil list, the composition of the Legislative Council (which the patriots desired to make elective that they might fill it with men of their own party), and the tenure of the judges, whom they wished to make irremovable, like the judges in England, in order to diminish the power of the Crown, besides minor and personal questions about which party feelings were aroused. Controversies about the land law also arose and set the seigniorial patriots among the French somewhat at cross purposes with the patriots pure and simple. The commercial interest, which was entirely British, clashed with the agricultural interest, which was mainly French. There was constant strife between the Upper Chamber, which was in the hands of the British, who filled it with placemen, and the Lower Chamber, which was in the hands of the French; the Upper Chamber perpetually putting its veto upon the legislation of the Lower Chamber. The French, untrained in English constitutional government, went beyond the bounds of constitutional opposition. Gallic temper often broke out, and governors, struggling painfully to maintain their authority, and at the same time to pour oil upon the waters, became the objects of fiery remonstrance, sometimes even of insult thinly veiled. The Home Government, looking on from afar, in the days before steam communication and ocean telegraphs, knew not what to make of the fray or how to deal with it. Its own policy was not clearly defined, nor did it know whether it meant really to bestow Parliamentary government on a dependency or not. So far was it from understanding the situation that in 1839 we find Lord Durham informing it, with the pomp of a momentous revelation, that the conflict in French Canada was one not of political opinion but of race. Moreover, power in Downing Street was always changing hands, and was wielded one day by a Tory and the next by a Liberal or a Tory of a more Liberal brand. Governors correspondingly different in character were sent out: now a military martinet like Haldimand, now a reactionary aristocrat like the Duke of Richmond, anon a conciliator like Prevost or Gosford. The governors who made themselves popular with the French were of course regarded as traitors and detested by the British. Sir James Craig, who is said to have usually addressed civilians as if they needed the cat-o'-nine tails, seemed to the British just the man for that country. There were still among the British political leaders some who clung desperately to the policy of ascendency, and contended that the Province ought to be Anglicised, and might be Anglicised if it were handled with resolution. Pre-eminent among them was Chief Justice Sewell, a sort of Canadian Fitzgibbon. These men often got the ear of the Governor, to whom their circle had almost exclusively social access, and, when the Home Government was Tory, the ear of the Home Government. As the net result, a loyal though liberal historian has to say that "the government of Canada was one continued blunder from the day in which Amherst signed the capitulation of Montreal to the union of the Provinces," and that it presented a painful contrast to the resolute treatment of Louisiana by the Americans, who had at once introduced their laws and language. It is doubtful whether his parallel is perfectly correct, but he is certainly right as to his facts.

The British minority was reinforced, its sense of superiority was increased, and the enmity between it and the French majority was aggravated by the settlement in the district south of the St. Lawrence, called the Eastern Townships, of a colony of English farmers whose improved and energetic cultivation presented a contrast to the slovenly agriculture of the French.[1] Angry questions as to the representation of the Eastern Townships in the Assembly and as to the extension of the French civil law to that district were at the same time added to the budget of discord.

Nevertheless, compared with the rule of the Bourbons, the British rule was beneficent, and the Province, however discontented, had improved. M. Papineau, the rebel that was to be, drew the contrast at the hustings between the government under which he was living and that of former days. "Then," said he, "trade was monopolised by privileged companies, public and private property often pillaged, personal liberty daily violated, and the inhabitants dragged year after year from their homes and families to shed their blood from the shores of the great lakes, from the banks of the Mississippi and the Ohio to Nova Scotia, Newfoundland, and Hudson's Bay. Now religious toleration, trial by jury, Habeas Corpus, afford legal and equal security to all, and we need submit to no laws but those of our own making. All these advantages have become our birthright, and will, I hope, be the lasting inheritance of our posterity. To secure

1 See Lord Durham's Report.

them let us only act as British subjects and freemen." An eminent American judge avowed to the writer that he saw with pleasure the extension of the British Empire, because with British dominion went the reign of law under which no man could be deprived of property or right otherwise than by legal process. In the hearts of the upper and more Conservative classes the British Crown had perhaps taken the place of the French Crown as an object of loyalty, though of a loyalty far less intense. There had been for a time difficulties with the French Church. The ticklish question had been raised whether the King of Great Britain had not either stepped into the place of the King of France and inherited the French King's control over ecclesiastical appointments, or even become ecclesiastically supreme as he was in England. But the point had been waived by the prudence of a government which felt its need of clerical support, and the French clergy were pretty well contented with their relation to the State. They were more than contented with the conduct of England in waging war against the Revolutionary Atheism of France, and gave thanks to God for having snatched the people of Canada from dependence on an impious nation which had overturned the altars.[1]

Thus it came to pass that, in 1812, when war broke out between England and the United States, the French Canadians were once more true to England. The seigniors were as much opposed as ever to Republicanism. The priests, though they might have less reason than before to dread the intolerance of Puritanism, had been set more than ever against democracy by its alliance with Atheism in their mother country, while the national aspirations which had now become strong in the French breast recoiled from the prospect of absorption in the population of the United States. In the person of De Salaberry, a brilliant captain appeared of the French race, but trained in the British service. His victory at Chateauguay over a vastly superior force was among the most famous exploits of the war. French Canada, the Americans probably expected, would fall at once into their arms. But they had overrated the attractiveness of Republican institutions to the Frenchman, and had falsely assumed that the British and their rule were as odious in the French Canadian's eye as in their own. Americans are fond of dilating on the

1 Garneau's History, vol. ii, p. 225.

harsh features of the English character, which they say make England hateful to all men of other races, and from which they flatter themselves that their own character has become in three generations entirely free. But they have twice offered French Canada liberation from the yoke, welcoming her at the same time to their own arms, and twice she has answered them with bullets. It was the saying of an eminent French Canadian that the last gun in defence of British dominion on this continent would be fired by a Frenchman. True, the saying was expressive less of loyalty to Great Britain than of desire to preserve under her protection a nationality separate from the United States, and perhaps a theocracy untouched by Republican influence; yet it could hardly have been uttered if England had been hateful. About British unsociability too much has been said. It is true that such characters as are suited for command are generally less amiable than strong. But in India, saving the sympathetic disturbance set up in Oude by the Sepoy mutiny, there has not been a political insurrection since the formation of the British Empire, and when Russian invasion threatened, all the feudatories came forward of their own accord with contributions to the defence. England was right in ceding the Ionian Isles, but no bitter recollection of her rule, it is believed, lingers there. The Corsicans put themselves into her hands, and the Sicilians after 1815 would gladly have remained under her protectorate. The Egyptians do not want to be rid of the British, though France wants to see them out of Egypt. How did France, the reputed paragon of sociability, get on with the Sicilians in the days of the Sicilian Vespers, with the Germans at a later date, or with the nations whose territories her armies occupied under Napoleon? How does she get on with the Algerian tribes? The Americans, happily for themselves, have not yet been tried in this way.

The war with the Americans over, civil strife began again. This is the proper phrase. The French, the mass of them at least, were not fighting against British government or connection, but against the ascendency of the other race in office and in the Legislative Council. Their feeling towards the British government was rather that of disappointed and weary suitors than of rebels; they mistrusted its knowledge more than its intentions. They cried like their forbears in France, "*Ah, si le Roi le savait!*" Matters, however, went from bad to worse. For four successive years the Assembly stopped the supplies, so far at least as lay in its power; for the Crown had a fixed civil list and certain revenues of its own, besides the privilege, in extreme need, of falling back on the Imperial treasury; it could even turn the tables on the Members of the Assembly by causing the Legislative Council to throw out the Bill for their pay.

Since the year 1830 revolution had once more broken loose in France, and the infection had spread to some of the French leaders and to some active spirits among the young lawyers and journalists. A few of the British in Lower Canada were also touched by it and joined the French patriots against their own race. Though there had been a good deal of talk about popular education, the French people were still very ignorant; out of eighty-seven thousand of them whose names were affixed to a petition only nine thousand could write; and their minds were thus open to any delusions which the leaders chose to propagate. Just at this time civil discord was approaching the revolutionary point in Upper Canada, and though the two movements were distinct and had different sources, there was a sympathy between them, and the leaders were in close communication. Papineau, a great popular orator, put himself at the head of the French malcontents, and Nelson at the head of the British. When the crisis was approaching the Home Government became alive to the danger. The tocsin, in fact, was rung in ninety-two resolutions passed by the Canadian Assembly, and demanding, under the guise of a series of reforms, a practical revolution. Lord Gosford was then sent out with two other commissioners to inquire and advise. He preached concord with much unction but with little success. He reported in favour of some practical reforms, but against the change which would have made the Assembly master of the Government, and on which that body had set its heart. To make the Assembly master of the Government would have been not only tantamount to abdication on the part of the Crown, but would have entailed the abandonment of the British minority to the mercy of the exasperated French. Resolutions in the sense of the Report were moved by Lord John Russell in the House of Commons and carried in spite of the opposition of Roebuck, Molesworth, and other Radicals who had espoused the cause of the Canadian patriots. This was the signal for insurrection. The French clergy either were off their guard, or, there being on this occasion no danger to their religion from New England Puritans or French Atheists, wavered between their love of order and their patriotism as Frenchmen. At all events, they interfered too late to prevent the rising, though in time to render it if possible more hopeless. All the British and even the Irish rallied at once round the Government. Nelson proved himself a man of leading if not of light, and, though untrained to arms, repulsed a British detachment which attacked a hamlet in which he was entrenched. Papineau ran away. Sir John Colborne, a resolute veteran of Wellington's school, who was in command, soon swept the rebellion out of existence, and flung the American desperadoes who had come to join it over the border. Some of the leaders were hanged; martial law reigned, and the Constitution of French Canada came to a disastrous end. The next stage in the political history of the Province is its union with British Canada, of which we shall presently take up the thread.

Among the documents in Christie's *History of Lower Canada* (vol. vi), is a paper on the troubled state of French Canada, by a military man, whether Sir John Harvey, successively governor of Prince Edward Island, New Brunswick, Newfoundland, and Nova Scotia, or by Lieut.-General Evans, is uncertain. The writer speaks with the frankness of his profession. "To a people," he says, "in no respect identified with their rulers, French in their origin, their language, their habits, their sentiments, their religion, – English in nothing but in the glorious Constitution which that too liberal country has conferred upon them, – the sole effect of this boon has been to enable them to display in a constitutional manner those feelings of suspicion, distrust, and dislike by which the conduct of their representatives would warrant us in believing them to be animated towards their benefactors. The House of Assembly of Lower Canada has not ceased to manifest inveterate hostility to the interests of the Crown, it has withheld its confidence from the local government, and has through this blind and illiberal policy neutralised, as far as it could, every benefit which that government has wished to confer upon the people; and that the popular representatives have acted in unison with the feelings of their constituents the fact of their having invariably sent back those members whose opposition to the government has been most marked may be thought sufficiently to prove. Ought not such a people to be left to themselves, to the tender mercies of their gigantic neighbours, whose hewers of wood and drawers of water they would inevitably become in six months after the protection of the British fleets and armies had been withdrawn from them? The possession of this dreary corner of the world is productive of nothing to Great Britain but expense. I repeat that the occupation of Canada is in no respect compensated by any solid advantage. Nevertheless, it pleases the people of England to keep it much for the same reason that it pleases a mastiff or a bull-dog to keep possession of a bare and marrowless bone towards which he sees the eye of another dog directed. And a fruitful bone of contention has it proved, and will it prove, betwixt Great Britain and the United States before Canada is merged in one of the divisions of that Empire, an event, however, which will not happen until blood and treasure have been profusely lavished in the attempts to defend what is indefensible, and to retain what is not worth having."

"This dreary corner of the world" may be relegated to oblivion with Voltaire's *quelques arpents de neige.* The rest of the quotation will provoke dissent. But the soldier has hit the mark by saying that the only use which the French Canadians had made of the Constitution given them by Great Britain was to renew in a constitutional form their struggle against the power which had conquered them with the sword. Not only were they enabled to renew the struggle but to renew it with success; for the rebellion in both provinces, though vanquished in the field of war, was victorious in the political field and ended in the complete surrender of Imperial power. It is the height either of generosity or of folly when you have beaten people with arms to bestow on them the means of beating you with votes.

The French are not to be blamed in the slightest degree for what they have done. Rather they are to be admired for their patriotic constancy and the steadiness with which their aim has been pursued. A British colony conquered by France would have acted just as they have acted: it would have used any political power which the conqueror gave it or which it had extorted from his fears as an instrument for breaking his yoke. The fact with which statesmen have to deal is that the power has been so used by the people of New France under the guidance of their clergy, and that Quebec at the present day, though kindly enough in its feelings towards Great Britain, is not a British colony, but a little French nation.

Chapter 6

History of Upper Canada

Upper Canada founded by the United Empire Loyalists / Their wrongs as a vanquished party shut out from amnesty / Constitution of British Canada / Simcoe its first Governor / Beginnings of political life and controversy / Governorships of Hunter and Gore / War of 1812 / The Tory "Family Compact" / Conflict between it and the Reformers / Leaders of the Reformers, Mackenzie, Rolph, and Bidwell / The clergy reserves and other political issues / Demand for responsible government / Governorship of Sir Francis Bond Head / Conflict between the Governor and the Reformers / Rebellion breaks out and is suppressed / End of the governorship of Sir Francis Bond Head

The chief sources of this historical sketch are MacMullen's *Canada,* Read's *Life of Simcoe,* Coffin's *War of 1812*, Sir Francis Bond Head's *Narrative,* Mr. Lindsey's *Life of W. Lyon Mackenzie,* Dent's *Upper Canadian Rebellion,* and Lord Durham's Report.

HAD THE Americans been as wise and merciful after their first as they were after their second civil war, and closed the strife as all civil strife ought to be closed – with an amnesty – British Canada would never have come into existence. It was founded by the Loyalists driven by revolutionary vengeance from their homes, who at the same time settled in large numbers in Nova Scotia, New Brunswick, and Prince Edward Island. These men were deeply wronged, and might well cherish and hand down to their sons as they did the memory of the wrong. They had done nothing as a body to put themselves out of the pale of mercy. They had fought as every citizen is entitled and presumptively bound to fight for the government under which they were born, to which they owed allegiance, and which as they thought gave them the substantial benefits of freedom. They had fought for a connection which, though false, at all events since the colony had grown able to shift for itself, and fraught with the peril of discord, was still prized by the colonists generally, as might have been shown out of the mouth of all the revolutionary leaders, including Samuel Adams, the principal fomentor of the quarrel. The constitutional means of redress had not been exhausted, nor was there any reason to despair of obtaining a repeal of the Tea Duty as a repeal of the Stamp Tax had been obtained. A group of Boston republicans, who had been bent from the first, notwithstanding their disclaimers, on bringing about independence, laboured to excite the people and prevent reconciliation. The intelligence and property of the colonies, the bulk of it at least, had been on the loyalist side till it was repelled by the blundering violence of the government and its generals; nor would it have been possible to fix upon a point at which the normal rule of civil duty was reversed and fidelity to the Crown became treason to the commonwealth. Outrages had been committed on both sides, as is always the case in civil war. England, at all events, was bound in honour to protect the refugees in their new home;[1] otherwise she might have listened to counsels of wisdom and withdrawn politically from a continent in which she had no real interest but those of amity and trade. If an empire antagonistic to the United States is ever formed upon the north of them, and if

1 Besides protecting the Loyalists in their new home, England voted £3,300,000 to indemnify them for their lost estates.

trouble to them ensues, they have to thank their ancestors who refused amnesty to the vanquished in a civil war.

British Canada, when it was severed from French Canada received by Pitt's Act the same Constitution. It was provided with a Governor, called in the case of the younger province Lieutenant-Governor, to represent the Crown; an Executive Council to represent the Privy Council; a Legislative Council nominated by the Crown to represent the House of Lords; and an Elective Assembly to represent the House of Commons. This was called "the express image and transcript of the British Constitution." But though it might be the express image in form, it was far from being the express image in reality of Parliamentary Government as it exists in Great Britain, or even as it existed in Great Britain at that time. The Lieutenant-Governor, representing the Crown, not only reigned but governed, with a ministry not assigned to him by the vote of the Assembly, but chosen by himself, and acting as his advisers, not as his masters. The Assembly could not effectually control his policy by withholding supplies, because the Crown, with very limited needs, had revenues, territorial and casual, of its own. Thus the imitation was, somewhat like the Chinese imitation of the steam-vessel, exact in everything except the steam. But in the new settlement there was other business than politics on hand, and perhaps Parliamentary Government, party, and the demagogue came quite as soon as they were needed.

British Canada had as her first Lieutenant-Governor, Simcoe, and save in one respect she could not have had a better. Local history still fondly seeks to identify the spot where he pitched his tent – a tent which had belonged to Captain Cook – when the shore of Lake Ontario, on which the fair city of Toronto now stands, was a primeval forest, and the stillness of the bay, now full of the puffing of steamers and the hum of trade, was broken only by the settling of flocks of waterfowl or by the paddling of the Indian's canoe. Simcoe had a good estate in England, and had sat in the House of Commons. He might have lived at home at his ease when he chose to live under canvas in a Canadian winter and struggle with the difficulties of founding a commonwealth in Canadian wilds. The love of active duty must have been strong in him. But the love of fighting Yankees was strong also, and it led him at last into relations with Indians hostile to the United States which alarmed the Home Government and cut short his useful career. As colonel of the Queen's Rangers in the revolutionary war he had served the Crown gallantly, and at the same time had commanded the respect of his opponents. His character in itself would have been enough to prove that a patriot might be opposed to the revolution. His intercourse with the better men on the other side reminds us of the letter of Sir William Waller, the Parliamentary general, to a Royalist friend at the outbreak of the Civil War in England, praying that the war, since it must come, might be waged without personal animosity and in a way of honour. The Duc de Rochefoucauld Liancourt, the paragon of French liberal aristocrats and of landlords, driven into exile by the revolution, looks in on Governor Simcoe and reports of him that he is "just, active, enlightened, brave, frank, and possesses the confidence of the country, of the troops, and of all those who join him in the administration of public affairs, to which he attends with the utmost application, preserving all the old friends of the King and neglecting no means of procuring him new ones. He unites," says the Duc, "in my judgment all the qualities which his station requires to maintain the important possession of Canada, if it be possible that England can long retain it." The governor's face, in his portrait, bespeaks force of character, honesty, and good sense. His good sense he showed by admitting, in spite of his prejudice against the Americans, settlers from the United States, though he was careful to guard his frontier with a line of U.E. Loyalists, placing the Americans in the rear. With all his fervent attachment to Great Britain, he knew at all events that Canada was on the American continent.

At Niagara, then the capital, in a log-house which De Liancourt describes as small and miserable, but which if it were now standing would be venerated by Ontario as much as Rome venerated the hut of Romulus, Simcoe assembled for the first time the little yeoman Parliament of British Canada with all the forms of monarchical procedure, and in phrase which not unsuccessfully imitated the buckram of a Speech from the Throne, announced to his backwoods Lords and Commons the reception of the "memorable Act," by which the wisdom and beneficence of a most gracious Sovereign and the British Parliament had "imparted to them the blessings of our invaluable Constitution," solemnly enjoining them faithfully to discharge "the momentous trusts and duties" thereby committed to their rough hands. The meeting being at harvest time, and the harvest being of more consequence than politics, out of the five legislative councillors summoned two only, and out of the sixteen assemblymen summoned five only, attended. The good sense of those present, however, seems to have risen to the level of their legislative functions. Probably it showed itself now and for some time afterwards by letting the governor legislate as he pleased. The session over, they wended their way homeward, some on horseback through pathless woods, camping out by the way, or using Indian wigwams as their inns, some in bark canoes along the shore of Lake Ontario and down the St. Lawrence. It was not easy, as Simcoe found, to get a Parliament together in those days.

This was the heroic era before politics, unrecorded in any annals, which has left of itself no monument other than the fair country won by those obscure husbandmen from the wilderness, or perhaps, here and there, a grassy mound, by this time nearly levelled with the surrounding soil, in which, after their life's partnership of toil and endurance, the pioneer and his wife rest side by side. "The backwoodsman," says history,[1] "whose fortunes are cast in the remote inland settlements of the present day, far removed from churches, destitute of ministers of the Gospel and medical men, without schools, or roads, or the many conveniences that make life desirable, can alone appreciate or even understand the numerous difficulties and hardships that beset the first settler among the ague-swamps of Western Canada. The clothes on his back, with a rifle or old musket and a well-tempered axe, were not unfrequently the full extent of his worldly possessions. Thus lightly equipped he took possession of his two hundred acres of closely-timbered forest land and commenced operations. The welkin rings again with his vigorous strokes, as huge tree after tree is assailed and tumbled to the earth; and the sun presently shines in upon the little clearing. The best of the logs are partially squared and serve to build a shanty; the remainder are given to the flames. Now the rich mould, the accumulation of centuries of decayed vegetation, is gathered into little hillocks, into which potatoes are dibbled. Indian corn is planted in another direction, and perhaps a little wheat. If married, the lonely couple struggle on in their forest oasis like the solitary traveller over the sands of Sahara or a boat adrift on the Atlantic. The nearest neighbour lives miles off, and when sickness comes they

1 MacMullen's *Canada*, p. 232.

have to travel far through the forest to claim human sympathy. But fortunately our nature, with elastic temperament, adapts itself to circumstances. By and by the potatoes peep up, and the corn-blades modestly show themselves around the charred maple stumps and girdled pines, and the prospect of sufficiency of food gives consolation. As winter approaches, a deer now and then adds to the comforts of the solitary people. Such were the mass of the first settlers in Western Canada."

The rough lot, we trust, was cheered by health and hope, while the loneliness and mutual need of support would knit closer the tie of conjugal affection. To the memory of conquerors who devastate the earth, and of politicians who vex the life of its denizens with their struggles for power and place, we raise sumptuous monuments: to the memory of those who by their toil and endurance have made it fruitful we can raise none. But civilisation, while it enters into the heritage which the pioneers prepared for it, may at least look with gratitude on their lowly graves.

With clergy the people in those days were very scantily provided,[1] and their work, with their home affections, must have been their religion, the solemn and silent forest their temple. When the clergyman came his life in going round to settlements through an uncleared country was, as survivors of the primitive era will tell you, almost as hard as that of the backwoodsman himself. In due time the English of Canada showed their kinship to those of New England by setting up common schools, and their civilisation, though backward and rude at first, developed itself generally on the lines of their race.

Simcoe was followed by Hunter and Gore, about whom not much is known, but who were evidently weaker men, and failed to restrain wrong-doing which Simcoe had restrained. Even of these, however, and of the whole line of Royal Governors in both Provinces, it may be said that whether they were strong or weak, wise or unwise, popular or unpopular, there rests not upon the name of any one of them the stain of dishonour.[2] Neither British Canada nor French

1 MacMullen's *Canada,* p. 248.

2 Peter Russell, who acted as administrator between the governships of Simcoe and Hunter, appears to have disgraced himself by rapacity in the matter of Crown lands. Parting presents to Governors were questionable, but probably had not been condemned in those days. No charge of actual corruption was ever made against a Royal Governor.

Canada in British hands ever had an Intendant Bigot. The errors and misdeeds of the Governors arose chiefly from their ignorance of the country which they were sent to rule. On their arrival they almost inevitably fell into the hands of the dominant clique. The Home Government, from which they took their orders, was if possible more ignorant than they were, and its councils changed with every change of a party administration. It was their doom, in short, to be the instruments of that futile and pernicious attempt of the Old World to regulate the lives of communities in the New World which is now happily drawing to its close. For the character of the people, and perhaps even for their material welfare, the imported rule of men of honour, had they only been better informed and more impartial, might in itself have been not less desirable than that of the party leaders who have succeeded them. But party government, we will hope, is not the end.

The colony was filling up with settlers from different quarters. There came in, besides Englishmen, Scotchmen who brought Presbyterianism and usually Liberal ideas with them, Americans who had lived under a Republic, and Irishmen, both Orange and Green. Political life began, though it was still of little importance compared with the axe and the plough. Even so early we hear of an 'independent' Member of Parliament who is killed in a duel, though we are not told that the duel was owing to his difference of opinion with the Treasury Bench. On the more active and democratic spirits the neighbourhood of the American Republic could not fail to tell. An independent Press was born in a log hut, the embryo editorials being no doubt written and printed by the same hand. Under Hunter and Gore abuses had grown up, especially in the land department and in the administration of justice. Reformers arose. Reform had its proto-martyr in Thorpe, an English barrister sent out to a Canadian judgeship, and apparently an upright man, who for protesting against wrong was deprived of his place through the influence of Governor Gore, misadvised probably by the Council. Willcocks, an immigrant journalist, whom the Governor had learned to regard as "an execrable monster who would deluge the Province with blood," also testified in prison to the liberty of the Press. But political conflicts were suspended by the War of 1812.

Into that war the weak and unconscientious Madison was forced by the violent party whose leading spirit was Henry Clay, not for the reasons alleged, about which nothing was afterwards said in the negotiations for peace, but mainly in the hope of conquering Canada, and furthering the ambitious ends of the party. England had the war with Napoleon on her hands; victory seemed likely to rest with the oppressor of nations, and the United States, it was thought, might share with him the glory and the booty. Let it never be forgotten that the best part of the American people opposed the war. Their attitude was marked by the comparative absence of attacks on Canada along the line of Vermont and Maine; though the loss and suffering fell most on the maritime states of New England, and little on the West, which had driven the country into the war. Unprincipled aggression met with its due reward. The American invaders were repeatedly beaten by handfuls of Canadians, and the names of Sir Isaac Brock, and his comrades-in-arms, including the Indian chief Tecumseh, were endeared by heroic exploits to the country which they successfully defended against tremendous odds. The first invader, General Hull, and his army capitulated to a Canadian force not half their number, and the Canadians conquered Michigan. On Queenston Heights, the scene of Brock's death and his army's victory, the idol of Canadian patriotism sleeps beneath a monumental column which challenges by its stateliness respect for Canadian art. Of the share which French Canada and De Salaberry had in the defence mention has already been made. As the war went on it became more ferocious, and the inhuman burning of Niagara by the Americans in mid-winter was avenged by havoc not less inhuman, and by the burning of the Capitol at Washington. The Americans learned in time to fight well, and the battle of Lundy's Lane, near the close, was the most desperate of all. Till midnight the struggle went on, the roar of the cannon and the rattle of the musketry contending with the thunder of Niagara, and the loss on both sides was terrible. The superiority of American resources also showed itself upon the lakes; the Canadian flotilla on Lake Erie was totally destroyed, and Toronto, then called York, twice fell into the hands of the enemy. When Napoleon had fallen, the hands of Great Britain were free, the better party among the Americans prevailed, and they were ready for peace. Their aggression would have ended more disastrously than it did had not Pakenham blindly dashed his army against the cotton bales of New Orleans, and had the large force which England was at last enabled to send to Canada been placed under the command of a better soldier than Prevost.

Americans say that the war did them good by consolidating the Union. A nation has hardly a right to consolidate its union by slaughtering and despoiling its unoffending neighbours. But slavery, from which the real danger of disruption arose, was not weakened in its political influence; on the contrary it was strengthened by the war. Whatever attraction American institutions might before have had for Canadians was counteracted or weakened by American aggression. Worst of all was the effect which the fratricidal conflict inevitably had in renewing and envenoming the schism of the Anglo-Saxon race. Before that time British Canadians and Americans had hardly looked upon each other as foreigners. Americans had freely settled and been received as citizens in British Canada. Two generations have not sufficed to efface the evil memories of 1812. Ministers of discord, seeking to fan the dying embers of international hatred, still appeal to the names of Brock and his companions-in-arms, whose glory they sully by such misuse.[1]

The war over, the political struggle began again – with all the more intensity, perhaps, because the war had unsettled the people and excited their combative propensities, while, farming having been neglected, depression ensued as soon as the military expenditure had ceased. In the course of the next fifteen years a regular Reform Party was born. It had reason enough for its existence. The Government with all its patronage and influence, including the disposal of the Crown lands, had fallen into the hands of a Ring called the "Family Compact" – a nickname borrowed, it seems, from the diplomatic history of Europe rather than suggested by the

1 Injustice has been done to the memory of General Proctor, whose name seems worthy to be coupled with that of Brock. He gained one brilliant victory. It appears to be admitted that his retreat before Harrison's immensely superior and far more effective army had become inevitable after the destruction of the Canadian flotilla on Lake Erie. Even if, as the court-martial on him pronounced, he did not conduct the retreat with judgment, there seems to be no shadow of a pretence for charging him with personal misconduct. The court-martial expressly acquitted him of any charge of that kind. His name was coupled with a misfortune, which was not his fault, and he seems not to have been popular in command; but there is apparently nothing to justify an impeachment of his courage.

number of family alliances among the members. The nucleus of the Family Compact was a group of United Empire Loyalists who might not unnaturally deem themselves a privileged class. To this was added a number of retired officers and other British gentlemen who had received grants of lands but found themselves ill-fitted for farming in the bush, and better fitted for holding places under Government, together with scions of genteel families in England, sent out sometimes for the family's good. The Compact formed a social aristocracy as well as a political ring. It had, like all such political bodies, a tail less aristocratic than itself. Its strongholds were Government House, the occupant of which was all the more under its influence because he had no other gentlemen with whom to associate; the Executive Council, which was entirely in its hands, and the Legislative Council or Upper House of Parliament, which it also engrossed, and through which it was enabled to veto any bills passed by the Elective Assembly. The Elective Assembly, it will be borne in mind, could not effectually coerce the Government and the Upper House, as the British House of Commons had done, by stopping the supplies, the Government having a fixed civil list and a territorial revenue of its own, with the Imperial treasury whereon to fall back in extreme need. In the Assembly itself the Family Compact was able to control many seats, and sometimes a majority, through the influence of the Government, aided by irregularities in the representation. Its adherents filled the Bench, the magistracy, the high places of the legal profession, and those of the Episcopal Church, which at that time was virtually established and endowed by the State. By grant or purchase, its members had got into their hands nearly the whole of the waste lands of the Province, they were all-powerful in the Chartered Banks, and at last shared among themselves almost all offices of trust and profit.[1] By the appropriation of the public lands the Compact not only robbed the commonwealth, but, as the lands were held for a rise, obstructed settlement and retarded the progress of the country. It enhanced its unpopularity by giving itself social airs, though the account of its grand mansions, its trains of lackeys and its banquets, found in some historians, are certainly overdone. Of its mansions some remain and are of modest dimensions, nor did its chief members leave great

1 Lord Durham's Report, p. 66.

wealth. The Compact showed its exclusiveness even towards British immigrants, excluding them by jealous restrictions from free practice in the legal and medical professions, "so that an Englishman emigrating to Upper Canada found himself almost as much an alien in the country as he would have been in the United States."[1] The politics of the Compact were Tory, of course, and it was ardently loyal to British connection, so long, at least, as Toryism reigned at home. Like its counterpart in England, it was closely allied with the Established Church. Not all its leaders were jobbers: some were sincere lovers of prerogative. Sir John Beverley Robinson, for example, Attorney-General, afterwards Chief Justice, and the ruling spirit of the Executive Council, was a high-minded as well as very able man, though it is impossible to disconnect his name from a system of administrative jobbery, or from some acts of partisan injustice. At his side was Dr. Strachan, Archdeacon and afterwards Bishop of Toronto, a clerical aspirant who had passed from Presbyterianism to Anglicanism, as was generally believed, with a view to the advancement of his fortunes – a man of remarkable force of character, able and shrewd, though not wise, the type of a clerical politician, and, like all clerical politicians, even more mischievous to the Church for whose interests he fought than to the State. Beside the Family Compact there was gradually formed a Conservative party, in which the Compact ultimately merged, of men who had no desire to abet the oligarchy in its abuses, but recoiled from revolution. The Reform party was in like manner divided into an extreme and a moderate wing. Of the moderate and constitutional wing the chief was Robert Baldwin, a man whose renown for integrity and wisdom is such as to make him a sort of Canadian Lord Somers. Of the extreme and covertly republican wing the chief man at the time was William Lyon Mackenzie, a wiry and peppery little Scotchman, hearty in his love of public right, still more in his hatred of public wrongdoers, clever, brave, and energetic, but, as tribunes of the people are apt to be, far from cool-headed, sure-footed in his conduct, temperate in his language, or steadfast in his personal connections. With Mackenzie were Dr. Rolph, a man of more solid ability, of deeper character and designs, whom his admirers call sagacious, his critics sly; and Bidwell, the son of a

1 Lord Durham's Report, p. 74.

refugee from American justice, but himself apparently a man of virtue as well as sense. War was declared on a number of issues – the constitution of the Legislative Council, which the patriots wanted to make elective and to purge of placemen; the administration of the Crown lands; the independence of the judges, which was compromised both by their liability to removal at pleasure and by their holding seats in Parliament; the control of the revenue and the civil list, besides a number of personal questions, such as always present themselves in the heat of party war. Among all the special subjects of controversy most stir was made by the Clergy Reserves. Pitt, as we have seen, had set apart an eighth, or, according to the clerical interpretation, a seventh of every land grant "for the support of a Protestant clergy." This, by tying up blocks of land all over the country and standing in the way of close settlement, created an economical grievance, besides the jealousy excited by the favour shown to a particular Church, and a Church which, looking down upon all her sisters, treated their members as dissenters. To complicate the question, the term "Protestant clergy" was ambiguous. The Presbyterians, then equal in number to the Anglicans, claimed a share on the ground that their Church in Scotland was recognised by the State; the other Churches not Roman Catholic claimed a share on the ground that they also were Protestant, while thorough-going Reformers and Roman Catholics united in demanding complete secularisation. But all the special grievances and demands of the Reformers were summed up and merged in their demand for "Responsible Government." By Responsible Government they meant that the government should be carried on, not by an Executive nominated by the Governor and independent of the vote of Parliament, but, as in England, by a Cabinet dependent for its tenure of office on the vote of the Commons. They meant, in short, that supreme power should be transferred from the Crown to the representatives of the people. It was nothing less than a revolution for which they called under a mild and constitutional name. Mackenzie, who had for some time been spitting fire through his journal, having been borne into the Assembly on the shoulders of the people, the battle began in earnest, and with all the bitterness which his tongue could lend to it. The oligarchy from the outset defended itself furiously with every weapon at its command. It had before harried Gourlay – a benevolent and inquiring Scotchman who came among its lieges taking notes and printing them – out of his mind. It had persecuted the elder Bidwell under an Alien Act. It shut up Collins, another patriot, in gaol on a charge of libel. It now, having a majority in the Assembly, five times lawlessly expelled Mackenzie and still more lawlessly voted him incapable of re-election. The hot-blooded youths of the oligarchy were hurried into actual outrage: they wrecked Mackenzie's printing press, and the party paid the fine by subscription. The Governors during this period were two soldiers, Sir Peregrine Maitland and Sir John Colborne, neither of whom understood politics. Sir Peregrine was weakly subservient to the oligarchy, and he got himself into a scrape by using military force in a civil case. Sir John Colborne was a strong and upright man as well as a good soldier, and was by no means inclined to wink at abuses; but he had a military leaning to prerogative, deemed it his duty to hold the fortress for the Crown, and was eminently devoid of popular arts. His gracious reply to an Address was, "I receive your Address with much satisfaction and thank you for your congratulations." His less gracious and more succinct form was, "Gentlemen, I have received the petition of the inhabitants." He welcomed a patriotic deputation with artillerymen standing to their guns and troops served with a double allowance of ball-cartridge. Mackenzie went to England, showing thereby, as in fact did the Reformers generally, that they did not regard the Home Government as wilfully oppressive, but the reverse, though it might be sadly misinformed. In England itself a revolution had by this time taken place. Since the close of the war with Napoleon, the current of political life, long frozen, had begun to flow. The winter of Liberalism had ended; its sun rose high again, and Parliamentary reform had come. The change extended to the Colonial Office, though there Liberalism was still limited by lingering tradition. Even from the Canningite Lord Goderich the agitator received a degree of attention which scandalised the Tories of the Canadian Assembly. Among other things Lord Goderich laid it down in his despatch that ecclesiastics, if they were to keep their seats in the Council, ought to abstain from interfering with secular affairs; intimating his opinion at the same time "that by resigning their seats they would best consult their own personal comfort and the success of their designs for the spiritual good of the people." The Legislative Council treated the despatch with open contempt. By the Liberal Lord Glenelg a catalogue of grievances drawn up by the Reformers with Mackenzie at their head was respectfully considered, and a reply was written promising important reforms and concessions, though not the one great concession, Responsible Government. The law officers of the Compact, Boulton and Hagerman, were also dismissed for rebellion against the liberal policy of the Crown, whereupon the loyalty of the Tories gave way and they began to throw out hints of "alienation" from "the glorious Empire of their sires," and of "casting about for a new state of political existence." On a libcral policy congenial to that which prevailed in England the Home Government was now bent. But to carry it out through a warrior like Colborne was impossible, and he was recalled, though only to command against the rebels in the French Province. Before leaving, however, he set the house on fire by authorising the creation of fifty-seven Rectories out of the disputed Clergy Reserves Fund. Though the number actually carved out was only forty-four, it gave to the Church a substantial slice of the endowment which she claimed. This measure produced intense exasperation.

The choice of a man to take Colborne's place, and give effect to the new policy, which the Colonial Office made was so strange that to account for it recourse has seriously been had to the hypothesis of mistaken identity.[1] Sir Francis Bond Head, a half-pay major, an assistant Poor-Law commissioner, the hero of a famous ride over the Pampas, and the writer of light books of travel, was awakened in the dead of night at his lodging in Kent by a King's messenger, who brought him the appointment of the Lieutenant-Governorship of Upper Canada, with a summons to wait on the Colonial minister

1 The story told by Mr. Roebuck and others to Sir Francis Hincks that Sir Francis Bond Head was mistaken for Sir Edmund Walker Head, afterwards Governor-General, is still current, but cannot be worthy of credence. Sir Edmund Head, having been born in 1805, was at this time only a little over thirty, and though known to his friends as a political student, he had made no mark as yet in public life. It was not till six years afterwards that he was appointed to the Poor-Law commissionership, when he came forward as a public man. If such a blunder was possible on the part of Lord Glenelg, it was not possible on the part of the permanent Under Secretary, who was then Sir James Stephen.

next morning. In justice to him be it remembered that he declined, and accepted only when pressed in a manner which made acceptance a duty. He was recommended no doubt by the manner in which he had done his work as Poor-Law commissioner, by his genial temper, his knowledge of the world, and the plucky and adventurous character shown in his ride, which was likely to make him a favourite with people whom the Colonial Secretary might think more backwoodsmen in character than they really were. Nor was he wanting in discernment or in force; he did a great service by forbidding the Canadian Banks to suspend specie payment in a commercial crisis, and inducing them to ride out, at a sound anchorage, the financial storm which was sweeping over the United States. But he was very impulsive, very vain, and under the influence of success became light-headed. Joseph Hume and other Liberals commended him to their brethren in Canada, perhaps taking on trust the nominee of a Liberal government. He brought with him as the chart for his course Mackenzie's catalogue of grievances, with Lord Glenelg's commentary promising, as has already been said, practical reforms and an administration in accordance with the reasonable wishes of the people, but not promising Responsible Government, that is, the surrender of the power of the Crown to the representatives of the people. If the Colonial Office itself was still undecided on the vital point, it could not find fault with a Governor for taking what to him was the natural line. If it was itself still with hesitating hand fingering the keys of the fortress, it could hardly expect its delegate, – such a delegate, above all, as the horseman of the Pampas, – to perform for it the act of capitulation. Sir Francis was appointed in 1836. In March 1837 Lord John Russell, speaking in the House of Commons, pronounced Cabinet Government in the colonies incompatible with the relations which ought to exist between the mother country and the colony. "Those relations," he said, "required that His Majesty should be represented in the colony not by ministers, but by a Governor sent out by the King, and responsible to the Parliament of Great Britain. Otherwise," he said, "Great Britain would have in the Canadas all the inconveniences of colonies without any of their advantages." This seems enough to justify the resistance of Sir Francis Bond Head to Responsible Government. Glenelg himself was verbose and ambiguous, but the upshot of his mandate was that "in the administration of Canadian affairs a sufficient practical responsibility already existed without the introduction of any hazardous schemes," and that the last resort of the Canadians, if they were discontented, was to carry their complaints to the foot of the throne, whose occupant (then King William IV) "felt the most lively interest in the welfare of his Canadian subjects, and was ever ready to devote a patient and laborious attention to any representations." Such was the atmosphere of constitutional fiction in which these statesmen lived!

Sir Francis laughed when, on entering Toronto, he found himself placarded as "the tried Reformer," he who had never given a thought to politics, who had scarcely ever voted at an election. By the Reformers he was received with glad expectation, by the Conservatives with sullen misgiving; but both parties soon found themselves mistaken. He showed his weak side at once by a theatrical announcement of his mission, and by indiscreetly communicating to the Assembly the whole of Lord Glenelg's letter of instructions. Presently he had interviews with the leading Reformers, Mackenzie and Bidwell. In them he thought he detected designs reaching beyond the redress of the particular grievances which they had laid before the Colonial Office – Republican designs in short, such as he deemed it his special vocation to combat. Nor was he far wrong, for their aim, once more be it noted, was nothing less than to take away the Government from the Crown and hand it over to the representatives of the people. It cannot be doubted that the example of the neighbouring Republic was in their minds. By Lyon Mackenzie the baronet and man of society was personally repelled. "The tiny creature," he says, "sat during the interview with his feet not touching the ground, and his face turned away from me at an angle of 70 degrees." That Mackenzie had been a "pedlar lad" and an "errand-boy" was all against happy relations with the Lieutenant-Governor. Head soon found himself in the arms of the Compact, and fighting against Responsible Government as democratic, American, and subversive of British institutions. This he now deemed his grand mission. Hard hitting ensued between him and the Reformers both in the Assembly and out of it. He even forgot his social tact and cut Toronto to the heart by telling her deputies that he would talk down to the level of their understandings. The Opposition played into his hands by identifying itself with Papineau and the agitators in the Lower Province, whose object clearly was revolution, and by giving publicity to an indiscreet letter of Joseph

Hume talking of "independence and freedom from the baneful domination of the mother country." These mistakes threw the force of the Conservative party decisively into the scale of the Government. Loyal addresses came in. The Lieutenant-Governor seized the advantage and went to the country crying Treason. The cry prevailed, with the help of Government influence unsparingly used, corruption, mob violence, and the inequalities of the representation. A large majority in favour of the Government was returned. Head was beside himself with exultation, and fancied that his spirited policy had put all his enemies under his feet and made him perfectly master of the situation. "In a moral contest," he wrote to the Colonial Office, "it never enters into my head to count the number of my enemies." "The more I am trusted," he said, "the more cautious I shall be; the heavier I am laden, the steadier I shall sail." The Colonial Office had begun to suspect what sort of an instrument it had in the man who wrote to it in this style, and told it that he was aware his gasconading answer to an address "might be cavilled at in Downing Street, as he knew it was not exactly according to Hoyle, but it must be remembered that revolutions could not be made with rose-water." Still it could not be denied that he had succeeded. The Colonial Office waited with mingled curiosity and anxiety for the result.

The result was that the Reformers were driven to despair, and the more violent of them to rebellion. Under the leadership of Mackenzie, the malcontents armed and drilled. Confident in the power of his moral thunderbolts, the Lieutenant-Governor scoffed at danger, sent all the regular troops to the Lower Province, neglected to call out the militia, or even to put his capital in a state of defence, and turned a deaf ear to every warning. Toronto all but fell into the hands of the rebels. Mackenzie, who showed no lack either of courage or of capacity as a leader, brought before it a force sufficient for its capture, aided as he would have been by his partisans in the city itself, and he was foiled only by a series of accidents, and by the rejection of his bold counsels at the last. Just in time however help arrived, the rebellion collapsed, and its leaders fled. A filibustering war was for some time kept up by the American "sympathisers" along the border, and the burning of the *Caroline*, a piratical steamer which the Canadians sent flaming over Niagara, gave rise to diplomatic complications. The American authorities were slow in acting; but they acted at last, and there is no reason to believe that the American people in general strongly sympathised with the rebellion in British Canada, much less with that in the French Province. After all, these raids, reprehensible as they are, may be regarded, like the trouble given to diplomacy about the Fisheries and Behring's Sea, as so many blind efforts of the New World to shake off European interference.

On the other hand, when it is said that the Canadian rebellion was put down by British bayonets, let it be borne in mind that in Upper Canada there was not a single British bayonet when the rebellion was put down. In both Canadas it was, in fact, not a rebellion against the British Government, but a petty civil war, in Upper Canada between parties, in Lower Canada between races, though in Lower Canada the British race had the forces of the Home Government on its side. "We rebelled neither against Her Majesty's person nor her Government, but against Colonial misgovernment," were the words of one of the rebel leaders in Lower Canada. The two movements were perfectly distinct in their origin and in their course, though there was a sympathy between them and both were stimulated by the general ascendency of Liberal opinions since 1830 in France, in England, and in the world at large.

The rebellion was the end of Sir Francis Bond Head. Now came Lord Durham, the son-in-law of Grey, and an Avatar, as it were, of the Whig Vishnu, to inquire into the sources of the disturbance, pronounce judgment, and restore order to the twofold chaos.

Chapter 7

The united provinces

Mission of Lord Durham / His report on the situation / Re-union of the two Provinces under a single Governor and legislature / Concession of responsible government / The change carried into effect by Lord Sydenham / Parties and politics under the new constitutional system / Governorship of Sir Charles Bagot / An attempt of Lord Metcalfe as Governor to restore the power of the Crown brings him into conflict with the Assembly and the people / Practical end of monarchical government in Canada / Governorship of Lord Elgin / Personal influence retained by him under the new system / The Rebellion Losses Bill / Secularisation of the clergy reserves / The reciprocity treaty / Failure of the policy of union to bring about British ascendency or assimilate the French element / Influence of the French in politics / Political combinations and parties / The "Clear Grits" and the struggle for representation by population / Series of ephemeral administrations / Political deadlock from which refuge is sought in Confederation / Other motives for that measure / Mood in which it was carried

The principal sources of this sketch, besides a number of pamphlets and State papers, are MacMullen's *History of Canada*, Scrope's *Life of Lord Sydenham*, Walrond's *Letters and Journals of Lord Elgin*, Dent's *Last Forty Years*, Collins's *Life of Sir J. A. Macdonald*, and Gray's *Confederation of Canada*.

LORD DURHAM was a splendid specimen of the aristocratic man of the people, such as perhaps only the Whig houses, after being out of office for half a century, could have produced. From the hotel where His Excellency put up all other guests were cleared out, and not even the mails were allowed to be taken on board the steamer which bore his person. Invested with large powers, he exceeded them in playing the despot. He issued an ordinance banishing some of the rebels to Bermuda, under penalty of death if they should return. This delivered him into the hands of Brougham, who bore him a grudge, and at once set upon him in the House of Lords, pointing out that His Excellency's ordinance could not be carried into effect without committing murder. The Prime Minister was compelled to disallow the ordinance. Durham after thundering very irregularly against the ungrateful Government which had thrown him overboard, flung up his commission, folded his tragic robe round him, and went home. He had time, however, to produce, with the help of Charles Buller, who was his secretary, a very able and memorable Report (1839).

His diagnosis was to the effect that the disease in Lower Canada arose from a conflict of races, while in Upper Canada it was political. The remedy proposed was to unite the Provinces and give them both Responsible Government. In Lower Canada the two races, Durham held, would never get on harmoniously by themselves. The causes of estrangement were too deep and the antipathy was too strong. The British minority would never bear to be ruled by a French majority. Rather than this they would join the United States, and "that they might remain English, cease to be British." Of fusion, according to Lord Durham, there was no hope. Opposed to each other in religion, in language, in character, in ideas, in national sentiment, hardly ever intermarrying, their children never taking part in the same sports, meeting in the jury-box only to obstruct justice, the two races were "two nations warring in the bosom of a single State." The rebellion had divided them sharply into two camps. "No portion of the English population had been backward in taking arms in defence of the government; with a single exception no portion of the Canadian population was allowed to do so, even where it was asserted by some that their loyalty induced them thereto." There was nothing for it but a union of the Provinces, in which a British majority should permanently predominate, and which should place the British minority of the Lower Province under the broad ægis of British ascendency. Durham flattered himself that by the same measure French nationality with all the political difficulties, and all the obstacles to economical improvement which it carried with it, would be gradually suppressed. "A plan," he said, "by which it is proposed to ensure the tranquil government of Lower Canada must include in itself the means of putting an end to the agitation of national disputes in the legislature by settling at once and for ever the national character of the Province. I entertain no doubt as to the national character which must be given to Lower Canada; it must be that of the British Empire, that of the majority of the population of British America, that of the great race which must in no long period of time be predominant over the whole North American Continent. Without effecting the change so rapidly or so roughly as to shock the feelings and trample on the welfare of the existing generation, it must henceforth be the first and steady purpose of the British Government to establish an English population with English laws and language in this Province, and to trust its government to none but a decidedly English legislature." Steady purpose of the British Government! Steady purpose of a Government which itself was changed on an average about once in every five years, and which neither had nor could have any purpose in reference to its far-distant and little-known dependency but to get along from day to day with as little trouble and danger as it could! Did not Durham himself say, that in the case of Lower Canada the Imperial Government, "far removed from opportunities of personal observation, had shaped its policy so as to aggravate the disorder;" that it had sometimes conceded mischievous pretensions of nationality to evade popular claims, and sometimes pursued the opposite course; and that "a policy founded upon imperfect information and conducted by continually changing hands had exhibited to the colony a system of vacillation which was in fact no system at all?" Durham took it for granted that the British majority would act patriotically together against the French. Strange that he, fresh from the field of a furious faction fight, should have been so forgetful of the ways of faction! Sir Francis Bond Head saw in this case what Lord Durham and Charles Buller did not see. "So long," he said, "as Upper Canada remains by itself I feel confident that by mere moderate government her 'majority men' would find that prudence and principle unite to keep them on the same side; but if once we were to amalgamate this province with Lower Canada, we should instantly infuse into the House of General Assembly a powerful French party, whose implacable opposition would be a dead, or rather a living weight, always seeking to attach itself to any question whatsoever that would attract and decoy the 'majority men,' and I feel quite confident . . . that sooner or later the supporters of British institutions would find themselves overpowered, not by the good sense and wealth of the country (for they would, I believe, always be staunch to our flag), but by the votes of designing individuals, misrepresenting a well-meaning inoffensive people." Apart from the writer's Toryism, this passage was prophetic. The British were sure to be split into factions, and their factions were sure to deliver them into the hands of the French. The only way of operating with success on two discordant races is to set an impartial power above them both, as Pitt meant to do when by his Act of Union he brought Ireland under the Imperial Parliament, though he could not help impairing the integrity of the Imperial Parliament itself by introducing the Irish Catholic vote. Head's own proposal to annex Montreal to British Canada was more sensible than the plan of union, though it would have left the British of Quebec city and the Eastern Townships out in the cold.

The reunion of the two Provinces had been projected before: it was greatly desired by the British of the Lower Province; and in 1822 a bill for the purpose had actually been brought into the Imperial Parliament, but the French being bitterly opposed to it, the Bill had been dropped. The French were as much opposed to reunion as ever, clearly seeing, what the author of the policy had avowed, that the measure was directed against their nationality. But since the rebellion they were prostrate. Their Constitution had been superseded by a Provisional Council sitting under the protection of Imperial bayonets, and this Council consented to the union. The two Provinces were now placed under a Governor-General with a single legislature, consisting like the legislatures of the two Provinces before, of an Upper House nominated by the Crown and a Lower House elected by the people. Each Province was to have the same number of representatives, although the population of the French Province was at that time much larger than that of the British Province. The French language was proscribed in official proceedings. French nationality was thus sent, constitutionally, under the yoke. But to leave it its votes, necessary and right as that might be, was to leave it the only weapon which puts the weak on a level with the strong, and even gives them the advantage, since the weak are the most likely to hold together and to submit to the discipline of organised party.

On the subject of Responsible Government the decisive words of the Durham Report are these: "We are not now to consider the policy of establishing representative government in the North American colonies. That has been irrevocably done, and the experiment of depriving the people of their present constitutional power is not to be thought of. To conduct the government harmoniously in accordance with its established principles is now the business of its rulers; and I know not how it is possible to secure that harmony in any other way than by administering the government on those principles which have been found perfectly efficacious in Great Britain. I would not impair a single prerogative of the Crown; on the contrary, I believe that the interests of the people of these colonies require the protection of prerogatives which have not hitherto been exercised. But the Crown must on the other hand submit to the necessary consequence of representative institutions; and if it has to carry on the government in unison with a representative body it must consent to carry it on by means of those in whom that representative body has confidence." In plain words, the Crown must let the House of Commons choose the ministers, and through them determine the policy. What was to be left to the crown? "Its prerogatives." What were they when it had surrendered supreme power? Canada would have seen perhaps if the imperious author of the Report had stayed to make the experiment of Responsible Government in his own person; and it is not unlikely that instead of the anticipated harmony, discord and perhaps collision would have ensued. Perfectly efficacious, Durham said, the system had been in Great Britain. But he forgot that it had not been really tried before the Reform Bill; that the Reform Bill had been only just passed; and that even in Great Britain the answer still remained to be given to the Duke of Wellington's question, how the Queen's Government was to be carried on.

In place of Durham, the experiment was made (1839-41) by Poulett Thomson, afterwards Lord Sydenham, a steady man of business and a prodigious worker, imperious only in his demands on official industry. He performed the function of capitulation on the part of the Crown with a good grace, and fairly smoothed the transition, though he did not escape abuse. His first ministry was formed of the men whom he found in office on his arrival, and who were Conservatives. But these men could not accommodate themselves to the new system. They fenced with the question of Responsible Government, and when they faintly affirmed the doctrine with their lips their hearts were evidently far from it. Nor could they fully take in the idea of a Cabinet, or understand the mutual responsibility of its members, the necessity for their agreement, and the duty incumbent on them of resigning when they differed vitally from their colleagues, or of going out of office with the rest. Mr. Dominic Daly, for instance, acted as if he deemed himself a fixture in office, whatever might be the fleeting policy of the hour. Mr. Draper, the Ajax of the Conservatives, being pressed on the vital point, enveloped himself in a cloud of words, and said "that he looked upon the Governor as having a mixed character; firstly, as being the representative of Royalty; and secondly, as being one of the Ministers of Her Majesty's Government and responsible to the mother country for the faithful discharge of the duties of his station, a responsibility which he cannot avoid by saying that he took the advice of this man or of that man." The Assembly, however, was not to be hoodwinked, nor was it to be appalled by the assertion, however unquestionably true, that by the acceptance of the new principle "the Governor would be reduced to a cipher, and that such a system would make the colony an independent state." It passed resolutions (1841) which affirmed plainly, though in Blackstonian phrase, that in all colonial affairs the Governor must be ruled by his advisers, that his advisers must be assigned him by the Assembly, and that the policy must be that of the majority. The men of the old dispensation had presently to retire and to make way for a ministry which had for its head Robert Baldwin the Reformer with whom was afterwards joined Lafontaine, a Frenchman who had been the political associate of Papineau though he himself just stopped short of rebellion. Even Dr. Rolph, the Upper Canadian rebel and exile, ultimately found a place in a Reform Government.

All however was not yet over. The advent of Peel to power in 1841 had placed the Colonial Office once more in Conservative hands. Sir Charles Bagot, the first Governor appointed by the Conservatives was a life-long Tory, but a well-bred and placid gentleman, who accepted with grace his constitutional position of figurehead, dispensed hospitality to politicians of all parties, and turned his energies to the encouragement of practical improvements, such as making roads, and to the laying of first stones, now one of the chief functions of British Royalty. But his conduct did not give satisfaction to Tories either in the colony or at home. Lord Stanley, the Colonial Secretary in Peel's second Ministry, by no means acquiesced in the view that his representative should be a cipher and the colony an independent State. Stanley's appointment was Lord Metcalfe (1843-5), a man of the highest eminence in the East Indian service, who in Hindostan, and afterwards in Jamaica, had governed on the most liberal principles, but had governed. In Canada also he meant to govern on liberal principles, but in Canada also he meant to govern. The East Indian official, accustomed to administer in his own person, was shocked to find that he was "required to give himself up entirely to the council," "to submit absolutely to their dictation," "to have no judgment of his own," "to be a tool in the hands of his advisers," and "to tear up Her Majesty's Commission by publicly declaring his adhesion to conditions including the complete nullification of Her Majesty's Government." Accustomed in the Indian Civil Service, the purest in the world, to appoint his subordinates by merit, he was shocked at being told that he must allow the patronage of the Government to be used for the purposes of the party in power and must proscribe all its opponents. He tried to make his own appointments, and brought on a storm. The Assembly carried a resolution affirming in effect that the prerogative of appointment, with all the rest, had passed entirely from the Crown to the Parliamentary Ministers, and the Ministry resigned.

The Governor, the Colonial Secretary approving his course, formed a makeshift Ministry of the men of the old school, and appealed from the majority to the country. The distinguished and high-minded civil servant now found himself, to his intense disgust, immersed in all the roguery, corruption, and ruffianism of a fiercely-contested election, forced to use government patronage as a bribery fund, and to pay for "Leonidas Letters" with appointments to public trusts. He and his Ministry came out of the fray with a small majority. His death cut the inextricable knot. With him expired Monarchical Government in Canada. Nothing but its ghost remained. Sir Edmund Head is said to have afterwards lingered wistfully in the Council Chamber and to have been shown the door by a Conservative minister.

Metcalfe was succeeded by Lord Cathcart, a soldier, sent out probably on account of the threatening aspect of the boundary dispute with the United States. Then came Lord Elgin (1849-54), in whom again we see the public servant of the Empire whose only rule has been administrative duty in contrast with the party leader and the demagogue. Elgin was a Conservative, and was sent out by a Conservative Government, but he was calm and wise. He accepted Responsible Government, and even flattered himself that under that system he exercised a moral influence such as would make up to the Crown for the loss of its patronage. This, with his personal gifts and graces, and while the system was still in the green wood, he may possibly have done. It is more certain that he gave an impulse to material improvements in the way of railways, canals, and steamboats, as well as to the advancement of education. In one case he accepted Responsible Government with a vengeance, for he gave his assent to the Rebellion Losses Bill. The bill was denounced by the Tories both in Canada and in the British House of Commons as a bill for rewarding rebels; a bill for indemnifying rebels it undeniably was. The Tories in Canada rose, pelted the Governor-General at Montreal with stones and rotten eggs, put his life in some danger, and raised a mob by which the Parliament House was burned down. Their opponents did not fail to taunt them with their failing loyalty; but it must be owned that they were sorely tried, and that the Rebellion Losses Bill was a humiliation. Such humiliations are the lot of an Imperial country retaining its nominal supremacy and its reponsibility in a hemisphere where it has resigned or lost all power. The Ashburton Treaty, made some years before, cutting Maine out of Canada's side, seemed to Canadians an instance of similar weakness on the part of the Home Government. They made too little allowance for the distracting liabilities of an Empire exposed to peril in every quarter of the globe.

There was still, however, a field for which Elgin was well suited, and in which he could act without the danger of "falling," to use his own words, "on the one side into the *néant* of mock majesty, or on the other, into the dirt and confusion of local factions." By the adoption of Free Trade in 1846 England had cut the commercial tie between herself and her colony, and deprived the colony of its advantage in the British market. Commercial depression in Canada ensued. Property in the towns fell fifty per cent in value. Three-fourths of the commercial men were bankrupt. The State was reduced to the necessity of paying all the officers, from the Governor-General downwards, in debentures which were not exchangeable at par. A feeling in favour of annexation to the United States spread widely among the commercial classes, and a manifesto in favour of it was signed not only by many leading merchants, but by magistrates, Queen's counsel, militia officers, and others holding commissions under the Crown. Elgin himself was astonished that the discontent did not produce an outbreak. There was, as he saw, but one way of restoring contentment and averting disturbance. This was "to put the colonists in as good a position commercially as the citizens of the United States, in order to which free navigation and reciprocal trade with the States were indispensable." To this view he gave effect by going to Washington and there displaying his diplomatic skill in negotiating the Reciprocity Treaty, which opened up for Canada a gainful trade, especially in her farm products, with the United States, and was to her, during the twelve years of its continuance, the source of a prosperity to which she still looks back with wistful eyes. The rush of prosperity at the time turned the head of the community, and caused over-speculation, which led to a crisis in 1857.

The grand revolution having been accomplished, the minor changes which were its corollaries followed in its train. After hesitation on the part of religious Reformers like Lafontaine, who cherished the idea of a provision for religion, the Clergy Reserves were secularised. The same stroke knocked off the fetters of the Church of England, gave her the election of her own officers, and set her free to win back the hearts which, as a domineering favourite of the State, she had estranged. Tithe in Lower Canada ought to have been abolished at the same time; but it was guaranteed, or was held to be guaranteed, by the Treaty of Cession, made with a most Christian dynasty which had ceased to reign and which has since been replaced by an Anti-Christian Republic. University tests were repealed, and the University of Toronto was thrown open: whereupon, Bishop Strachan gave way to his resentment, and instead of sticking to the ship in which he had still the advantage of possession and of social primacy, went off in a cockboat and founded a new Anglican University. Other sectarian universities had been founded while that of Toronto was confined to Anglicanism, and the net result has been six or seven degree-giving bodies in a Province the resources of which were not more than equal to the support of one university worthy of the name. At length, happily for the advancement of high education, learning, and science in Ontario, university consolidation has begun.

The Upper House of the Legislature was made elective, with the same suffrage as that of the Lower House, but with larger constituencies, and a term of eight years. Municipal institutions on the elective principle were given to Upper Canada. In Lower Canada the seigniories, with all their vexatious incidents, were swept away, not however without compensation to the seigniors, theories of agrarian confiscation not having then come into vogue.

The French speedily verified the prediction of Sir Francis Bond Head, and belied the expectation of Durham and Buller. "They had the wisdom," as their manual of history before cited complacently observes, "to remain united among themselves, and by that union were able to exercise a happy influence on the Legislature and the Government." Instead of being politically suppressed, they soon, thanks to their compactness as an interest and their docile obedience to their leaders, became politically dominant. The British factions at once began to bid against each other for their support, and were presently at their feet. Nothing could show this more clearly than the Rebellion Losses Bill. The statute proscribing the use of the French language in official proceedings was repealed, and the Canadian Legislature was made bilingual. The Premiership was divided between the English and the French leader, and the Ministries were designated by the double name – "the Lafontaine-Baldwin," or "the Macdonald-Taché." The French got their full share of seats in the Cabinet and of patronage; of public funds they got more than their full share, especially as being small consumers of imported goods they contributed far less than their quota to the public revenue. By their aid the Roman Catholics of the Upper Province obtained the privilege of Separate Schools in contravention of the principle of religious equality and severance of the Church from the State. In time it was recognised as a rule that a Ministry to retain power must have a majority from each section of the Province. This practically almost reduced the Union to a federation, under which French nationality was more securely entrenched than ever. Gradually the French and their clergy became, as they have ever since been, the basis of what styles itself a Conservative party, playing for French support by defending clerical privilege, by protecting French nationality, and, not least, by allowing the French Province to dip her hand deep in the common treasury. On the other hand, a secession of thorough-going Reformers from the Moderates who gloried in the name of Baldwin, gave birth to the party of the "Clear Grits," the leader of which was Mr. George Brown, a Scotch Presbyterian, and which having first insisted on the secularisation of the Clergy Reserves, became, when that question was out of the way, a party of general oppostion to French and Roman Catholic influence. The population of Upper Canada having now outgrown that of Lower Canada, the Clear Grits demanded that the representation should be rectified in accordance with numbers. The French contended with truth that the apportionment had been irrespective of numbers, and that Upper Canada, while her population was the smaller, had reaped the advantage of that arrangement. Mortal issue was joined, and "Rep. by Pop." (Representation by Population) became the Reform cry. The war was waged with the utmost vehemence by Mr. Brown and his organ, the *Globe,* which became a power, and ultimately a tyrannical power, in Canadian politics. But the French, with the British faction which courted their vote, were too strong. A change had thus come over the character and relations of parties. French Canada, so lately the seat of disaffection, became the basis of the Conservative party. British Canada became the stronghold of the Liberals. But the old Tories of British Canada, true at least to their antipathies, combined with the French against the Liberals in the amalgam styled Conservative.

Irish influence, almost as sectional as the French, was now beginning to grow powerful. The famine of 1846 had thrown upon the shores of Canada thousands of miserable exiles, stricken with pestilence as well as with famine. At the moment when Canada lost her commercial privileges as a colony, she was called upon to perform the most onerous of colonial duties to the mother country, and the duty was nobly performed, the medical profession taking the lead in heroic philanthropy. Abortive insurrections in Ireland added some political exiles. Among the number was D'Arcy M'Gee, a Fenian leader who, in a happier political climate, doffed his Fenianism while he retained his enthusiasm and his eloquence, and for doffing his Fenianism was murdered by his quondam fellow-conspirators. There was now an Irish as well as a French vote to be played for. Had not the difference of race generally prevailed, as we have said, over the identity of religion, there might have been a coalition of the two Roman Catholic races, which would almost have reduced the other races to political servitude.

A struggle of principle is sure to leave some men of principle as well as mark upon the scene. Such were Robert Baldwin on one side, and Draper on the other. But when these have passed away faction, intrigue, cabal, and selfish ambition have their turn. What else can be expected with party government when the great issues are out of the way and nothing but the prizes of office remains? Already, in Lord Elgin's time, politics had entered on a phase of party without principle. He had pensively remarked that in a community "where there was little if anything of public principle to divide men, political parties would shape themselves under the influence of circumstances, and of a great variety of affections or antipathies – national, sectarian, and personal." "You will observe," he says, "when a Ministry is trying to recruit itself by coalition, that no question of principle or of public policy has been mooted by either party during the negotiation. The whole discussion has turned upon personal considerations. This is, I fancy, a pretty fair sample of Canadian politics. It is not even pretended that the divisions of party represent corresponding divisions of sentiment on subjects which occupy the public mind." He complains that his Ministers insist on appealing to low personal motives, as if they did not believe in the existence of anything higher, that unprincipled factiousness is taken for granted as the rule of conduct on all hands, and that he is himself in danger of being besmirched by its mire. A period of tricky combinations, perfidious alliances, and selfish intrigues now commenced, and a series of weak and ephemeral governments was its fruit. The Hincks-Morin, the MacNab-Morin, the Taché-Macdonald, the Brown-Dorion, the Cartier-Macdonald, the Sandfield Macdonald-Sicotte, the Sandfield Macdonald-Dorion, the Taché-Macdonald (second) administrations followed each other like the shifting scenes of a farce, their double headships indicating the necessity of compounding with the French, whose vote was the great card in the game. Unfortunately they left their traces. "A political warfare," said Senator Ferrier (a Montreal merchant) afterwards in the debate on Confederation, "has been waged in Canada for many years of a nature calculated to destroy all moral and political principle, both in the Legislature and out of it." In such a competition, unscrupulous craft, with a thorough knowledge of the baser side of human nature, is sure to prevail, and to mount to the highest place. It did prevail; it did mount to the highest place, and became the ideal of statesmanship to Canadian politicians.

It was in the course of this unimpressive history that the one remaining prerogative of the Crown was exercised by the Governor-General for the last time.[1] In 1858, Mr. George Brown, the leader of the "Clear Grits" put the Conservative Ministry in a minority on the question of the choice of a site for the Capital, the Queen having given her decision in favour of Ottawa. Though the combination against the Government was fortuitous, and the question not one of principle, the Ministry resigned; it was surmised because they thought it politic to appear as martyrs to their loyal respect for the Sovereign's judgment. The Governor, Sir Edmund Head, sent for Mr. Brown but refused him a dissolution, on the ground that the Parliament was newly elected, that there was no reason for supposing that public opinion had changed, and therefore that there was no justification for throwing the country again into the turmoil of an election. Mr. Brown's fortuitous majority deserting him, his Ministry at once fell. The Governor was of course fiercely denounced by the Grits for partisanship; but supposing he still held the prerogative of dissolution, it would seem that he did right; he certainly did what was best for the country. A farcical sequel to this episode was the "Double Shuffle," a name applied to a piece of legerdemain by which the old Ministers, on resuming their places, contrived to bilk the constitutional rule which required them to go to their constituencies for re-election. Public morality was outraged. The courts of law, by an extremely technical construction, sustained the trick. But nothing smarter was ever done by any Yankee politician.

1 It has been since exercised on one occasion by a Lieutenant-Governor of a Province.

At last there came a Ministry with a majority of two, which afterwards dwindled to one, so that the fate of the administration might hang upon the success of a page in hunting up a member before a division, and the dangerous opportunity was afforded to each individual politician of saving the country by his single vote. Dissolutions only made faction more factious. Finally there was a deadlock. The wheels of the political machine ceased to turn, and the most necessary legislation was at a stand. As a door of escape from the predicament into which their factiousness and selfishness had brought the country, the politicians bethought them of a confederation, including all the North American Colonies of Great Britain. In this the antagonism between British and French Canada, which was the immediate source of the dilemma, would be merged, and altogether there would be a fresh deal. The idea of such a confederation was not new. Lord Durham had recommended it in his Report: even before his day, Judge Haliburton had ventilated the idea in *Sam Slick*; while Mr. George Brown, finding that he could not carry his project of Representation by Population, had been proposing that the Union between Upper and Lower Canada should be reconstituted on a federal footing, so that they might be made independent of each other in their local affairs. The three Maritime Provinces – Nova Scotia, New Brunswick, and Prince Edward Island – had, as has been already said, meditated a Legislative Union among themselves; and, though a difficulty about the choice of a capital had come in the way, it is likely that in time they would have carried the project into effect.

Another inducement to confederation at this juncture was the belief that it would bring to all the Provinces an increase of military strength and of security against invasion. On this head there was at the time some ground for alarm on account of the critical position into which Canada as a dependency of Great Britain had been drawn in relation to the United States. Before the American Civil War Canada had been, like the mother country, an enemy of the Slave Power; one of the first acts of her yeoman legislators in the Upper Province had been the abolition of slavery; and she had prided herself on being the refuge of the slave. At the opening of the conflict between Slavery and Freedom her heart had been where it was natural that it should be. But after the *Trent* affair she had been drawn, together with the aristocratic party in England, into an attitude of hostility to the North. Her citizens had taken to drilling, and she had sounded the trumpet of defiance. Her Government had strictly discharged their international obligations, but the Confederates had violated the neutrality of her territory in the case of the St. Alban's raid, and some of her own citizens who were hot sympathisers with the Slave Power had hardly kept their sentiment within the bounds of the Queen's proclamation. The Union was now triumphant and had a large and victorious army at its command. There was reason to fear that its ire, kindled by the conduct of Great Britain in the matter of the *Alabama,* and by the stinging language of the British Press, might find vent in an attack on the dependency. There had in fact been a Fenian raid encouraged by the laxity of the American Government, if not by its connivance, and somebody having blundered, a number of Canadians had in the disastrous affair of Ridgeway fallen in defence of the frontier. The second Fenian raid in 1870 was a mere imposture got up to make the money flow again from the pockets of Irish servant girls; but the first was rendered formidable by the presence among the raiders of Irishmen who had fought in the American Civil War. It was a natural impression, though some saw through the fallacy at the time, that the political union of the Provinces would greatly add to their force in war. The Home Authorities also applauded the project, in the hope that the colonies would become better able to defend themselves, lean thenceforth less heavily for protection on the arm of the overburdened mother country, and be less of an addition to her many perils. Some years before, Lord Beaconsfield, then Mr. Disraeli, Imperialist as he was, had written in confidence to the Minister for Foreign Affairs urging him to push the Fisheries question to a settlement while the influences at Washington were favourable, and remarking that "these wretched colonies will all be independent too in a few years and are a millstone round our necks."[1] What Mr. Disraeli said in the ear was said on the housetop by the *Edinburgh Review,* which after averring that it would puzzle the wisest to put his finger on any advantage resulting to Great Britain from her dominions in North America, and glancing at the "special difficulties which beset her in that portion of her vast field of empire," pronounced it not surprising that "any project which

1 See Lord Malmesbury, *Memoirs of an Ex-Minister*, vol. ii, p. 344.

may offer a prospect of escape from a political situation so undignified and unsatisfactory should be hailed with a cordial welcome by all parties concerned." If the same thing was not said by other statesmen it was present in a less distinct form to the minds of some of them: at least they were very anxious that the millstone should be a millstone no more, but be able to provide for its own defence at need and perhaps to help the mother country. Colonial Reformers like the Duke of Newcastle, Mr. Adderley, and Mr. Godley who clung to the political connection, were just as desirous of relieving the mother country of the military burden and of training the colonies to self-reliance and virtual independence as were the men of the so-called Manchester School, who advocated complete independence. Cobden and Bright, it may be remarked by the way, though their opinion was avowed, never took a very active part in the discussion.

A third motive was the hope of calling into existence an intercolonial trade to make up for partial exclusion from that American market which Canada had been enjoying to her great advantage during the last twelve years. To the anger which the behaviour of a party in England had excited in America, Canada owes the loss of the Reciprocity Treaty, and the bitter proof which she has since had of Lord Elgin's saying that free navigation and reciprocal trade with the States are indispensable to put her people in as good a position as their neighbours. If Great Britain can with justice say that she has paid heavily for the defence of Canada, Canada can with equal justice reply that she has paid heavily, in the way of commercial sacrifice, for the policy of Great Britain.

Under the pressure of necessity the faction-fight was suspended, and a coalition government, after some haggling, was formed (1864) with Confederation as its object, the Grit leader, Mr. George Brown, and two of his friends entering it, with Sir John A. Macdonald and his Conservative colleagues, under the figure-headship first of Sir Etienne Taché and, on his death, of Sir Narcisse Belleau. The spectacle was seen, as a speaker at the time remarked, of men who for the last twelve years had been accusing each other of public robberies and of every sort of crime seated on the Ministerial benches side by side. Delegates, comprising the leading men of both parties, were appointed by the Governors of Canada, Nova Scotia, New Brunswick, and Prince Edward Island, at the instance of the several legislatures. They met and drew up a scheme which, having been submitted to the legislatures, was afterwards carried to London, there finally settled with the Colonial Office, and embodied by the Imperial Parliament in the British North America Act, which forms the instrument of Confederation. The consent of the Canadian Legislature was freely and fairly given by a large majority. That of the Legislature of New Brunswick was only obtained by heavy pressure, the Colonial Office assisting, and after strong resistance, an election having taken place at which every one of the delegates had been rejected by the people. That of the Legislature of Nova Scotia was drawn from it, in defiance of the declared wishes of the people and in breach of recent pledges, by vigorous use of personal influence with the members. Mr. Howe, the patriot leader of the Province, still held out and went to England threatening recourse to violence if his people were not set free from the bondage into which, by the perfidy of their representatives, they had been betrayed. But he was gained over by the promise of office, and those who in England had listened to his patriot thunders and had moved in response to his appeal, heard with surprise that the orator had taken his seat in a Federationist administration. Prince Edward Island bolted outright, though high terms were offered her by the delegates,[1] and at the time could not be brought back, though she came in some years afterwards, mollified by the boon of a local railway for the construction of which the Dominion paid. In effect, Confederation was carried by the Canadian Parliament, led by the politicians of British and French Canada, whose first object was escape from their deadlock, with the help of the Home Government and of the Colonial Governors acting under its directions.

The debate in the Canadian Parliament fills a volume of one thousand and thirty-two pages. A good deal of it is mere assertion

1 In the autumn of 1866, Mr. J. C. Pope (Premier of Prince Edward Island) went to England "and an informal offer was made through him by the delegates of the other provinces, then in London, settling the terms of Confederation, to grant the Island $800,000 as indemnity for the loss of territorial revenue and for the purchase of the proprietors' estates, on condition of the Island entering the Confederation."–*History of Prince Edward Island,* by Duncan Campbell, p. 180.

and counter-assertion as to the probable effects of the measure, political, military, and commercial. One speaker gives a long essay on the history of federations, but without much historical discrimination. Almost the only speech which has interest for a student of political science is that of Mr. Dunkin, who, while he is an extreme and one-sided opponent of the measure, tries at all events to forecast the working of the projected constitution, and thus takes us to the heart of the question, whether his forecast be right or wrong. Those who will be at the trouble of toiling through the volume, however, will, it is believed, see plainly enough that whoever may lay claim to the parentage of Confederation – and upon this momentous question there has been much controversy – its real parent was Deadlock.

Legally, of course, Confederation was the act of the Imperial Parliament, which had full power to legislate for dependencies. But there was nothing morally to prevent the submission of the plan to the people any more than there was to prevent a vote of the Colonial Legislatures on the project. The framers can hardly have failed to see how much the Constitution would gain in sacredness by being the act of the whole community. They must have known what was the source of the veneration with which the American Constitution is regarded by the people of the United States. The natural inference is that the politicians were not sure that they had the people with them. They were sure that in some of the provinces they had it not. The desire of escaping from the political dilemma, however keenly felt by the leaders, would not be so keenly felt by the masses, and the dread of American invasion would scarcely be felt by them at all. There was no such pressure of danger from without as that which enforced union on the members of the Achæan League, on the Swiss Cantons, on the States of the Netherlands, on the American Colonies; while the British Colonies in North America were already for military purposes as well as for those of internal peace united under the Imperial Government, so that the main purpose of a federal union was already fulfilled. Without worship of universal suffrage or of the people, it may be said that the broader and deeper the foundation of institutions is laid the better, and that the sanctity once imparted by the fiat of a king can now be imparted only by the fiat of the whole nation. A compact invalid in its origin may, no doubt, be made valid by acquiescence; but the Constitution of the

Canadian Confederation is valid by acquiescence alone. It is said that at general elections which followed, federation was practically ratified by the constituences: but at a general election different issues are mixed together; various questions, local and personal as well as general, operate on the voter's mind; the legislative questions are confused with the question to whom shall belong the prizes of office; party feeling is aroused; a clear decision cannot be obtained. The only way of obtaining from the people a clear decision on a legislative question is the plebiscite. Unless the single issue is submitted a fair verdict will never be returned. If some day Canadians are called upon to make a great sacrifice of wealth and security in order that they may keep their own institutions, the reply perhaps will be that the institutions are not their own but were imposed upon them by a group of politicians struggling to escape from the desperate predicament into which their factiousness had drawn them, employing in some cases very questionable means to arrive at their end, and bringing to bear upon Canada the power of a distant government and Parliament, which, worthy as they might be of reverence, were those of the British, not those of the Canadian people.

So far as political affinity was concerned the Maritime Provinces were ready for Confederation. To each of them had been given the same Constitution as to the two Canadas. Each of them had a Governor, an Executive Council, an Upper House of Parliament nominated by the Crown, and a Lower House elected by the people. The political history of each of them had followed the same course. In each of them an official oligarchy had entrenched itself in the Executive Council and the Upper House. In each of them its entrenchments had been attacked and at last stormed by the popular party which predominated in the Elective House. In Prince Edward Island with the struggle for responsible government had been combined a war with an absentee proprietary of original grantees, which was at last settled under an Act of the Imperial Parliament, such as was in those times deemed a startling infringement of proprietary rights, though it was mild indeed compared with the Irish land legislation of the present day. Patriots in the Maritime Provinces had in fact acted in sympathy with patriots in Canada, and the leaders of either party in each battlefield had kept their eyes fixed upon the other. Sir Francis Head, for instance, watched anxiously the progress of the struggle in New Brunswick, and in the surrender of the Colonial Office and its representative there read the general doom. Everywhere the war had been waged on nearly the same issues, the chief being the control of the civil list, and everywhere its result had been the same. Responsible government had prevailed, and the Crown, under a thin veil of constitutional language, had given up its power to the people. About the time when in Canada Sir Charles Metcalfe was striving to recover power for the Crown a desperate attempt of the same kind had been made by Lord Falkland in Nova Scotia. But Lord Falkland, like Sir Charles Metcalfe, succumbed to destiny, whose Minister in his case was the great orator and patriot, Joseph Howe.

Chapter 8

The federal constitution

The monarchical element of the Constitution / The Governor-General / His loss of political power / His social and other functions / The office devoid of constitutional value / Baronetcies and knighthoods / Futility of attempts to introduce aristocracy into the New World / Canada in reality a Federal Republic / Deviations of the Canadian Constitution from the American model / Powers of the central government and legislature / The veto power / The Canadian Senate compared with the American Senate, and with the British House of Lords / The Canadian House of Commons and its composition / Localism in elections / Party government / Weak points of the elective system / Provincial governments and legislatures / The interpretation of the Constitution / The Supreme Court / The Civil Service / The Judiciary / Canada practically independent of the mother country / Canada affords no precedent for Irish Home Rule / A written constitution a necessity of democracy / Ottawa as the seat of government

The Canadian Constitution is to be studied in the British North America Act of 1867, on which abundant commentaries have appeared by Messrs. Todd, Bourinot, O'Sullivan, Watson, and Doutre. To the works of these learned and eminent writers the reader is referred for such details as do not come within the scope of this very general sketch. The debate on Confederation in the Canadian Parliament (Quebec, 1865) may be consulted by the diligent reader. Extracts from the principal speakers are given in Colonel Gray's work on Confederation.

IN DUTIFUL imitation of that glorious Constitution of the mother country, with its division of power among kings, lords, and commons which, though it really died with William III, still exists in devout imaginations, the Constitution of the Canadian Dominion has a false front of monarchy. The king who reigns and does not govern is represented by a Governor-General who does the same, and the Governor-General solemnly delegates his impotence to a puppet Lieutenant-Governor in each province. Everything is done in the names of these images of Royalty, as everything was done in the names of the Venetian Doge and the Merovingian kings; but if they dared to do anything themselves, or to refuse to do anything that they were told to do, they would be instantly deposed. Religious Canada prays each Sunday that they may govern well, on the understanding that heaven will never be so unconstitutional as to grant her prayer. Like their British prototype, they deliver from their thrones speeches which have been made for them by their Prime Ministers, to whom they serve as a ventriloquial apparatus. Each of them, to keep up the constitutional illusion, is surrounded by a certain amount of state and etiquette, the Governor-General, of course, having more of it than his delegates. At the opening of the Dominion Parliament by the Governor-General there is a parade of his bodyguard, cannon are fired, everybody puts on all the finery to which he is entitled, the knights don their insignia, the Privy Councillors their Windsor uniform, and the ladies appear in low dresses. At the opening of a Provincial Parliament the ceremony is less impressive, and in some cases is reduced to a series of explosions mimicking cannon.

The last prerogative which remained to the Governor-General was that of Dissolution. We have seen that Sir Edmund Head exercised his own judgment in declining to dissolve Parliament at the bidding of Mr. George Brown. But this power of control seems since to have been abandoned like the rest. The Governor-General now appears to feel himself bound to dissolve Parliament at the bidding of his Minister, without any constitutional crisis requiring an appeal to the country, or cause of any kind except the convenience of a Minister who may think the moment good for snapping a verdict. We here see that a political cipher is not always a nullity, but may sometimes be mischievous. That the existence of a Parliament should be made dependent upon the will and pleasure of a party leader, and should be cut short as often as it suits his party purposes, is obviously subversive of the independence of the legislature. Such an arrangement would never be tolerated if it were openly proposed. But it is tolerated, and with perfect supineness, when, instead of the name of the Prime Minister, that of the Governor-General is used. The robe of the Queen's representative in this and other cases forms the decorous cover for the practices of the colonial politician. In the case before us the arbitrary power grasped by the party leader under constitutional forms in the Colony seems even to have exceeded that grasped by the party leader in the mother country. In the mother country some good authorities at least still maintain that the Crown has not entirely resigned the prerogative, and that the Sovereign may refuse a dissolution, except in case of a Parliamentary crisis, such as renders necessary an appeal to the people, or when the House of Commons has been deprived of authority by the close approach of its legal end. At all events, in England tradition has not wholly lost the restraining power which it had when government was in the hands of a class pervaded by a sense of corporate responsibility and careful not to impair its own heritage. An American or Canadian politician in playing his game uses without scruple every card in his hand; traditions or unwritten rules are nothing to him; the only safeguard against his excesses is written law. The Americans are surprisingly tolerant of what an Englishman would think the inordinate use of power by the holders of office; but then they know that there is a line drawn by the law beyond which the man cannot go, and that with the year his authority must end. The politician in Canada, not less than in the United States, requires the restraint of written law.

A Governor-General has been made to read a speech from the Throne commending to the nation a commercial policy which was not only opposed to his own opinions as a free trader, but laid protective duties on British goods. Nor is it possible to doubt that in appointments his personal conscience and honour are treated as entirely out of the question. A Governor-General, about whose own keen sense of right there could be no question, has thus been made to place upon the Bench of Justice, manifestly for a party purpose, a man upon whose appointment the whole profession, without distinction of party, cried shame. To the appointment of his own representatives, the Lieutenant-Governors or to those of Senators, the Governor-General, it is generally believed, has not a word to say.

We had a decisive proof of the Governor-General's impotence in the case of Mr. Letellier de St. Just, who was deposed from the Lieutenant-Governorship of Quebec. Mr. Letellier had been appointed by a Liberal Government. He quarrelled with a Provincial Ministry of the opposite party for breach of rules, turned it out, and called in other advisers, who, upon an appeal to the Province, were sustained, though by a bare majority. The Quebec Conservatives were infuriated at the loss of the Provincial patronage. In the Dominion Senate, where their party had a majority, they at once got a vote of censure passed on the Lieutenant-Governor. They had not at that time a majority in the House of Commons, but a general election having soon after given them a majority, they passed a vote of censure in the Lower House also. The party leader thereupon, as Prime Minister, "advised" the Governor-General to dismiss Mr. Letellier. It was simply an act of party vengeance, Mr. Letellier having done nothing which was not strictly within the letter of the Constitution, and having been sustained by the people of his province. The Act of Confederation required that for the dismissal of a Lieutenant-Governor a cause should be assigned. The only cause assigned was, that after the adverse vote of the Dominion Parliament "his usefulness had ceased." Evidently this was no cause at all, but a mere mockery. What the law required was the assignment of a specific breach of duty, of which it could not be pretended that the Lieutenant-Governor had been guilty. The votes of the Senate and the House of Commons were nothing but manifestations of party resentment. Their character was marked by the manner in which they had been passed; not in the same session, so as to represent the judgment of Parliament, but in different sessions, the vote of the House of Commons being delayed till the result of the election had given the party power in that House. It was evident that the conscience of the Governor-General recoiled from this treatment of his own representative, whose rights and character he was specially bound in honour to guard. He referred to the Colonial Office, but the Colonial Office bade him obey his constitutional advisers. He might have done the Colony a great service, though at some risk to himself, had he told the Minister that on questions of policy he was ready to be guided by others, but that on questions of justice, especially in a case where his own deputy was concerned, he had a conscience of his own, and that he would do what honour bade him or go home. The Minister would probably have given way, and at all events a most wholesome lesson would have been read. But grandees do not run risks. *Noblesse oblige* is the reverse of the truth. The nobleman is rather apt to feel that even if he does what would compromise another, his rank will carry him through.

The Governor-Generalship, it is said, saves Canada from presidential elections. Presidential elections are an evil, and as at present conducted by popular vote they are a morbid excrescence on the American Constitution, since the farmers intended the electoral college really to elect, though it is strange that they should not have foreseen that election by a college chosen for the nonce would result in a mandate. But the Governor-Generalship is not the Presidency of Canada: the Prime Ministership is the Presidency, and the general election in which the Prime Ministership and Cabinet offices are the prize is little less of an evil than the presidential election. The same answer meets the allegation that the Governor-Generalship or the monarchical element which it represents is a pledge of political stability. The Government of Canada has of late years presented an appearance of stability, the account of which will be given hereafter. But in Australia ministers, notwithstanding the presence of a governor, are as fleeting as shadows chasing each other over a field, and the same was the case in Canada before Confederation. The real government is liable to constant change, which is no more tempered or countervailed by the permanency of the Governor than by the permanency of the Sergeant-at-Arms. An American government is comparatively stable, having a fixed tenure for four years.

The constitutional hierophants of Ottawa, such as Mr. Alpheus Todd, assure the uninitiated in solemn tones that in spite of appearances which may be deceptive to the vulgar, the Governor-Generalship is an institution of great practical value, as well as of most awful dignity. Highly deceptive to the vulgar, it must be owned, the appearances are.

If it is said that the service is not political but social, and that the little Court of Ottawa is needed to refine colonial manners, the answer is first, that the benefit must be limited to the Court circle; and secondly, that colonial manners do not stand in need of imported refinement. Nobody who lives long on the American Continent can fail to be struck with the fact that vulgarity is but the shadow of caste. The manners of men who have raised themselves from the ranks of industry are in all essential respects perfectly good, so long as the men are allowed to remain in their native element of equality and not infected with aristocratic notions or set striving to imitate an alien model. If there is anything in Canadian manners which is traceable to the Court at Ottawa, it is not that which is best in them. Indeed, if the stories which sometimes get abroad of Ottawa balls and suppers are true, Ottawa refinement itself occasionally stands in need of refining.

The example of an expensive household or of profuse entertainments is of questionable value. One Governor-General was specially noted for the profusion of the entertainments by which he courted popularity, as well as by the increase which he made in the cost of his office to the country; and it is said that officials with small salaries at Ottawa rue his fancy balls to this hour.

The same Governor-General also courted popularity by oratorical tours, or, to use the common phrase, by going on the stump. The orations necessarily consist largely of flattery, and the effect of flattery on a young nation is pretty much the same as on a young man.

When Royalty became a denizen of Government House an attempt was made by some zealous officials to introduce monarchical etiquette. An enthusiastic professor of deportment went over privately to consult the Lord Chamberlain, and published a manual for the instruction of ignorant Canadians. The keynote is struck by the exordium, "What on this earthly sphere is more enchantingly exclusive than Her Majesty's Court" – a doubtful assertion, perhaps, since the powers of wealth have triumphantly forced their way into those precincts. "The impression," proceeds the Professor, "made by the debutante is a lasting one in England, consequently art is brought to bear, and the curtseys, the walk, the extending the arm for the train, and each physical movement are practised repeatedly before some competent teacher of deportment, who charges well for the lessons." Imagine the ladies of a commercial colony fired with this ambition! The genius of the Continent rejected etiquette as it had rejected Pitt's proffered boon of a hereditary peerage. When an edict went forth that at Court balls ladies should appear in low dresses, unless they could obtain from their physicians a dispensation on the ground of health, a comic journal had a print of a bare-footed servant girl asking the master of the ceremonies whether nakedness at that extremity of the person would not do as well.

As an object of social worship the representative of Royalty keeps his place. Like Royalty itself, he is taken about to open institutions or exhibitions; words of approbation which he may be pleased to utter are recorded as oracles, and sacrificial banquets are offered to him. What is the social value of such a worship every one must determine for himself. In England it seems that the worship goes on while the smallest and most necessary payment for the support of the idol raises a storm of popular anger.

The practical aim of a Governor-General is social popularity combined with political peace. So long as he simply gives way in everything to the politicians, he will have a quiet course, and at the end of it he will go away amidst general plaudits with the reputation of having "governed" Canada well. Discerning eulogists will even point out to you the particular gifts of mind and temper which have enabled him to administer his province with so much success. He is then qualified in the eyes of the Home Government for a higher post, and India will be fortunate if she does not some day get from this manufactory of spurious reputations a less competent Viceroy than Lord Lansdowne. Connection and responsibility end together with the parting salute.

As an authoritative informant of the Home Government about Canadian affairs and sentiment the Governor-General, besides being a newcomer to the country, lies under the twofold disadvantage of being a personage to whom it is difficult to speak the truth, and of being always in an official capital where, on certain subjects, not much truth is spoken. If, like Haroun Alraschid, he could go about in disguise conversing with his lieges, he might learn and impart to the Colonial Office what would be worth knowing. As it is, when we read the disquisitions of an ex-Governor-General on the country which was the scene of his administration, we at once become sensible of the happy environment in which during his tenure of office he has lived.

There are those who think that figments, though worse than useless in any other department, are useful in politics, and that there is an occult virtue in the practice of fetichism and hypocrisy. Only let those theorists remember that the reverence which is bestowed on the false is withdrawn from the real ruler, and that servile worship of a fetich and manly respect for lawful authority are not always found dwelling in the same breast. Democracy has its perils, Heaven knows. Let us look them in the face and deal with them as best we may. To hide them from us by throwing over them the veil of a mock monarchy is not to help us in our endeavour.

The same people will also believe in the usefulness of baronetcies and knighthoods, which have survived the catastrophe of the abortive Canadian peerage, and of which the Governor-General is the supposed conduit, though it is surmised that of late the party leader has virtually got this prerogative also into his hands, and added it to his general fund of influence. Let us have titles of honour by all means, so long as they denote a public trust. Let the Councillor of State or the Judge be styled Honourable, and the Mayor His Worship. Let scientific and military eminence be marked by their appropriate decorations. There is no reason why Democracy should deny herself such emblems of civil dignity and incentives of generous ambition any more than there is a reason why she should deny herself rational and symbolic state. She too must have her æsthetics. But titles of chivalry do not denote a public trust. In the age of chivalry they had a meaning; now they are merely personal decorations, and if they serve any public object it is that of introducing into the Colonies, in the supposed interest of British aristocracy, sentiments at variance with those on which, in such communities, public effort and public virtue must be based. They can feed, to put it plainly, nothing but flunkeyism. Some of the worthiest men in Canada have refused them. They are given sometimes with little discernment; they have even served to gild dishonour. Baronetcies, the fashion of creating which has of late been revived, are open to the further objection which was urged with decisive force against the creation of an hereditary peerage in a country where there are no entailed estates. We may some day have a baronet blacking shoes. To make a Canadian politician a baronet is to tempt and almost to constrain him to use his political opportunities for the purpose of accumulating a fortune to bequeath to his son. This is no imaginary danger. Nor when honour has been forfeited can the title and its influence be annulled.

Aristocracy had its uses in its time. That it served as an organising force in a barbarous age, no one versed in history will deny. The feudal lord was not a sybarite with a title; sheathed in iron, he lived, as a leader, a magistrate, and a rural law-giver, laborious days. Possibly the services of the institution may not yet be exhausted in the lands to which it is native: there it may at all events be destined to smooth a transition. But it has no business in the New World, and the attempt to import it never has done and never can do anything but mischief. To make a colony an outpost of aristocracy for the purpose of maintaining that institution at home is to sacrifice the political character of an American community to the interest of a European caste.

The Lieutenant-Governorships are bestowed by the party leader invariably on his partisans and usually on worn-out politicians. That they form a decent retirement for those who have spent their energies in public life but on whom the community would not consent to bestow pensions, forms the best defence for their existence. Political value they have none. The theory is that Government House in each province forms a centre of society: but the men after their stormy lives are generally too weary for social effort and the salary is not sufficient for hospitality on a large scale. Men of wealth and high social position, who might fulfil the social ideal, are not likely to take the appointments. As one of them said bluntly, they do not want to keep a hotel for five years.

Passing through the false front into the real edifice we find that it is a federal republic after the American model, though with certain modifications derived partly from the British source. The Dominion Legislature answers to Congress, the Provincial Legislature answers to the State Legislature, the Dominion Prime Minister and Cabinet answer to the President and his Cabinet, the Provincial Prime Ministers and their Cabinets to the Governor and Officers of States. The relations of the Province and the Dominion to each other are in the main the same as those of the State and the Federation. Were a Canadian Province to be turned at once into a State of the Union the change would be felt by the people only in a certain increase of self-government. The political machinery would act as it does now.

The deviations in the Canadian copy from the American original are chiefly in the direction of an increase of the Federal power. The framers of the Canadian Constitution fancied that American secession was an awful warning against leaving the Federal Government too weak. In this they were mistaken, for slavery and slavery alone was the cause of secession, and had the Federal Government possessed authority to deal with the Southern institution and proceeded to exert it, that would only have precipitated the catastrophe. Perhaps, however, the Canadian legislators were also swayed by the centralising tendency and sentiment of the monarchy with which they were connected. Their bias at all events was in favour of central power. Some of them would have preferred a legislative union had they been able to overcome the centrifugal nationalism of Quebec. To the Federal Government and Legislature in Canada belong criminal law and procedure. To the Federal Government belongs the appointment of all the judges. To the Federal Legislature belong the regulation of trade and the law of marriage. The Federal Government has the direct command of the Militia, whereas in the United States the President can only call upon the State Government for military aid. It has by the Constitution a political veto on all State legislation, whereas in the American Republic State legislation can be cancelled only on legal grounds by the Supreme Court. And whereas by the American Constitution all powers not given to the Federation are left in the States, by the Canadian Constitution all powers not given to the provinces are left in the Federation. This last distinction is important. The origin of it was, that the sovereign power which gave birth to the Confederation had its seat not, as in the case of the Americans, in the several federating communities, but in the Crown and Parliament of Great Britain.

About the nature and importance of the national veto on provincial legislation doubts have recently been raised from a motive which will presently be explained, but there were no doubts at the time. Mr. (afterwards Sir John) Rose said in the debate: "The other point which commends itself so strongly to my mind is this, that there is a veto power on the part of the General Government over all the legislation of the Local Parliaments. . . . I believe this power of negative, this power of veto, this controlling power on the part of the Central Government, is the best protection and safeguard of the system; and if it had not been provided I would have felt it very difficult to reconcile it to my sense of duty to vote for the resolutions. But this power having been given to the Central Government it is to my mind, in conjunction with the power of naming the local governors, the appointment and payment of the judiciary, one of the best features of the scheme, without which it would certainly, in my opinion, have been open to very serious objection." This plainly refers to a power of political control to be exercised in the interest of the nation, not to a mere power of restraining illegal stretches of jurisdiction, a function which belongs not to a government but to a court of law. Again, Mr. Mackenzie, afterwards Premier, said: "The veto power is necessary in order that the General Government may have a control over the proceedings of the Local Legislature to a certain extent. The want of this power was the great source of weakness in the United States, and it is a want that will be remedied by an amendment in their Constitution very soon." This could not refer to a mere power of restraining excesses of jurisdiction on the part of State Legislatures, since such a power is already possessed and constantly exercised by the Supreme Court. In like manner Mr. Dorion, Mr. Joly, and other opponents of the scheme assume that the veto is general, and regard it accordingly with suspicion. The point of these remarks will hereafter appear.

Thus, constitutionally, the Canadian Dominion is less federal and more national than the American Republic. Practically the reverse is the fact, because in the case of the American Republic the unifying forces, economical and general, of which the power increases with the advance of commerce and civilisation, have free action, the barrier of slavery being now removed; whereas in the case of Canada their action is paralysed by geographical dispersion, commercial isolation, and the separatist nationality of French Quebec.

The American President is elected by the people at fixed periods, and for a term certain. He and his Cabinet have no seats in Congress, nor has he any part in legislation except his veto and such influence as his position in the party may enable him to exercise behind the scenes. The framers of the American Constitution were full of Montesquieu's false notion about the necessity of entirely separating the executive from the legislative, and probably also of that supersensitive dread of the presence of placemen in the popular assembly which in England gave birth to the Place Bills. The Canadian Premier, like the British Premier, is elected by the people at periods rendered uncertain by the power of dissolution, and for so long only as he can keep his majority in the House of Commons. On the other hand, he and his Cabinet have seats in Parliament, where, with their majority at their back, they initiate the most important part of legislation and control the whole of it. Assuming that government is to be by party, the Canadian and British system has clearly the advantage in respect to the conduct of legislation. The American House of Representatives is apt for want of leadership to become a legislative chaos. Order and the progress of business are secured only by allowing the speaker, who ought as chairman to be neutral, to act as the party leader of the majority, and control legislation by a partisan nomination of the committees. A speaker having thought it right to confine himself to his proper duties, anarchy prevailed and legislation was at a standstill till a masterful and unscrupulous partisan got into the chair, when legislation and expenditure marched with a vengeance. The advantage, we say, depends on the existence of government by party; for, were party out of the way, there seems to be no reason why a legislative assembly with a competent chairman should not get on with its business as well as an assembly of any other kind. Another plea which may be made for the Canadian system is that by a sure and constitutional process it brings the executive into agreement with the legislature and with the people by whom the legislature is elected, whereas when President Andrew Johnson entered upon a course of policy directly at variance with the policy of Congress no remedy could be found except the very rough remedy of impeachment. It is on this account that some Canadians boast that their system is more democratic than that of the Americans, and taunt the American Republic with being monarchical and even autocratic.

On the other hand, the American system gives the country a stable executive independent of the fluctuating majorities of the legislative chamber and of those shifting combinations, jealousies, and cabals which in France, and not in France alone, have been making it almost impossible to find a firm foundation for a government. The American Executive for the four years of the Presidential term is independent; it would be so at least were it not for the baleful influence of the power of re-election. As it is, the veto is sometimes exercised most uprightly and with the best effect, while the Presidential Government, raised in some measure above the party strife, enjoys a dignity and a measure of national respect which to the party Premiership are denied. A Canadian Premier always engaged in party fighting and manœuvring, perpetually on the stump, stoops to acts which, if done by an American President, would cause great scandal. The American system moreover has the advantage of sometimes admitting to the Cabinet and to the highest service of the State men of high administrative ability who are not party managers and rhetoricians. Such selections indeed have been not unfrequently made. Turgot would probably have been a bad Parliamentary leader and a failure on the stump: he could hardly have made his way into a Parliamentary Cabinet; but in an American Cabinet, supposing his name had become known as an administrator and a master of political science, he might have found a place. Of the Presidents themselves, several have been men who, though attached to the party by which they were nominated, had not spent their lives in the party war, and their patriotism and breadth of view have been greater on that account.

When we come to compare the Canadian Senate with its American counterpart, though the form and the nominal power are the same, the actual difference is great indeed. The American Senate, elected by the State Legislatures, is in the full sense of the term a co-ordinate branch of the Federal Congress with the House of Representatives, rejects the Bills passed by the House with perfect freedom, and with equal freedom initiates legislation on all subjects except finance. It has a veto on appointments, and can in this way put strong though irregular pressure on the Executive. It has a veto on all treaties, as Foreign Governments which have the misfortune to negotiate with that of the United States know to their cost. Of late, under a violent stress of party exigency, it has been bringing a stain upon its record. It has been consenting to a Tariff Bill, the folly of which no man of sense can fail to see, and doing in regard to the admission of new States and the decision of Senatorial elections what no party exigency can excuse. Faction corrupts all that it touches. There is also a growing belief that wealth exerts an undue influence both directly and indirectly in Senatorial elections. Still the power of the Senate remains the same; its authority is generally regarded by Americans as the sheet-anchor of the State, and a seat in it is, after the Presidency, the highest prize of American ambition. The Canadian Senate nominated by the Crown is, on the contrary, as nearly a cipher as it is possible for an assembly legally invested with large powers to be. The question as to the constitution of the Upper House when it came before the framers of the Dominion

Constitution was not mooted in Canada for the first time. Under the old Constitution, first of the separate then of the United Provinces, the Legislative Council, as the Upper House was then called, had been nominated by the Crown. This system had been pronounced a failure and a change to the elective system was one of the reforms which followed the transfer of supreme power from the Crown to the people. Lord Elgin was in favour of the change, though he saw as he thought that among its advocates, with some whose aim was Conservative, there were others whose aims were "subversion and pillage." He expressed his belief "that a second legislative body returned by the same constituency as the House of Assembly under some differences with respect to time and mode of election would be a greater check on ill-considered legislation than the Council as it was then constituted;" and he predicted that Robert Baldwin, who opposed this with other organic changes, and having got what he imagined to be the nearest thing to the British Constitution wished to cast anchor, would, if he lived, find his ship of State among unexpected rocks and shoals. His own ideas, perhaps, were not very clear. He wished to introduce the elective principle, yet in such a way as not to exchange "Parliamentary Government," which was his idol, for "the American system," which he abjured; but in what essential respect a system with two elective Chambers and with supreme power vested in the representatives of the people would differ from the American system he might have found it difficult to explain. In 1856, however, as has been already said, the change was made and the system adopted was that of election by popular vote, the suffrage being the same as that for elections to the House of Commons, but the electoral divisions much larger, and the term eight years instead of four. The alternative of election by Provincial legislatures of course could not present itself under the legislative union. The experiment of an Upper Chamber elected by the people appears not to have been successful, the labour of canvassing the extended electoral divisions being found so oppressive by candidates that the best men declined to come forward. It is curious that the Fathers of Confederation when they came to debate the constitution of their Upper House seemed to think that their only choice was between the retention of election by popular suffrage and a return to the system of nomination by the Crown. It did not occur to them apparently that as they were about to erect

Provincial legislatures corresponding to the State legislatures of the Americans they might vest in these the election of the Senate. Their chief reason for rejecting the elective principle and going back to nomination appears to have been that if the Senate felt the sap of popular election in its veins, its spirit would become too high, it would claim equality as a legislative power with the House of Commons, perhaps even in regard to money bills, and collision between the Houses would ensue. But these are perils inseparable from the system of two Chambers. Wherever the power is divided between two assemblies, collision may at any time arise, and if the collision is prolonged deadlock may ensue. There has been legislative deadlock or something very like it at Washington when one of the political parties has had a majority in the House of Representatives and the other in the Senate. You cannot have the advantages of union and division of power at the same time. To construct a body which, without claiming co-ordinate authority, shall act as a Court of legislative revision, and as the sober second-thought of the community, is practically beyond the power of the political architect. He must try to ensure sobriety where he places power. To suppose that power will allow itself on important matters to be controlled by impotence is vain. Evidently the image of the House of Lords hovered before the minds of the builders of the Canadian Constitution. But the House of Lords has never acted as a court of legislative revision or as an organ of the nation's sober second-thought. It has acted as the House of a privileged order, resisting all change in the interest of privilege. It resisted Parliamentary reform till it was overborne by the threat of a swamping creation of peers. All the power which it retains is the power of hereditary rank and wealth. Nothing analogous to it exists or can exist in Canada, and in framing Canadian institutions it ought to have been put out of sight.

Nomination having been chosen it followed that the appointments should be for life: nothing else could give the nominees of the Crown even a semblance of independence. But the result is a nullity, or rather an addition to the number of vicious illusions, since the sense of responsibility in the Lower House may be somewhat weakened by the impression, however false, that its acts are subject to revision. The Senate is treated with ironical respect as the Upper House and surrounded with derisive state. The decorations of its Chamber surpass those of the Commons' Chamber as the decorations of the Lords' Chamber surpass those of the Commons' Chamber at Westminster. The members sit in gilded chairs, are styled Honourable, and on all ceremonial occasions take precedence of the holders of real power. But these, like the observance paid to the Governor-General and his Vicegerents, are merely the trappings of impotence. The Senate neither initiates nor controls important legislation. After meeting for the Session it adjourns to wait for the arrival of Bills from the Commons. About once in a Session it is allowed to reject or amend some measure of secondary importance by way of showing that it lives. It is supposed to be sometimes used by the Minister who controls it for the purpose of quashing a job to which he has been obliged to assent in the Lower House. Measures of importance may sometimes be brought in first in the Upper House, for the sake of saving time, but they never originate with it. At the end of the Session the measures passed in the Lower House are hurried through the Upper House with hardly time enough for deliberation to save the semblance of respect for its authority. Its debates are rarely reported unless piquancy happens to be lent to them by personal altercation. Nobody dreams of looking to it for the second-thought of the nation, or imagines that in any political emergency it could serve as the sheet-anchor of the State. Men of a certain class may seek seats in it for the sake of the title, the trappings, and whatever of social grade may be attached to membership. To some possibly the annual payment of a thousand dollars and mileage may be an attraction. But Senatorships are not sought from the promptings of a generous ambition or a desire to render active service to the country. Almost the only serious business of the Senate is sitting in judgment, as the House of Lords used to do, on divorce cases, an incongruous function, exercised because the French Catholics will not allow the Dominion to have a regular Divorce Court.[1] The experience which led under the Union to the reform of the old nominee Legislative Council and the judgment of Lord Elgin on that subject are confirmed; and it is proved that under the elective system nothing which is not based on election can have power.

It is true that the work of those who instituted the nominee

1 Thanks to the exertions of Senator Gowan, something more of the character of a regular Divorce Court has recently been given to the Senate.

Senate has hardly had a fair chance. They may have reckoned on a broad, tolerably impartial, and patriotic exercise of the power of appointment. They may have had before their minds an assembly comprehending representatives of national eminence in all lines, not the agricultural and mercantile only, but the professional, the scientific, the educational, and opening its doors to men capable of doing good service in special departments of legislation, as well as of lending by their character and attainments dignity to the Legislature, but without inclination or aptitude for the party platform or the turmoil of popular elections. Even the Bonapartes tried to make their Senate respectable by giving it a character of this kind. But of the seventy-six Senators of Canada, all but nine[1] have now been nominated by a single party leader, who has exercised his power for a party purpose, if for no narrower object. "My dear P____, I want you before we take any steps about T. Y____'s appointment to see about the selection of our candidate for West Montreal. From all I can learn W. W____ will run the best. He will very likely object; but if he is the best man you can easily hint to him that if he runs for West Montreal and carries it, we will consider that he has a claim to an early seat in the Senate. This is the great object of his ambition." This letter, from a Prime Minister to a local party manager, illustrates at once the sort of work which a Canadian Prime Minister does and the principle upon which he uses his power of appointment to the Senate. Money spent for the party in election contests and faithful adherence to the person of its chief, especially when he most needs support against the moral sentiment of the public, are believed to be the surest titles to a seat in the Canadian House of Lords. If there is ever a show of an impartial appointment it is illusory. When the expenditure of money is a leading qualification, commerce is pretty sure to be well represented. But no one will pretend that the general emincence of Canada is represented by its Senate. No intellectual or scientific distinction finds a place, while illiteracy scarcely excludes those who have served a party leader well. The age of the members as a body would in itself preclude active work. It will be seen from the letter just quoted that

1 This includes some members of the old Legislative Council, in the selection of whom the Act enjoined that consideration should be shown to both political parties.

the Prime Minister treats the Governor-General as a perfect cipher in regard to these appointments, and looks upon the patronage as entirely his own. Propose that a party leader shall in his own name nominate one branch of the Legislature and you will be met with a shout of indignation; but under the name of the Crown a Prime Minister is allowed to nominate a branch of the Legislature without protest of any kind. Such is the use of fictions!

A life tenure, though it makes a nominee more independent than a tenure for a term of years, does not make him entirely independent of the power which created him, though it does make him entirely independent of the people and of public opinion. He is still eligible for political office as well as for a baronetcy or a knighthood. He has sons and nephews. The other day a controversy having arisen about the quality of cloth furnished to the Militia for uniforms, it transpired that the contractor was a member of the Senate. In the case of the British House of Lords general independence is secured, apart from any mode of political appointment, by hereditary rank and wealth, and there is usually nothing to be feared but the bias of the privileged order.

That of seventy-six members all but nine would ever be the nominees of a single party leader the framers of the Constitution can hardly have anticipated. But they did anticipate a preponderance of different parties in the two Houses which might bring on a collision and a deadlock. Against this they tried to provide by an expedient borrowed from the British method of constitutionally coercing the House of Lords. To swamp an adverse majority in the Senate a Minister is allowed to create three or six extra Senators. The device is both clumsy and invidious, besides being open to exception as a recognition of the party principle. But weighted down as the scale now is with the following of a single politician, an additional creation of six would have no perceptible effect upon the balance. If the other party should come into office, and the Senate under the influence of the Outs should be inclined to give trouble to the Ins, there is no way of bringing it to its senses short of a revolution. Instead of being a mere cipher, it may possibly become an active source of evil if it ever allows itself to be used as an engine by the man to whom the majority of its members owe their nominations, for the purpose of embarrassing the Government when he is out of power.

In imitation of the Constitution of the United States, which recognises the federal principle by giving two Senators to each State without regard to population, the Canadian Act of Federation assigned an equal number of senators (24) to each of the great divisions of the Dominion, Ontario, Quebec, and the Maritime Provinces. Provision was made for the extension of the principle to provinces thereafter to be admitted.

As the Senate was to be distinctively federal, representing the provinces, the House of Commons was to be national, representing the people of the whole Dominion. In the House of Commons and the Ministers whose tenure of office depends upon its vote supreme power centres. In this the Canadian Constitution is a faithful copy of that of Great Britain. But copying the Constitution of Great Britain not for Canada only, but for all communities like Canada, is perilous work unless they understand their model more distinctly than it is understood at home. The House of Commons was not originally intended to be the Government or even the Legislature. The Government resided in the Crown, and the House of Commons was merely the representation of the people summoned by the Crown to grant it money, and at the same time to inform it about the state and wants of the country. Through its hold over the purse it gradually drew to it supreme power and in effect became the State. But it at the same time ceased to be in reality a popular assembly, and became, though in irregular and illegitimate ways, a representation of the wealth and high political intelligence of the nation. In this phase of its existence it was oligarchical, no doubt, and legislated in the interest of a class, but it was a powerful and dignified assembly capable of governing the country. It was enabled to be what it was because England had a large leisure class at liberty to devote itself to public life and to serve the country without wages. It is now as a consequence of democratic change rapidly losing this character, and it is at the same time becoming an anarchy and a bear-garden incapable either of legislation or of government, incapable even of putting down the feeblest rebellion or preserving the integrity of the nation. A commercial colony has no such class as that which supplied the members of the House of Commons in the palmy days of that body. It has very few men of wealth and leisure, still fewer of those who, having inherited wealth, are at liberty from their youth, if they possess the sense of duty or the ambition, to devote themselves to politics. The chiefs of commerce, the leading manufacturers and the bankers, the lawyers and physicians who are in good practice, the most substantial and the wealthiest members of the community generally, cannot afford to leave their business and spend four months of every year in rather petty politics at Ottawa, to say nothing of the drafts made upon their time by canvassing, correspondence with constituents, and the fell demands of the stump. It is necessary therefore to have recourse for politicians to an inferior class of men, and too often to those who have failed in other industries or prefer living on the public to living by the sweat of their brows. Go to one of these assemblies, look behind the thin line of ability or of political experience presented by the front bench, and you will see the connection of effect with cause. Business interests and the necessity of looking after legislation which affects their trades will draw to Parliament a certain number of commercial men, and these probably will be about the best material that you will get, though they are not likely to be statesmen, while they are likely to have interests of their own. This is not a criticism upon the work of the framers of the Canadian Constitution alone; it applies to the whole system of governing through supposed imitations of the British House of Commons.

When you have in making up your legislature to call in the country lawyer, the country doctor, the storekeeper, the farmer, the payment of members plainly becomes a necessity. The salary of a thousand dollars and mileage is small, but it is enough to tempt a man hanging rather loose upon industry, or a country practitioner with little practice. Advocates of the system assume the case to be, that the electors having chosen a poor man for his worth it is requisite in order to secure to them his services to give him a salary, whereas the fact may be, that the salary induces the poor man to compass heaven and earth in order to press himself on the electors. To French members, whose habits are very frugal, the indemnity is said to be sometimes a livelihood, and there is reason to believe that their unwillingness to risk the loss of it forms something of a practical check upon the Minister's use of the power of dissolution. Public men of the higher stamp have been heard to condemn the system as apt to call into activity local intriguers who devote themselves to capturing beforehand the favour of the constituency, and close the avenue against worthier candidates whom the election day might otherwise bring forward. The revolutionary party in England appears to have taken up payment of members as a democratic measure. It is democratic with a vengeance, and is a pretty sure way of turning the highest of callings into a trade not so high. Still where there is no leisure class, or where the leisure class is excluded from public life, as a needy man cannot live on his sense of duty, you have to choose between paying him regularly and letting him pay himself in irregular ways. Of the two evils the first is clearly the less.

Among the American errors, of which even Liberals who took part in founding the Canadian Confederation promised themselves to steer clear, was universal suffrage. Canadian suffrage in those days was comparatively conservative, the qualification being practically ownership of a freehold, which was not beyond the reach of any industrious and frugal man. But the inevitable Dutch auction has been going on, alike in Dominion and in Provincial politics, and it is evident that to universal suffrage – to manhood suffrage at least – Dominion and Provinces will soon come. Already they have come to its very verge. Thus power will be transferred from the freehold farmers to people far less conservative, and at the same time from the country to the city. It has already been mentioned that the public school system does its work but imperfectly in educating the dangerous class. As in Great Britain so in Canada, the politicians who style themselves Conservatives vie in the competition with those who call themselves Liberals, and like their compeers at Westminster "dish the Whigs." It was a Conservative Minister that extended the franchise to Indians, who, it was anticipated, would have patriotism and intelligence enough, if proper inducements were held out to them, to vote for the Government candidate. The same Minister attempted, probably with the same strategical motive, to give the franchise to women, but the conservatism of his French supporters, in regard to the relations of the sexes, forced him to withdraw his proposal.

Canadian politics are also exemplifying a weakness of democracy which though little noticed by political writers is very serious – its tendency to narrow localism in elections. In the United States the localism is complete, and the ablest and most popular of public men, if he happens to live in a district where the other party has the majority, is excluded from public life. In England, before the recent democratic changes, places were found on the list of candidates for all the men of mark, wherever they might happen to live, and a good many non-residents are still elected, though localism has evidently been gaining ground. In Canada there is a chance still for a non-resident if he holds the public purse, perhaps if he holds a very well-filled purse of his own, but as a rule localism prevails. Even the Prime Minister of Ontario, after wielding power and dispensing patronage for eighteen years, encounters grumbling in his constituency because he is a non-resident. A resident in one electoral division of Toronto would be rather at a disadvantage as a candidate in another division, though the unity of the city, commercial and social, is complete. The mass of the people into whose hands power has now passed naturally think much less of great questions, political or economical, than of their own local and personal interests; of these they deem a local man the best champion, and they feel that they can correspond more freely about them with him than with a stranger. Besides they like to keep the prize among themselves. Such, in the exercise of supreme power, are the real tendencies of those whom collectively we worship as the people. That the calibre of the representation must be lowered by localism is evident; it will be more lowered than ever when the rush of population, especially of the wealthy part of it, to the cities shall have concentrated intelligence there and denuded of it the rural districts. The Hare plan, of a national instead of a district ticket, would immensely raise the character of the representation if it could be worked; but it assumes a level of intelligence in the mass of the people far above what is likely for many a generation to be attained. In the meantime as, on the one hand, the local man represents the choice of nobody outside his own district, and on the other hand men are excluded by localism whom the nation at large would elect, the net outcome can hardly be with truth described as an assembly representing the nation.

But the most important point of all in the case of Canada, as in that of every other Parliamentary country, is one to which scarcely an allusion was made in the debate on Confederation, and of which the only formal recognition is the division of the seats in the Halls of Parliament. Regulate the details of your Constitution as you will, the real government now is Party; politics are a continual struggle between the parties for power; no measure of importance can be carried except through a party; the public issues of the day are those which the party managers for the purposes of the party war make up; no one who does not profess allegiance to a party has any chance of admission to public life. Let a candidate come forward with the highest reputation for ability and worth, but avowing himself independent of party and determined to vote only at the bidding of his reason and conscience for the good of the whole people, he would run but a poor race in any Canadian constituency. If independence ever presumes to show its face in the political field the managers and organisers of both parties take their hands for a moment from each other's throats and combine to crush the intruder, as two gamblers might spring up from the table and draw their revolvers on any one who theatened to touch the stakes. They do this usually by tacit consent, but they have been known to do it by actual agreement. What then is Party? We all know Burke's definition, though it should be remembered that Burke on this, as on other occasions not a few, fits his philosophy to the circumstances, which were those of a member of a political connection struggling for power against a set of men who called themselves the King's friends and wished to put all connections under the feet of the King. But Burke's definition implies the existence of some organic question or question of principle, with regard to which the members of the party agree among themselves and differ from their opponents. Such agreement and difference alone can reconcile party allegiance with patriotism, or submission to party discipline with loyalty to reason and conscience. Organic questions or questions of principle are not of everyday occurrence. When they are exhausted, as in a country with a written constitution they are likely soon to be, what bond is there, of a moral and rational kind, to hold a party together and save it from becoming a mere faction? The theory that every community is divided by nature, or as the language of some would almost seem to imply, by divine ordinance, into two parties, and that every man belongs from his birth to one party or the other, if it were not a ludicrously patent example of philosophy manufactured for the occasion, would be belied by the history of Canadian parties with their kaleidoscopic shiftings and of Canadian politicians who have been found by turns in every camp. Lord Elgin, coming to the governorship when the struggle for responsible government was over, and a lull in organic controversy had ensued, found, as his biographer tells us, that parties formed themselves not on broad issues of principle, but with reference to petty local and personal interests. On what could they form themselves if there was no broad issue before the country? Elgin himself complained, as we have seen, that his ministers were impressed with the belief that the object of the Opposition was to defeat their measures, right or wrong, that the malcontents of their own side would combine against them, and that they must appeal to personal and sordid motives if they wished to hold their own. That is the game which is played in Canada, as it is in the United States, as it is in every country under party government, by the two organised factions – machines, as they are aptly called; the prize being the Government with its patronage, and the motive powers being those common more or less to all factions – personal ambition, bribery of various kinds, open or disguised, and as regards the mass of the people, a pugnacious and sporting spirit, like that which animated the Blues and Greens of the Byzantine Circus. This last influence is not by any means the least powerful. It is astonishing with what tenacity a Canadian farmer adheres to his party Shibboleth when to him, as well as to the community at large, it is a Shibboleth and nothing more. Questions of principle, about which public feeling has been greatly excited, questions even of interest which appeal most directly to the pocket, pass out of sight when once the word to start is given, and the race between Blue and Green begins. Questions as to the character of candidates are unhappily also set aside. It is commonly said that Canada produces more politics to the acre than any other country. The more of politics there is the less unfortunately there is of genuine public spirit and manly readiness to stand up for public right, the more men fear to be in a minority, even in what they know to be a good cause. People flock to any standard which they believe is attracting votes; if they find that it is not, they are scattered like sheep. Political aspirants learn from their youth the arts of the vote-hunter; they learn to treat all questions as political capital, and to play false with their own understanding and conscience at the bidding of the wirepullers of their party. The entrance to public life is not through the gate of truth or honour. These are not peculiarities of Canada; they are things common to all countries where the party system prevails, and peculiar only in their intensity to those countries in which party is inordinately strong.

It is a necessity of the party system that the Cabinet is made up not of eminent administrators, but of men who are masters of votes or skilful in collecting them. One minister represents the French vote, another the Irish Catholic vote, a third the Orange vote, a fourth the Temperance vote. The Ministry of Finance in a commercial country is consigned to a star of the philanthropic platform. Next to gathering votes by management the chief attribute of statesmanship is effectiveness on the stump. Hardly a public man in Canada has a high reputation as an administrator. The Prime Minister notoriously pays little attention to his department. He speaks on great public questions, such as the fiscal system, only to show that he has not much given his mind to them. His title to his place is that of unique experience and unrivalled dexterity in the collection and combination of votes. In all this Canada only resembles other Parliamentary countries, but in analysing a particular set of institutions it is necessary to recall the general facts.

The absence in the debate on Confederation of any attempt to forecast the composition and action of Federal parties fatally detracts from the value of the discussion. If Australia or any other group of Colonies thinks of following the example of Canada, a forecast, as definite as the nature of the case will permit, of Federal parties will be at least as essential to the formation of a right judgment as the knowledge of anything relating to the machinery of the Constitution.

Party government necessarily brings with it a party Press, with its well-known characteristics, in which the party Press of Canada has certainly not been behind its compeers. Of late an independent journalism has been struggling into existence and giving some expression to opinions unsanctioned by the party machines. Questions, such as that of the Jesuits' Estates Act, on which the politicians were tongue-tied, have in this way been freely treated, and men who would never receive a party nomination have been enabled on such questions to take a share of public life.

The best apology for Party is one which at the same time, in the case of Canada as in every other case, discloses an almost fatal weakness in the whole elective system of government. The system theoretically assumes that the electors will lay their heads together to choose the best men. Practically, it is impossible for the electors to do anything of the kind. They are a multitude of people unknown for the most part to each other, without anything to bring them together, and without any power of setting a candidature on foot. The best qualified are not likely, perhaps they are of all the least likely, to come forward of themselves. An organisation of some sort there must be to bring a candidate forward and collect votes for him, and it is difficult to devise any other sort of organisation than Party. The inevitable results of this, however, are the domination of faction, with all its malignity, its violence, its corruption, its calumny, its recklessness of the common weal; the ascendency of the Caucus and of Mr. Schnadhorst; government of the people by the people, and for the people, in name, government of the Boss, by the Boss, and for the Boss, in reality. The consequence in England is nearly half the House of Commons trooping out behind a party leader, and under the lash of the party whip, to vote against their recorded convictions for the dismemberment of their country. The fruits of the system in Canada, and everywhere else, are of the same kind. In Canada, as elsewhere, though there are honourable men in public life, the standard of morality which ought to be the highest in politics is in politics the lowest. The community is saved by its general character, by its schools, its churches, its judiciary; by the authority which chiefs, generally worthy, and always more or less able, exercise over industrial and commercial life. By its elective polity it would scarcely be saved.

The partition of power giving the civil law to the Provinces and the criminal law to the Dominion, whereas by the American Constitution both are given to the States, does not seem very reasonable in itself. The same legislative intellect is required in both cases, nor is the boundary between the two lines clearly defined. But this was a necessary concession to Quebec, who clings to her French law as a pledge of her national existence. It has been already mentioned that the absence of divorce courts is a concession to the same influence.

The structure of the provincial governments and legislatures generally, with their constitutional Lieutenant-Governors, their Parliamentary Premiers and Cabinet, is the same as that of the Dominion government and legislature, though on a small scale. Like the Governor-General, the Lieutenant-Governor is a figurehead, and constitutional writers who say that he has the assistance of an Executive Council to aid and advise him in administering public affairs, might say the same thing with equal truth of his flagstaff. Identical also is the procedure, and so is the ceremony, so far as any ceremony is retained. But Ontario, Manitoba, and British Columbia – democracy apparently becoming more intense as it goes west – have done away with the Upper House. In other provinces, as in Nova Scotia, efforts have been made to abolish the Upper House, as a waste of public money, but the House clings to its existence. Members nominated on the special condition that they shall vote for abolition, when they have taken their seats, find reasons for endless delay. No proprietor of a rotten borough ever clung to his political property with more tenacity than a democrat clings to any anomaly in which he has an interest. The change to a single house, if not material in itself, brings clearly to view the fact that a heavy responsibility is cast on these bodies of municipal legislators, which by a single vote can in one night enact the most momentous change in anything connected with civil right or property, totally alter the law of wills, or profoundly modify the relations between the sexes by the introduction of female suffrage. The Legislature of Ontario once broke a will at the solicitation of parties interested, though the Courts of Law found a reason for treating the Act as void. The Governor of a State in the American Union has a real veto, which he exercises freely. A governor put his veto not long ago on a Bill passed in a moment of heedlessness, which would have subverted the civil status of marriage. Moreover no amendment can be made in the Constitution of an American State, no extension of the State franchise can take place, without submission to the people. This is a great safeguard. The general disposition of the people is against change. In other respects the experience of Switzerland in regard to the Referendum is confirmed by that of the United States. At all events the people are not accessible to personal influence or cajolery as individual legislators are, while the issue being submitted to them separately, and not mixed up with other issues, as is the case at general elections, can be better grasped by their intelligence. Nominally the Lieutenant-Governor of a province has a veto, really he has none; and once more we see the pernicious effect of constitutional figments in veiling real necessities. Political architects in the United States, looking democracy in the face, attempted at all events to provide the necessary safeguards. At first, under the Canadian Constitution, the same man could sit both in the

Dominion and the Provincial Legislatures. Provincial Legislatures were led by men who sat in that of the Dominion. But, by a self-denying ordinance (1872), the wisdom of which was perhaps as questionable as that of self-denying ordinances in general, it is now forbidden to any man to sit in more Legislatures than one. This change increases the demand on the not very abundant stock of legislative capacity in the country, lowers the quality of the Provincial Legislatures, and enhances the peril of committing vital questions to their hands. The farmer, the country practitioner, or the village lawyer, are good representatives, we are told, of the average mind; they may be, but to solve aright problems at once the most difficult and the most momentous something more than the average mind is required. Perhaps the advocate of the party system may find a specious argument in the subordination which it entails of the rank and file of a legislative assembly on each side to the party leader, who is likely to be a man of superior intellect and knowledge. The leaders are usually lawyers, and acquainted with the British statute book, which forms a lamp to guide their feet in the legislative path. Yet lawyers complain of the Ontario statute book, and the need of a government draftsman seems to be felt.

The function of interpreting the Constitution in the last resort, and keeping each of the Powers within its proper bounds, discharged in the United States by that august tribunal the Supreme Court, is discharged in the case of Canada, as of the other colonies, by that still more august tribunal, the Judicial Committee of the British Privy Council, with its romantic range of jurisdiction, now deciding who shall take a Hindoo inheritance and offer the family sacrifice to a Hindoo deity, now pronouncing on the validity of an excommunication laid on by the Roman Catholic Church of Quebec. In the integrity and ability of the Judicial Committee absolute confidence is felt; but a doubt is sometimes raised whether judges ignorant of Canada can place themselves exactly at the right point of view, and complaints are heard of the distance and the expense. To spare suitors in these respects was partly the object in giving Canada a Supreme Court, which intercepts not a little of the litigation; and which, if the Canadian Confederation ever becomes independent, will be to it what the Supreme Court is to the United States. The Judicial Committee, though a legal, not a political tribunal, perhaps does not leave considerations of statesmanship entirely out of sight.

In deciding questions between the Dominion and the Provinces it seems to have leant to the side of Provincial autonomy, as most conducive to the peace of the Confederation, much as in ecclesiastical cases it leans to comprehension in the interest of the stability of the Church.

The American Constitution is subject to amendment, as we know, though by a very guarded process. So much of the Canadian Constitution as is composed in the Act of Confederation can be amended only by the same authority by which the Act was passed, that of the Imperial Parliament. This amounts almost to practical immutability, for the Imperial Parliament, sinking beneath the burden of its own business, has no time or thought to bestow on the improvement of colonial institutions. That power of Constitutional amendment, without which there cannot be full liberty of self-development, Canada can hardly hope to acquire without the severance of the political connection.

More than one good thing in her polity Canada has derived from her specially English traditions. She has in the first place a permanent Civil Service which saves her from the Spoils System introduced in the United States by that incarnation of faction and mob-rule, General Jackson, whose victory at New Orleans, as it made him President and filled American politics with his spirit, though he lost not a score of men in the action, is the most dearly bought victory in history. Party in Canada does not, as in England, quite keep its hands off the Civil Service. It practically takes the appointments, for though there is an examination system, this is so managed as to be like the sugar-tongs which the Frenchman held, in compliment to the habit of his English hosts, while he slipped his fingers between them to take up the sugar. Vacancies are also made for partisans by superannuations, and a Collectorship of Customs has just been kept open for two years to suit the political convenience of the Government. Still Canada, compared with the United States, is free from the Spoils System. To the heads of her permanent Civil Service she owes it that while government, in the persons of the Parliamentary heads of departments, is on the stump, or dickering for votes, she enjoys the general benefits of a regular and intelligent administration. In the second place, election petitions are tried as in England by the judges, and with the same good results, while in the American House of Representatives contested elections are decided as they were in England in the days before the Grenville Act, by a party vote. In the third place, the judges themselves are appointed by the Executive for life, instead of being, as they are in most American States, though not in all or in the case of the Supreme Court, elected by the people for a term of years; a system of which the Americans themselves feel the evils, and which they are disposed to modify by lengthening the judge's term. In England Party has now resigned to professional merit most of the appointments to the judiciary. This is not the case in Canada, though a few impartial appointments have been made.

The Americans, when their Confederation was framed, wisely closed all pecuniary accounts between the Federal Government and the States, and absolutely separated the Federal Treasury from those of the States. The Canadians not so wisely left the account open and permitted; subventions to be granted by the Central Government to the Provinces. The consequences are, as might have been expected, continual demands for increased subventions, under the too-familiar name of "Better Terms," the opening of a sluice of Federal corruption, and the weakening of Provincial independence.. Each Province, especially Quebec and the poorer Provinces, instead of practising economy and helping itself, is always looking for Government doles. Mr. George Brown, one of the chief framers, foresaw this, and was for defraying the whole of the local expenditures of the local governments by means of direct taxation, but the Sons of Zeruiah were too strong for him. "Whether the constitution of the Provincial Executive savours at all of Responsible Government or not," said Mr. Dunkin in the Debates on Confederation, "be sure it will not be anxious to bring itself more under the control of the Legislature, or to make itself more odious than it can help, and the easiest way for it to get money will be from the General Government. I am not sure, either, but that most members of the Provincial Legislature will like it that way the best. It will not be at all unpopular, the getting of money so. Quite the contrary. Gentlemen will go to their constituents with an easy conscience, telling them, 'True, we had not much to do in the Provincial Legislature, and you need not ask us very closely what we did; but I tell you what, we got the Federal Government to increase the subvention to our Province by five cents a-head, and see what this gives you – $500 to that road – $1000 to that charity – so much here, so much there. That we have done; and have we not done well?' I am afraid in many constituencies the answer would be, 'Yes, you have done well; go and do it again.' I am afraid the provincial constituencies, legislatures, and executives, will all show a most calf-like appetite for the milking of this one magnificent government cow." Practically the cow has been Ontario, the wealthiest by far as well as the most populous of all the Provinces, but politically weaker, because more divided by faction, than Quebec.

The Imperial Government retains a veto on all Dominion legislation, though not on the legislation of the Provinces, which is liable to disallowance by the Dominion Government alone. But so far as the internal legislation of Canada is concerned, the Imperial veto is like that veto of the British Sovereign on British legislation, which since the time of William III has slept the sleep that knows no waking. Competent judges seem to think that, let Canada do what she will within herself, even if she chose to indulge in a civil war, the Colonial Office will interpose no more. She has legalised marriage with a dead wife's sister, while in the United Kingdom such marriages remain illegal. She has adopted a tariff adverse to the mother country. It is only when Canadian legislation comes into direct collision with British rights, as in the case of copyright, that restraint is attempted, and even in the case of copyright it is not patiently borne.

Foreign relations, of course, with the power of peace and war, remain in the hands of the Imperial Government. But Canada has gone a long way towards the attainment of diplomatic independence in regard to commercial policy. She is allowed to negotiate commercial treaties for herself under the auspices of the British Foreign Office, and subject to Imperial treaty obligations. In the everlasting imbroglio about the fisheries her Government has a voice which, it naturally uses in the way dictated by its own interests, political as well as commercial. A motion was made two sessions ago for the appointment of a representative of Canada, who would practically have been an ambassador, at Washington, but was defeated by the Government majority.

England sends out a general to command the militia, but the last two generals have had troubled lives, and nativism is claiming the appointment as its own. The disposal of the forces belongs to the Canadian Government.

It seems almost incredible that either the relation of a Canadian province to the Dominion, or that of the Dominion to the Imperial country, should have been seriously cited as a precedent for the relation which Mr. Gladstone's Bill would have established between the Sovereign Parliament of Great Britain and his vassal Parliament of Ireland. Break the whole of the United Kingdom to pieces, give each piece the rights of a Canadian Province, put a federal government like that of the Dominion over them all, and you will have a counterpart of the Canadian polity. No Canadian Province would rest content with such a position as that of a vassal community paying tribute, but with only a local assembly and no share in the councils of the nation, although the Canadian Provinces were drawn together by a common desire for closer union, at least on the part of their political leaders, whereas Ireland would set out with revolt burning in her veins. The only analogy capable of being cited on the Irish question which Canada presents is the relation between the Roman Catholic majority and the Protestant minority in Quebec, and this is not in favour of leaving the Protestant minority in Ireland to the tender mercies of a Roman Catholic Parliament there.

In passing it may be remarked that before analogies are drawn for the guidance of statesmen in dealing with such problems as that of Ireland, either from Canadian or American institutions, and before it is assumed that federation is the universal cure, it would be well to consider how far such a thing as a genuine federation now exists. The Achæan League was a federation, inasmuch as it was a combination for mutual defence, the States still remaining separate; so originally was the Swiss Bund. But the Swiss Bund now is a nation with a federal structure. So is the American Republic. Railways, telegraphs, commerce between States, the action of federal parties, and other unifying influences, whatever the Constitution may say, have made the Americans a nation. There will presently be a national marriage law, and it will very likely be followed by a uniform commercial code, the want of which is greatly felt by commercial men or companies doing business over the whole Union or in several States. Against the course of nature the Jeffersonian Democrat protests in vain. Mr. Parnell has announced that his aim is to put Ireland on the footing of a State in the American Union. Let him first ascertain what practically as well as constitutionally that footing is. The Central Government of Canada, as we have seen, has national powers, such as that of criminal legislation, and by the Constitution it has a national veto. Germany is a nation in process of construction. Austria and Scandinavia are uneasy wedlocks without union.

The Canadian Constitution belongs mainly, not wholly, to the written class. Its framers declared that the Government under it was "to be administered according to the well-understood principles of the British Constitution," thereby recognising "understandings" as a virtual part of it. The most important understanding, of course, was that the Sovereign, in whom the Government was solemnly proclaimed to be vested, should not govern at all. We have had occasion in reference to the exercise of the prerogative of dissolution to notice how precarious is an understanding in a land where tradition has no force and every one goes to the full length of his tether. A written Constitution strictly limiting everyone's powers appears to be an exigency of democracy with which the British democracy itself will have some day to comply.

Ottawa, which was chosen as the capital of the United Canadas, and retained as that of the Confederation, is an official city, and can never be anything else. Its only commerce is lumber, which, as the forests are cut down, is a receding trade, and there is nothing to draw general residence to it. Its climate combines the extremes of heat and cold. When selected it was simply the nearest lumber village to the Pole. The motives for the selection appear to have been three – fear of the rivalry among the great cities, Quebec, Montreal, and Toronto, fear of mobs such as that which had burned the Parliament House at Montreal, and fear of American invasion if the capital were too near the frontier. For the fear of mobs there was little ground, and against American invasion the distance of a few days' march would scarcely be a sufficient barrier. The best reason was the beauty of the site, on a bluff over the Ottawa river, of which the buildings are not unworthy. Washington, till lately, was in like manner a merely official city without commerce or society; but it is now becoming the social centre of the continent, while the haggard ugliness of thirty years ago is being changed into remarkable beauty. Politics and politicians, especially politicians of the rural class, need the tempering criticism and the refining influence of general society, while the combination of interests and ideas – political, commercial, literary, professional, and social – in London or Paris, in a school of public character and thought. The Supreme Court which sits at Ottawa is said to suffer by the absence of resident Bar. A mistake was made in not following the American example and federalising the district in which the capital stands. It is an anomaly that the federal capital should be in provincial jurisdiction, and that the Legislature should be dependent on provincial authorities for the maintenance of order at its doors. It is from Ottawa evidently that the journals and reviews in England mainly receive their accounts of men, affairs, and sentiment in Canada. With all respect for "our own correspondent" we may be permitted to observe that the official world of Ottawa is naturally loyal to itself, and that not all Canada is official.

If the North-West prospers and is peopled, the centre of political power will shift to the centre of the continent, and Ottawa as a capital will then be misplaced. But before this can happen other changes will most likely come.

Chapter 9

Fruits of confederation

Doubtful increase of military security / The incorporation of the North-West / Resistance of the French half-breeds to the annexation / Federal railroads, the Intercolonial and the Canadian Pacific / Adoption of a Protective tariff under the name of "National Policy" / Effects of that measure, particularly in regard to the settlers of the North-West / Apparent failure of Confederation to produce national unity / Aspiration of French Canada to separate nationality continued and increased / Question of the Jesuits' estates / Renunciation of the national veto on provincial legislation / Want of national union and of Dominion parties entails government by corruption / The Pacific Railway scandal / Injury to the political character of the people / Conflict of sectional with national interests / The financial condition of the Dominion / The Exodus from Canada to the United States

Books consulted: Collins's "Life and Times of Sir J. A. Macdonald," Stewart's "Canada under the Administration of Earl Dufferin," Collins's "Canada under the Administration of Lord Lorne," The Statistical Year Books of Canada, Morgan's "Dominion Annual Registers," and Mr. A. Blue's valuable issues of the Ontario Bureau of Industries and Statistics.

AMONG THE ostensible objects of Confederation the most immediate perhaps were military strength and security against American aggression. Sceptics, among whom were two British officers,[1] pointed out at the time that if the number of the militia would be increased by Confederation, the length of frontier to be defended would be much more increased, and that though a bundle of sticks might, as Federationists said, become stronger by union, the saying might not hold good with regard to a number of fishing-rods tied together by the ends. The Dominion since its extension to the Pacific has a frontier, for the most part perfectly open, of something like 4000 miles, while the garrison is broken into four sections, far beyond supporting distance of each other. The frontier of Manitoba and the North-West Territories, which for 800 miles is a political line, has to defend it the militia which can be furnished by a population of 150,000. In the days of her glorious defence against American invasion, Canada was comparatively compact. Moreover, she was a fastness of forest; she had no great cities on her frontier at the mercy of the invader; nor had the invader railroads to enable him to bring his superior forces to bear, though as we have seen they began to tell as the war went on. Neither was there then a great mass of French Canadians on the south side of the line in close connection, local and social, with their brethren on the north. The Canadians of that day as backwoodsmen were rough soldiers ready-made. They were less democratic than they are now, and followed more willingly perhaps than their descendants would the royal officers who were set over them, or their own gentry. They had in this respect the same sort of advantage over the Republicans at the beginning of the war as the Cavaliers had over the Roundheads and the Southerners over the North, till the Roundheads and the North learned the necessity of discipline. The regular force of the Dominion consists of schools of cavalry, infantry, and artillery, limited by law in the whole to a thousand men. The embodied Militia are in number 38,000, partly French. Half of this body is each year called out for a fortnight. City regiments voluntarily drill once a week during half the year. The enrolled Militia, comprising all men of military age, exists only on paper, though by Canadian politicians,

1 "Confederation of British North America," by E. C. Bolton and H. H. Webber, Royal Artillery. London, 1866.

speaking to the British public and anxious to please their hearers, it has been represented as an organised force ready at any moment to spring to arms. In the North-West there are a thousand Mounted Police, who, however, are confined by law to the Territories. There is a Military College at Kingston of high repute; but there is no army staff, commissariat, or provision for field hospitals. The men may be the worthy descendants of those who fought at Queenston Heights or Chateauguay, but supposing each of them to be a Paladin it must be left to soldiers to judge what force Canada would be able to put into the field within the time allowed by the swift march of modern war. The Duke of Wellington said that to defend herself successfully, Canada must command the Lakes, and in the War of 1812 loss of the command of the Lakes, after strenuous efforts to keep it, was at once followed by disaster. But Canada has no vessels of war on the Lakes; thanks to her commercial isolation, she has very little lake or river shipping of any kind. At sea she would have to trust entirely to the British fleet. It is true the American army is also very small, while the American militia is probably not better drilled than that of Canada. But it has been seen that money will buy men. The Americans have among them a good many immigrants trained under the military system of Europe, and they showed in their Civil War that they could quickly turn wealth into military power. In vain does Imperial eloquence appeal to an industrial community on this Continent to keep up a regular army. It is not solely or principally the dislike of expenditure that stands in the way; it is the whole character of the people; it is their character, political and social, as well as commercial; for they would fear that the army would become their master and that they would have an aristocracy of scarlet over their heads. That their fears would not be idle even the present bearing of some wearers of uniform shows. And who is the enemy? A community allied to the Canadians by blood, in which half of them have relatives, with which in all things saving government and the customs line they are one. Imperialist writers, while in trumpet tones they call Canada to arms, admit that the American Republic will in the natural course of events one day acquire the Protectorate of her Continent. Is the difference between tutelage and union so momentous that a people, who are or are destined to be under tutelage, can be expected to live armed to the teeth against their own sons, brothers, and cousins for the purpose of averting union? Might it not even occur to them when they were told to beat their ploughshares into swords that union was the higher condition of the two? "Only one absurdity can be greater – pardon me for saying so – than the absurdity of supposing that the British Parliament will pay £200,000 for Canadian fortifications; it is the absurdity of supposing that Canadians will pay it themselves. Two hundred thousand pounds for defences! and against whom? against the Americans? And who are the Americans? Your own kindred, a flourishing people, who are ready to make room for you at their own table, to give you a share of all they possess, of all their prosperity, and to guarantee you in all time to come against the risk of invasion or the need of defences if you will but speak the word." So, writing to the Colonial Secretary, said Lord Elgin, Governor-General of Canada, and an ardent upholder, if ever there was one, of British connection.

Unity of command the Provinces had before as British dependencies under the general whom the Home Government might send out. Perhaps they were more sure of having it in their former state than they are in a state in which jealousies and rivalries among themselves might possibly interfere with devotion to the common cause.

After Confederation the British troops were withdrawn. The flag of conquering England still floats over the citadel of Quebec, but it seems to wave a farewell to the scenes of its glory, the historic rock, the famous battlefield, the majestic river which bore the fleet of England to victory, the monument on which the chivalry of the victor has inscribed together the names of Wolfe and Montcalm. For no British redcoats muster round it now. The only British redcoats left on the Continent are the reduced garrison of Halifax. The beat of England's morning drum will soon go round the world with the sun no more. But as its last throb dies away will be heard the voice of law, literature, and civilisation still speaking in the English tongue. The noblest of England's conquests is that which will last for ever.

Those who crow over what they imagine to be the collapse of the movement in favour of Colonial Emancipation and against Imperial aggrandisement which prevailed thirty years ago forget how much that movement effected. They forget that it brought about not only the cession of the Ionian Islands, which was its immediate fruit, but the withdrawal of the troops from the Colonies, the proclamation of the principle of Colonial self-defence, and a largely increased measure of self-government.

The framers of Confederation, however, promised themselves not only increase of military strength but a North-American empire to be formed by incorporating the North-West, British Columbia, and Newfoundland, so that their realm should stretch from sea to sea and over the great adjacent island on the east. As regards the North-West and British Columbia their hope was fulfilled. The Hudson's Bay Company found itself constrained by Imperial pressure and the precarious character of its chartered rights to sell in 1869 its almost measureless domain, much of which, however, is as hopelessly sterile as Sahara, for £300,000 and some reservations of good land. Possession was not taken without resistance. In the North-West was a population of French half-breeds belonging to the Catholic Church in whom their kinsmen and fellow-Catholics fondly saw the germ of a French and Catholic nation which should in time occupy that vast region to the exclusion of British and Protestant colonisation. Moreover the Half-breeds felt that their hunting and trapping-grounds would be threatened and their very primitive industries supplanted by the advance of the agricultural settler. Their leader, Louis Riel, upon the approach of the first Canadian governor of the territory called his people to arms, set up a provisional government, and put to death, with circumstances of great atrocity, Scott, a British Protestant and an Orangeman who resisted his assumption of power. At the approach of Sir Garnet Wolseley, Riel collapsed and presently fled, aided, as was afterwards discovered, with money for his flight by the Canadian Government, which, placed between the devil of Orange wrath and the deep sea of French sympathy with the leader of French race and religion, had no desire in deciding on the fate of the rebel chief to choose between two modes of destruction for itself. The struggle was renewed in 1885, when the Half-breeds, having been exasperated by the disregard of their prayers respecting some land claims, to which the Ottawa Government, absorbed in the party struggle, found no time to attend, and being also probably alarmed by the advance of an alien civilisation, welcomed back Riel as their chief and once more rose in arms. That he had been amnestied in the meanwhile did not prevent Riel from playing the same game over again. The rising of the Half-breeds was quelled, and Batoche, their hamlet-capital, was taken by a Canadian force under General Middleton, after a resistance which the candour of history must allow to have done credit to the valour of those poor people, considering that they could put into the field only a few hundred men of all ages, a man of ninety and a boy of sixteen being found among the slain, that only a part of them were armed with rifles, and that even these were short of ammunition. Riel suffered death and deserved little sympathy, since he had not only broken his amnesty but been willing to sell himself and his cause to the Government. Quebec, however, boiled over with sympathy for him, which would perhaps have proved more formidable had not he by playing the prophet given offence to the priesthood. The Liberal Opposition in the Dominion Parliament, misled by the temporary ferment, and thinking to gain the French vote, took up Riel's cause and pleaded for his exemption from punishment on the two grounds, not very consistent with each other, that he was insane and that his offence was political. That a man who had conducted with no small address an arduous enterprise and retained complete control over his followers was insane in such a sense as to make him irresponsible for his actions could be believed by no human being, even if there was a streak of madness in Riel's general character; while it was evident that if every offence which could be styled political was to go unpunished, society would be at the mercy of any brigand who chose to say that his object in filling it with blood and havoc was not booty but anarchy or usurpation. Some of the best men in the Opposition refused to vote with their leader, and the Government, standing to its guns, gained a well-merited victory. Among the troops sent to the North-West were two regiments of French militia. But these were not sent to the front. Of the two colonels, one left the army in the field and went home, while the other telegraphed to the Minister of Militia his advice that the troops should be employed in guarding the forts and provisions, and that men fighting in the same way as the rebels should be sent to make the war. It is but fair to suppose that what these gallant officers wished to shun was not powder but political ruin. The suppression of this petty insurrection cost the Dominion \$8,000,000, besides the loss of life, a fine paid for the supineness or the political distractions of the Government, which when the Rebellion had broken out issued a Commission to inquire into the Half-breed claims.

The French yet cling to the hope of making the North-West their own. Their Archbishop still reigns, not without opulence and state, in St. Boniface, the transriverine suburb of Winnipeg, and they have an immigration agency managed by priestly hands. But the balance of destiny has clearly turned against them; as pioneers they are no match for their rivals. The Legislature of Manitoba has passed an Act abolishing the official use of the French language and the Separate Schools for Catholics. The Half-breeds are not a strong race, nor is immigration doing much to recruit their numbers. The next generation will probably see their few thousands merged in a great inflow of English-speaking settlers.

When the North-West is peopled, and filled perhaps with a population partly drawn from the United States and other quarters not Canadian, it being locally far removed and commercially disunited from the eastern parts of the Dominion, what will be the effect on the cohesion and stability of Confederation? That is a question which the politicians of to-day have probably put off to the morrow.

Newfoundland, the oldest of British Colonies, has hitherto refused, in spite of all overtures, to come into Confederation, and her decision seems now to be final. The owners of her boats, who are the owners of her fishermen, probably think that their interest is better served by remaining apart; perhaps she also looks with alarm on the growth of Confederation debt. The Confederation, on the other hand, by taking her in would annex a very bitter local feud between Orangemen and Catholics, commit itself to the naval defence of an island, add to the Fisheries question with the United States a similar but more dangerous question with France, in which she would have her own French against her, and open a new field of political corruption.

To link together the widely-severed members of the Confederation two political and military railways were to be constructed by united effort as Federal works. The first was the Intercolonial, spanning the vast and irreclaimable wilderness which separates Halifax from Quebec. This has been constructed at a cost of $40,000,000, and is now being worked by the Government at an annual loss, the amount of which it is difficult to ascertain, but which is reckoned by an independent authority at $500,000. The Canadian Pacific has also been constructed at a cost to the Dominion in money, land grants, guarantees, completed works and surveys of something like $100,000,000, though it was promised by the original project that there should be no addition to taxation. Of the military value of these lines, and of their availability as a route for the transmission of troops from England to India, it is for military men to judge. At the time when the Intercolonial was projected, the two British officers of artillery, whose pamphlet has been already cited, pointed out that the line would be fatally liable to snow-blocks. It would be awkward if, at a crisis like that of the Great Mutiny or that of a Russian invasion in India, the reinforcements were blockaded by snow in the wilderness between Halifax and Quebec. We need hardly take into account such a chance as that of the closing of Halifax harbour by ice, which happens not more than once in thirteen or fourteen years. It is a more serious consideration that the line where it approaches the northern frontier of Maine runs, if the enemies are the Americans, within easy reach of a raid. Still more exposed to hostile attack is the Canadian Pacific, which runs along the northern shore of Lake Superior, the southern shore of which is in the hands of the Americans, and for 800 miles across the prairie country where the frontier is perfectly open. In the mountain region there are points at which, if an enemy could get at it with dynamite, it might, as the writer has been assured on competent authority, be blocked for months. Against snow-blocks and against avalanches, which are frequent, careful provision on a large scale is being made; but landslides also are frequent in that region, where it has been jocosely said "the work of creation is not quite finished." One of them blocked the course of the great Thompson River for forty-eight hours. But the fact is constantly overlooked in vaunting the importance of this line to the Empire that its eastern section passes through the State of Maine, and would, of course, be closed to troops in case of war with any power at peace with the United States.[1] In sending troops to India there

1 The *Quarterly Review*, for example, spoke of the Canadian Pacific Railway as running from "start to finish" over British ground, though the line was at that very moment applying for bonding privileges to the Government of the United States. I take the opportunity of repeating that the statement of the *Quarterly*, that I had been going about the United States trying in vain to persuade the Americans to annex Canada, is baseless. The only occasion on which

would be two transhipments, a consideration the importance of which again it is for the War Office to determine.

As a commercial road the Intercolonial is a failure, for the simple reason that there is not, nor is there likely to be, any trade of the slightest importance between Canada and the Maritime Provinces of the Dominion. Small must be its receipts for local traffic between Quebec and Halifax or St. John. Its commercial usefulness will be reduced, if possible, still lower if not altogether destroyed, now that the Canadian Pacific, its reputed consort in the great Imperial scheme, cuts it out by taking the route, 200 miles shorter, through the State of Maine; nor can the condition to which it will probably be reduced by commercial depression fail to tell upon its efficiency even as a military road. What are the success and prospects of the Canadian Pacific as a commercial road we shall be better able to say when the earnings of the original and national line between Ottawa and the Pacific coast are distinguished from those of the Eastern and American extensions, which are no part of the original and national enterprise. So far as the profits of the Canadian Pacific Railway are made at the expense of the Grand Trunk they are made at the expense of a road which has done a great deal more for Canada than the Canadian Pacific Railway itself, and in which £12,000,000 sterling of British capital are invested. As a colonisation road its achievements are very doubtful. It has strung out the settlers along a line of 800 miles, carrying them far away from their markets and their centres of distribution, raising their freights, and, what is worst of all, depriving them of the advantages of close settlement which in a wintry climate are particularly great. Many emigrants it carries all

I spoke publicly of the political relations of Canada with the United States was at a debating society in New York, where I had been invited to take part in the discussion; and what I said on that occasion was, in effect, that political union was a question for the future, while the improvements of commercial relations was the question of the present. The story published in the *Quarterly* about a rebuke administered to me for my Annexationist sentiments by General Sherman, at the banquet of the Chamber of Commerce of New York, is also pure fiction. The General spoke before me, he spoke to his own toast, and my speech on that occasion was confined to the commercial question, the political question being mentioned only to exclude it.—G.S.

down the line to British Columbia, whence, there being hardly any land for them to take up, they pass into the Pacific States of the Union. In one of the emigrant trains there were found ten persons bound for British Columbia and fifty-eight bound for places in the United States. Besides this, the monopoly granted to the Company in consideration of the sacrifice of commercial to military and political objects in the laying out of the line long weighed like lead upon the rising community. To this, in conjunction with the tariff and with some unfortunate land regulations made both by the Company and the Government, it is due that whereas Dakota and Manitoba started eighteen years ago on nearly equal terms, Dakota has a population of over 500,000, while that of Manitoba is about 150,000. At one time Manitoba was brought to the verge of despair: men who had been members of a Conservative Government were leaving her for the United States. Yet the Ottawa Government, in pursuance of its political aims obstinately maintained the monopoly by the exercise of its veto, and was supported in so doing by its compliant majority in the Dominion Parliament. Suddenly, on a transparently hollow pretext, it changed its course. The province petitioned the Crown for a hearing before the Privy Council, and it is commonly believed that the British Government then sent the Ottawa Government a hint, to which the Ottawa Government gave ear. Manitoba would otherwise have escaped ruin only by secession, and a Canadian Government which boasts that by its statesmanship the Confederation is held together, and excuses the most equivocal practices by that plea, would itself have been the immediate author of dissolution.

There is one point of view in which the history of the Canadian Pacific Railway is most instructive. It was originally proclaimed as a purely national and imperial enterprise which was to assure the perpetual separation of Canada from the United States, frustrating for ever the designs of American ambition, and in which no Yankee was in any way whatever to take part. So everybody said and Sir George Cartier swore. An American firm was in the syndicate; an American, now Vice-President of the United States, was the first Vice-President of the Company; a genuine American was the first manager and is now President. The line runs through the State of Maine; it connects the Canadian with the American railway system not there only but at the Sault Ste. Marie and at its Pacific terminus.

It is an applicant for bonding privileges at Washington, and in danger of being brought under the Inter-State Commerce Act. It is in fact, or soon will be, as much an American as a Canadian line. The C.P.R. even discriminates in its freights, involuntarily no doubt, against Canadians and in favour of Americans.[1] Such is the outcome of designs for the suppression of geography and nature.

In opening a trade among the Provinces, a natural trade at least, these inter-provincial railroads have failed, for the simple reason that the Provinces have hardly any products to exchange with each other, and that means of conveyance are futile when there is nothing to be conveyed. "I take," says Mr. Longley, the Attorney-General of Nova Scotia, "the solid ground that naturally there is no trade between Ontario and the Maritime Provinces whatsoever. Without the aid or compulsion of tariffs scarcely a single article produced in Ontario would ever seek or find a market in Nova Scotia or the other Maritime Provinces. In like manner, unless under similar compulsion, not a product of the Maritime Provinces would ever go to Ontario. Twenty years of political union and nine years of an inexorable Protectionist policy designed to compel inter-provincial trade have been powerless to create any large trade between these two sections, and what it has created has been unnatural, unhealthy, and consequently profitless." As illustrations, Mr. Longley points out that Ontario sent to the United States $7,000,000 worth of barley, timber to the same value, and $4,000,000 worth of animals and their produce, but to the Maritime Provinces none; while, on the other

1 The following is from an official source: "1st. The rate on wheat from Winnipeg to St. John, N.B., is 50 cents, and to Halifax, 63½ cents per 100 pounds. These are rates for traffic when carried by the C.P.R. alone. 2d. The rates on wheat from Minneapolis to Portland, Me., is 42½ cents, Boston, 42½ cents, and New York 37½ cents per hundred pounds. These rates apply where traffic takes the route from Minneapolis *via* the "Soo Line" and C.P.R., and were made effective Jan. 1st inst. Prior to that date each of the above rates was 5 cents less per 100 pounds. 3d. The first-class rate on general merchandise from St. John, N.B., to Winnipeg is $2.64 per 100 pounds, and from Montreal $2.08 per 100 pounds. These rates apply *via* the C.P.R. 4th. The rates on first-class merchandise from Portland and Boston to Minneapolis is $1.05 per 100 pounds, *via* C.P.R. and "Soo Line."

hand, Nova Scotia sent to the United States also in spite of heavy duties $2,000,000 worth of fish, $600,000 worth of minerals, and $500,000 worth of farm products; sending none to Ontario. "Of the genuine natural products," continues Mr. Longley, "Nova Scotia sends practically nothing to Ontario. If the exports of Nova Scotia to Ontario are carefully studied, it will be found that they consist chiefly of refined sugar and manufactured cotton, the product of two mushroom industries called into existence by the Protective system, and which do not affect one way or another the interests of 500 individuals in the entire province of Nova Scotia." To any one who may ask why this state of things exists, "God and nature," he says, "never designed a trade between Ontario and the Maritime Provinces. If I have a barrel or ton of any commodity produced in Nova Scotia, and I desired to send it to Toronto or Hamilton, the cost of sending it thither, unless it were gold, would probably be more than the value of the commodity. But I can at any moment put it on board of one of the numerous vessels or steamers which are daily leaving every port in Nova Scotia for Boston and send it to that city for twenty or thirty cents. If I desired to go to Toronto and Hamilton to sell it I should have to mortgage my farm to pay the cost of the trip, whereas I can go to Boston and back for a few dollars." Much more would he have to mortgage his farm if he carried his bales to Calgary or Vancouver. The moral drawn by Mr. Longley is, "that the Maritime Provinces have no natural or healthy trade with the Upper Provinces, but with the New England States; that the Upper Provinces have no natural trade with the Maritime Provinces, but with the Central and Western States adjoining them; that Manitoba has no natural trade with the larger provinces of Canada, but with the Western States to the south of her; that British Columbia has no trade with any part of Canada, but with California and the Pacific States. In other words, that inter-provincial trade is unnatural, forced, and profitless, while there is a natural and profitable trade at our very doors open and available to us." The harvests of the North-West, as they cannot be moved south, go along the Canadian Pacific Railway to the sea. If an Asiatic trade comes to Vancouver the tea will be carried across the Continent. But this is not inter-provincial trade, nor, being merely of a transitory kind, can it add much, beyond the railway freight, to the wealth of the Dominion. The French province, the people of which live on the produce of their own farms and clothe themselves with the produce of their own spinning, is uncommercial, and lies a non-conductor between the more commercial members of the Confederation.

To force trade into activity between the Provinces and turn it away from the United States, giving the Canadian farmer a home market, and consolidating Canadian nationality at the same time, were the ostensible objects of the adoption in 1879 of a Protective tariff. The real object perhaps was at least as much to capture the manufacturer's vote and his contributions to the election fund of the party in power. Protectionists boast and enlightened men speak sadly of the course which opinion has been taking on this subject. It is true that through the extension of the suffrage the world has passed from the hands of Turgot, Pitt, Peel, and Cavour into those of a multitude ignorant of economical questions, swayed by blind cupidity, the easy dupe of protectionist sophistry; and that fallacies which it was hoped had been for ever banished have thus regained their power. But in the United States and Canada it is less mistaken opinion that has been at work than the influence of sinister interest. The Canadian politicians who framed the Protective tariff were not and had never professed to be believers in Protection. If they had been identified with any fiscal policy it was that of Free Trade, at least between Canada and her own Continent. Their watchword had been reciprocity of trade or reciprocity of tariffs, in other words, the enforcement of Free Trade by Retaliation, which, though the purists of Free Trade may condemn it, is not protectionism but the reverse. If they had formed their design, they masked it till the election was over and declared that what they meant was not protection but readjustment, for which and for an increase of taxation to fill a deficit there were good grounds. They so far paid homage to their old principles as to keep in their Tariff Act a standing offer to the United States of reciprocity in natural products, though, as the Americans could not in common justice to their own interests allow their manufactures to be excluded, this was little better than a mockery. But even this they afterwards threw overboard, and one of them declared broadly that free trade even in farm products is an evil, so that Kent had better keep her hops and Worcestershire her apples all to herself; for this would not be more absurd than the refusal of Manitoba to sell hard wheat, or of Ontario to sell her superior barley across the Line, and take American products or manufactures in payment. The upshot is that on the neck of the Canadian as of the American Commonwealth now rides an association of protected manufacturers making the community and all the great interests of the country tributary to their gains. Before a general election the Prime Minister calls these men together in the parlour of a Toronto hotel, receives their contributions to his election fund, and pledges the commercial policy of the country. Then British journals in their simplicity advise Canada to meet the M'Kinley Act by a declaration of Free Trade.

It would be a waste of words to argue over again to any intelligent reader the questions whether Canada, or any other country, can be enriched by taxation, and whether natural or forced industries are the best. That to which attention should be called is the difference between the case of Canada and that of the United States, the example of which Canada follows. The United States are a continent extending from regions almost arctic to regions almost tropical, embracing an immense variety of production, producing nearly everything in short, except tea and spices, with a market of 63,000,000. The largest measure of Free Trade ever passed was the American Constitution, which forbade a customs line to be erected between States. This it is – not the protective tariff on the seaboard – that has been the source of American prosperity. In like manner it was not Napoleon's continental system that gave his Empire such a measure of prosperity as it enjoyed, but the large area which it included, and over which there was Free Trade. The Canadian Dominion lies all in a high latitude, and its range of production is limited. The market, instead of being 63,000,000, is under 5,000,000, and these 5,000,000 are divided into four or five markets widely distant from each other, and most of them sparse in themselves. The effect might have been easily foretold. A number of factories have been forced into existence, and have prospered as forced industries prosper. Of the cotton mills only one or two, it is believed, have paid dividends, several are in liquidation, and the owners of others have been trying to find English purchasers at a discount of 50 per cent. The loyal attempt to foster the iron and steel industry of Canada, by a duty excluding British manufactures, for which a Canadian Finance Minister was rewarded with a baronetcy, has totally failed. Of course there is continual running to Ottawa for larger draughts of the fatal stimulant, when the first draught has failed. "The imposts," says an ex-President of the Toronto Board of Trade, "are a mass of incongruous absurdities; the duties on raw materials are now as high in some cases as those on the manufactured articles. In attempting to extend to all industries the benefits of protection, the height of the ridiculous was reached when the duty was largely increased upon umbrellas and parasols for the special behoof of one small concern which failed within the year." A patriot writes to the Minister of Finance to say that he proposes to foster home industries and consolidate the nation by starting a canned-soup factory, but he must have a duty of 20 per cent on canned-soup, and a protective duty on tomatoes. About the stomachs of the consumers nothing is said. Combines are now being formed to keep up prices. A spasmodic demand for labour and an artificial rise in wages have been followed by short time. In the first days of the system the Minister of Finance made a triumphal progress through the factories to witness and glorify the work of his own hands; he has not repeated his tour. What are the fruits of the policy to the public need hardly be told. A great wholesale dealer in woollens and cottons, in a debate at the Toronto Board of Trade, deprecating free trade with the United States, said that if American goods were admitted free, the capital invested in Canadian manufactories under the protective tariff would not be worth more than a third of its face value; the inference from which was that the interest on the other two-thirds, if paid at all, must be paid by the community. This, however, applies only to the forced industries. Those of the Canadian manufacturers who feel that their industries have a natural and sound basis disclaim the desire of protection, and ask only a fair field. In no trade probably would American competition be keener than in the manufacture of agricultural implements. Yet the other day a firm of large manufacturers in that line declared for free trade with the United States. The agricultural implement business, they said, had been overdone, they wanted more people to whom to sell, and they would not be afraid of American competition. Another large manufacturer in the same line, spoke to the same effect, pointing out, by the way, that the immense territory which in Canada had to be covered in order to embrace a sufficient market, was a heavy addition to the manufacturer's expense. These are not by any means the only firms which take that view. It is the hothouse plants that shrink from the open air; and while all possible consideration is due to those who have been induced by Parliament to invest, it is hard that the community should be required for ever to expiate the mistake.

The isolation of the different Canadian markets from each other, and the incompatibility of their interests, add in their case to the evils and absurdities of the protective system. What is meat to one Province is, even on the protectionist hypothesis, poison to another. Ontario was to be forced to manufacture; she has no coal; yet to reconcile Nova Scotia to the tariff a coal duty was imposed; in vain, for Ontario after all continued to import her coal from Pennsylvania. Manitoba and the North-West produce no fruit; yet they were compelled to pay a duty in order to protect the fruit-grower of Ontario 1500 miles away. Hardest of all was the lot of the North-West farmer. His natural market, wherein to buy farm implements, was in the neighbouring cities of the United States, where, moreover, implements were made most suitable to the prairie. But to force him to buy in Eastern Canada 25 per cent was laid on farm implements. As he still bought in the States, the 25 per cent was made 35 per cent. Handicapped with 35 per cent on his implements, and at the same time with railway monopoly, as well as with the general imposts of tariff, he has to compete with the farmer of Minnesota or Dakota, buying in a free market, and enjoying freedom of railway accommodation. An attempt was made to show that manufactories had been called into existence in Manitoba, and that she was exporting their products; but the list was found to embrace the work of lime kilns, blacksmiths' forges, photography, and re-shipments of old railway engines.

The British reader will not be surprised to hear that the arguments used by the defenders of the system are only such as have been a hundred times confuted. In the case of Canada, as in other cases, the protectionist makes no attempt to lay down his principle by defining native industries, or to say what is the proper area for its application; why Ontario should not benefit by protection against New Brunswick, as well as against New York, or New York benefit by protection against her sister States. The statement that England nursed her manufactures by protection is still repeated, and so is the plea for infant industries, babes who, when they come to manhood, instead of giving up their pap and swaddling-clothes, take you by the throat and demand more. The protectionists loudly profess loyalty, which with them means high duties on American goods. Their organs labour to keep up hatred of the people of the United States, just as the organs of protectionism in the United States labour to keep up hatred of England. But the main strength of protectionism in Canada, as in the United States, lies in its Lobby and in the money which it subscribes for elections. International hatred, directed in Canada against her American neighbours, and political corruption, are two inseparable companions of the system. A third is smuggling, which is rife all along the Canadian border, to the detriment of lawful trade, and with the usual effect on the morality of the people.

For the fusion of population between the Provinces, Confederation seems to have done as little as for the creation of inter-Provincial trade. Reciprocal trade indeed is almost necessary to fusion. In the census return for 1881, which is the last, it appears that in that year there were of natives in Ontario, 105 settled in Prince Edward Island, 310 in New Brunswick, and 333 in Nova Scotia; in all, 748 natives of Ontario settled in the Maritime Provinces. Much the same state of things is found in Quebec, with the exception of two counties which border on a district of New Brunswick, with an identical population. On the same day there were of persons of United States birth, 609 in Prince Edward Island, 5108 in New Brunswick, 3004 in Nova Scotia; or, roughly speaking, thirteen times as many natives of the United States in the Maritime Provinces as there were natives of Ontario. It is found, moreover, that in 1861, before Confederation, and when there was no Intercolonial railway, there were 6700 natives of the Maritime Provinces in Ontario; twenty years afterwards there were only 7200. In Quebec, among the people of eight or ten populous counties, not a man from the Maritime Provinces was to be found, immigration had actually declined in spite of the official connection. Meantime it appears that there are 1,000,000 immigrants from Canada in the United States.

Without commercial intercourse or fusion of population, the unity produced by a mere political arrangement can hardly be strong or deep. It will, for the most part, be confined to the politicians, or to those directly interested in the work of Dominion parties. No inhabitant of Nova Scotia or New Brunswick calls himself a Canadian. The people of British Columbia, priding themselves on their English character, almost disdain the name. Manitoba and the

North-West have been largely colonised from Ontario, yet Manitobans tell you that though their personal and family connections are cherished, as a community they are severed from Eastern Canada. All the Provinces are under the British flag. All are united by the sentiments common to British Colonies and by historical associations. This they were before Confederation. That Confederation has as yet increased the community of feeling or strengthened the moral bond there is nothing in the attitude of the Provinces towards each other, political or general, to prove.

So much as to the British Provinces. Of Quebec something has been already said. If there is a word hateful to French ears it is amalgamation. Not only has New France shown no increase of tendency to merge her nationality in that of the Dominion; her tendency has been directly the other way. She has recently, as we have seen, unfurled her national flag, and at the same time placed herself as the French Canadian nation, under the special protection of the Pope, who accepts the position of her ecclesiastical lord. At her head, and to all appearances firmly seated in power, is the chief of the Nationalist and Papal party, who bids Blue and Red blend themselves in the tricolor and restores to the Jesuits their estates. The old Bleu or Conservative party, associated with the clergy of the Gallican school, which by its union with the Tories in the British Provinces linked Quebec politically to the Dominion, has fallen, as it seems, to rise no more. What life is left in it is sustained largely by Dominion subsidies of which the Ottawa Government makes it the accredited channel. "The complete autonomy of the French Canadian nationality and the foundation of a French Canadian and Catholic state, having for its mission to continue in America the glorious work of our ancestors," are the avowed aims of the Nationalist and Ultramontane press. Greybeards of the old Conservative school protest that all this means nothing, that no design of autonomy has been formed, and that it is unjust to speak of French nationality and theocracy as dangers to Confederation. Whether the design has been distinctly formed or not matters little if the tendency is manifestly there and is gaining strength every day. Let those who prophesy to us smooth things take stock of the facts. When one community differs from another in race, language, religion, character, spirit, social structure, aspirations, occupying also a territory apart, it is a separate nation, and is morally certain to pursue a different course, let it designate itself as it can. French Canada may be ultimately absorbed in the English-speaking population of a vast Continent; amalgamate with British Canada so as to form a united nation it apparently never can. In the Swiss Confederation there are diversities of race, language, and religion, but the union is immemorial; it was formed and is held together by the most cogent pressure from without; its territory is compact and surrounded by a mountain wall; the races and religions are interlocked, not confronted like two cliffs, and the division into small cantons tends to avert a broad antagonism of forces. After all, Switzerland has had its Sonderbund, and the Jesuit, whose intrigues gave birth to the Sonderbund, is now dominant in Quebec. Quebec sends her representatives to the Federal Parliament. But their mission is not to take counsel with the other representatives of the nation so much as to look to the separate interest of Quebec, and above all to draw from the treasury of the Dominion all that can be drawn in aid of her empty chest. They let pass no opportunity of doing their duty to her in that line. On one occasion they stayed out of the House haggling with the Government till the bell had rung for a division, when the Government gave way. Quebec, as revelations going on at this moment show, is politically corrupt, and by her corruption she may be held in the Union, but of what benefit the Union will be to her partners, or how they will be indemnified for the expense, it is not easy to see. Her people, saving the Protestant traders of Montreal and the remnant of British commerce at Quebec, being very poor, their contribution to the common revenues is small. The creative genius of Lord Lorne, besides a Royal Society and a Royal Academy, bestowed on Canada a National hymn. The hymn should have been written in alternate stanzas of French and English.

The beauty of the French language, the brilliancy of French literature, the graces of French character, the value of the contributions made by France to the common treasure of civilisation, on which Governors-General preaching harmony dilate, are by nobody denied. But supposing Quebec to be the depositary of all French gifts, mere vicinity to them is little worth when the separation in all other respects is as complete as if seas rolled or Alps rose between. France may enrich the store of humanity, but the store of the Dominion, material or moral, is not enriched by simple want of homogeneity and harmony among its members.

The last deliverance on this subject from the French side is *La Question du Jour,* by M. Faucher de Saint-Maurice. The author puts the question, "Shall we remain French?" and answers it with a thundering "Yes," hurling his anathemas at all whom he suspects of a desire to bring about denationalisation. A curious and instructive part of the pamphlet is that which, in portraying the emotions of Quebec on the occasion of the Franco-German war, displays the passionate attachment of New France to her own mother country. "At the thought of the struggle in which the land of our fathers is engaged the French blood stirred in our veins, as though it had never been chilled, and we shouted for the flag of our mother country as if it had never ceased to wave over our heads." "We admire the United States, whose prosperity dazzles us, but France alone is the object of our passionate love." "Our thoughts and our hearts belong to our mother country." We have seen that Sir George Cartier, of all French men the most British, spoke in a similar strain. In the event of a war between Great Britain and her most probable enemy, on which side are we to suppose that the hearts of the French Canadians would be? After reckoning up all the elements of French population and strength, including 108,605 "Acadians" in the Maritime Provinces, M. Faucher de Saint-Maurice concludes by saying, "With courage, with perseverance, with union, with effort, and above all with a constant devotion to our religion and our language, the future must be ours. Sooner or later, marching on together, we shall arrive at the position of a great nation. The logical conclusion of my work can only be this – One day we shall be Catholic France in America." This writer, at all events, has formed his design.

The coping-stone and the symbol of nationality in the Constitution, it has been already said, was the national veto on Provincial legislation, that vast power, as Sir Alexander Galt,[1] one of the Fathers of Confederation, called it, and that palladium, as he deemed it, of Protestant and civil rights in Quebec, which might otherwise be exposed without defence to Ultramontane aggression. Yet this coping-stone of nationality, this palladium of civil right, both the parties have abandoned or reduced to nullity under the pressure of the French-Catholic vote. In the transfer of Quebec from

1 *Church and State*, by Sir Alexander T. Galt, K.C.M.G., Montreal, 1876.

France to Britain the revenues of the parish clergy were secured with the religion of the people, but the estates of the religious orders were left to the pleasure of the Crown, and the Solicitor-General Wedderburn advised that while the other religious orders might be allowed to exist, that of the Jesuits, on account of its anti-national character, could not. The Crown as a matter of humanity, allowed the remaining Jesuits subsistence on the estates for their lives. In 1773 the Order was suppressed by the Pope. The estates then, at all events, fell to the Crown, which held them for the purposes of education, and ultimately transmitted them to the Province impressed with that trust. But the restored Order laid claim to the estates. The claim would have been met by any Government in Europe with derision. But Quebec had fallen under Jesuit influence. An Act was passed (1888) by the Provincial Legislature in which Protestantism has a merely nominal representation, assigning to the Jesuits the sum of $400,000 by way of compensation for the estates. To give colour to the transaction the sum of $60,000 was assigned to Protestant education. The Pope's name was introduced in the Act as arbiter of the arrangement. Apologists in Parliament pretended that this was a mere expedient of conveyancing; but if it had been nothing else it would most certainly have been avoided. There could be no doubt about the spirit and intention of the Act; had there been any it would have been set at rest when Mr. Mercier, as we have already said, before an assembly of Roman Catholic Bishops and Clergy, boasted that he had emulated the glorious deeds of the American Revolutionists by undoing the wrong done by George III. The Act was a rampant assertion of Roman Catholic ascendancy by the endowment out of a public fund of an Order formed specially for the subversion of Protestantism, and at the same time a recognition of the Pope as the ecclesiastical sovereign of Quebec. Morally, if not legally, it was an excess of jurisdiction, since religion is not in the list of subjects with which the Provincial Legislatures are authorised by the Constitution to deal, while the endowment out of the public treasury of a professedly propagandist Order was certainly a religious measure and one of an extreme kind, as we should soon have been made to understand had the legislature of Ontario endowed a Protestant mission for the subversion of the Roman Catholic Church. Yet such is the power of the French vote that both parties fell on their faces before it. The position of the

Government was the worst, since the hollowness of its affected respect for Provincial self-government was betrayed by its own recent conduct in vetoing a Railway Act of the Manitoba Legislature, the legality of which could not be questioned, in the interest of its auxiliary, the Canadian Pacific Railway. But a Liberal party, voting for the public endowment of Jesuitism, also cut a strange figure. Only thirteen members out of a total of 215 in the Dominion House, however, dared to uphold the national character of Confederation, British ascendancy, the rights of the Civil Power, and the separation of the Church from the State. After the division, the members who had voted for the endowment of Jesuitism lulled their consciences, as they sometimes do, by singing "God save the Queen." Indignation, however, was aroused, great meetings were held at Toronto and elsewhere in Ontario to protest against the Act, and the most powerful movement that has yet been witnessed outside the party machines was organised under the name of Equal Right, and is still on foot. It aims at the repression of priestly influence in politics, and of French encroachment at the same time; and its first fruits have been the abolition of Separate Schools and the discontinuance of French as an official language in Manitoba. It is not religious or directed in any way against the faith or worship of the Roman Catholics, but political and purely defensive. It is religious at least only in so far as the Church, not less than the State, has an interest in that entire freedom of each from the interference of the other which is a great organic principle of society in the New World.

The Maritime Provinces and those of the West have been imperfectly incorporated, if they can be said to have been incorporated at all, into the old political parties which have their basis in the two Canadas, and were formed before Confederation upon questions and in interests with which the other Provinces had no concern; the Conservative party being a combination of the reactionary clericism of Quebec with the Toryism and Orangeism of Ontario, the Liberal party being a counter-combination of the Liberals of Ontario with the misnamed *Parti Rouge* of Quebec. It can hardly be said that in the remoter Provinces a Dominion party, otherwise than as a combination for securing local advantages through the Dominion Government, exists. When the writer asked a denizen of the Pacific Coast what were the politics of his Province, the answer was, Government appropriations. Once more let Australians who propose to follow the example of the British

North-American Provinces by forming an Australian federation remark that this, under our present system, means the creation of Federal parties, and that unless a basis of principle for Federal parties can be assigned, Government appropriations will be the basis. "There is a perfect scramble among the whole body to get as much as possible of this fund for their respective constituents; cabals are formed by which the different members mutually play into each other's hands; general politics are made to bear on private business, and private business on general politics; and at the close of the Parliament the member who has succeeded in securing the largest portion of the prize for his constituents renders an easy account of his stewardship, with confident assurance of re-election." This picture, though drawn by Lord Durham of the legislature of a single colony, would be found to be heightened in its colours as well as extended in its scale when the constituencies were Provinces, and the members were the representatives of Provincial interests. It would be so at least unless such momentous issues and such a pervading spirit of Federal patriotism were awakened as have not yet been witnessed in the Canadian Confederation.

In the want of a real bond among the members of Confederation, the anti-national attitude of Quebec, the absence of real Dominion parties, and the consequent difficulty of holding the Dominion together and finding a basis for the administration must be found the excuse, if any excuse can be found, for the system of political corruption which during the last twenty years has prevailed. "Better Terms," that is, increased subsidies to Provinces from the Dominion treasury, Dominion grants for local railways and other local works and concessions to contractors, together with the patronage, including, as we have seen, appointments to the Senate, have been familiar engines of government. It was a Conservative member of the Senate who the other day, when the usual batch of railway grants was pushed through at the end of the Session, could not refrain from protesting against a vast system of bribery. Post offices and local works of all kinds are held out by Government candidates as bribes to constituencies with an openness which would almost have scandalised a French constituency under the Second Empire, and it is painful to see how paltry an inducement of this kind will prevail. "The people of ____ County want railways and other public works, and they all know that the policy of the Government regarding railways is liberal. If a Government supporter is elected, any reasonable request will be granted. It rests entirely with the Government candidate what will be done." Such is the language held. The result of an election won by the Protectionist Government the other day in Victoria County, was reported to the English Press as highly significant, and as showing that the people were against Reciprocity; but the fact was apparent from the returns that the Government had gained its majority of 133 by two subsidies to local railways.[1] Nova Scotia and New Brunswick, as they suffer particularly

1 Here are two specimens, which will probably be enough. The first is an extract from a circular letter of a Roman Catholic bishop to the electors of Antigonish, Nova Scotia, in favour of Sir John Thompson, Minister of Justice, and a member of the Bishop's communion. The second is the address (in French) of a Quebec member of the Dominion Parliament to his constituents.

"Seventeen months ago you needed postal communication and facilities in various localities, and already you have no fewer than five new post-offices opened. You needed improvement in our railway tariff. Through Mr. Thompson's strenuous efforts you have obtained these. If you needed money to repair most useful public works or to complete others and to originate more, already no less than $34,346 has been placed at your disposal for that purpose, yet this magnificent sum is doubtless but an instalment of the amount which we may expect under the auspices of this most efficient benefactor, to be expended for our advantage. Lastly, he has been mainly instrumental in persuading the Cabinet to undertake and build a railway through Cape Breton as a Government measure. He has thus conferred an inestimable boon to Eastern Nova Scotia, as well as on that fine island in whose prosperity we all feel the liveliest interest. In view of the foregoing undeniable facts, I ask you, gentlemen, have you not every reason to be proud of your admirable representative and deeply grateful for what he has already achieved in your behalf, and confident that your public works, whether begun or only in contemplation, will be satisfactorily completed by him more likely than by men who now ask you to oust him. Indeed it is simply incredible that Hon. A. McGillivray is now under the impression that he can without office and in the cold shades of opposition serve you better than he can, an incomparably abler man, in the commanding position of Minister of Justice. It is plainly therefore your duty as patriotic citizens to resist such conduct and to vote one and all for the Minister of Justice, who so eminently deserves your confidence and esteem, and not to give him his discharge. In the existing circumstances it would be an act of senseless ingratitude, a public calamity, and a lasting disgrace, for which I trust you will never be guilty of making yourselves answerable. In a word, to do yourselves full credit you ought not only to return Mr. Thompson, but to return him by an overwhelming majority. Gentlemen, I confidently leave the issue in your hands, and remain your devoted well-wisher and servant in Christ."

"Les deux grandes questions politiques qui intéressent le comté sont la construction de nos chemins de fer et les travaux publics. Au sujet du chemin de fer, j'ai fait un travail plus qu'ordinaire afin d'obtenir les subsides nécessaires à sa construction. J'ai envoyé vingt-deux requêtes à tous les honorables curés du comté afin de les faire signer, lesquels requêtes demandaient un subside de $100,000. Vingt requêtes m'ont été retournées couverte de dix-huit cents signatures; deux ne m'ont pas été renvoyées, je ne sais pourquoi. Il est vrai que la demande de $100,000 n'était pas suffisante selon ce que j'ai appris plus tard, et j'ai modifié ma demande en la portant à $239,000.

"Tous les députés Canadiens m'ont donné leur appui, et dix-huit Sénateurs ont signé ma demande que j'ai adressée au Conseil Privé. Jusqu'au dernier moment l'on m'a fait les plus grandes promesses. Sir Hector me disait toujours: 'Mon cher Couture, ne crains rien; les subsides ne sont pas encore votés, mais nous n'oublierons pas ton comté.' Jusqu'au dernier moment j'ai supporté le Gouvernement, même j'ai voté contre mes convictions, confiant dans les promesses qui m'etaient faites.

"Quand aux travaux publics, j'ai demandé tellement que mes confrères me reprochaient de vouloir enlever les deux tiers des subsides du Dominion. J'ai demandé $40,000 pour le comté, et j'avais encore les mêmes promesses des Ministres. À la fin voyant que rien ne venait j'ai commencé à m'apercevoir que l'on voulait me jouer, et j'ai cru me rendre aux vœux du comté en refusant d'approuver une conduite aussi déloyale, et j'ai voté contre le Gouvernement. Je savais que le comté me reprocherait pas d'avoir voté contre un gouvernement qui ne voulait rien m'accorder. C'est sur la question des quinze million au Pacifique que je me suis séparé du gouvernement. Je croyais que ces gens en avaient eu assez; il est vrai qu'ils donnaient des garanties en terre au gouvernement, mais je savais que la crême de ces terres était vendue."

from the commercial atrophy produced by severance from their natural markets, are specially open to the influence of the Treasury, and before an election a Nova Scotian, who is master of such arts, is actually brought over from England, and put for the time into the Ministry, that he may secure to the Government the votes of his Province. This he does by promises the fulfilment of which, it was reckoned at the time, would cost several millions. If you express surprise at the result of an election in one of the Maritime Provinces, the explanation which you get is four Government grants or promises of grants for piers, wharves, or local works of some kind. The Government, which, it is justly said, ought in the matter of public works to act as trustee for the whole people, in effect proclaims that public works will be regulated by the interest of constituencies whose support it receives. That "the whole North-West of Canada has been used as one vast bribery fund" is a statement just made by a leading member of the Opposition, who can point to at least one recent and most flagrant instance in proof of his sweeping accusation. But what corruption can be more pestilential or more dangerous to the commonwealth than the surrender of the commercial policy of the country to private interests, in return for their votes and the support of their money in elections? No president of the United States, being a candidate for election, could without total wreck of his character and prospects, assemble the protected manufacturers in a room at an hotel and receive their contributions to his election fund.

In Quebec it is an eminent Conservative journalist and politician of that Province who says that the electors are wholly demoralised; that if all the constituencies are not equally rotten, the symptoms of the evil are everywhere to be seen; that the electors, those who are well off not less than the poor, compel the candidates to bribe them; that the franchise is a merchantable commodity; that many will not go to the polls without a bribe. The clergy denounce the practice from the altar, but in vain. In truth the priests, who, instead of leaving the voter free, and bidding him make an independent use of his vote, coerce him in their own interest, are not in the best position for reading him homilies on electoral duty. The truth is, that under a theocracy the people are not citizens: they do not understand the political franchise or value it; and when you preach to them about its responsibilities, you preach in vain. They not unnaturally regard it as a thing to be used in their own interest, and if they like, to be sold. The Conservative politician just cited is now producing in a series of papers startling proofs in support of his allegation.

Once the character of the means by which Government is maintained appeared too plainly, with a result fatal for a time to the Ministry by which the system was being carried on. This was in the case of the Pacific Railway Scandal, the echoes of which reached as far as England. The Prime Minister and two of his colleagues were convicted of having received from the grantee of a railway charter, whose position was virtually that of a contractor, a large sum of money to be used in elections. It was pretended by the Ministers that the money was a political subscription to the Party fund; but it was well known that the commercial gentleman from whom it was received took no interest in politics, and could have had only his commercial object in view. It was also pleaded that there was nothing wrong in the charter granted him, and this was true; but it was evident that the Government, when it had taken his money, would be in his hands. Public indignation was strongly aroused, and for the moment overcame party feeling; the Government, deserted by its majority, fell; and the country, on an appeal being made to it, emphatically ratified the verdict of the House of Commons. The conduct of the Governor-General was, in his own opinion at least, and in that of the courtly pundits of Ottawa, constitutional in the highest degree. He continued to treat the accused Ministers as his constitutional advisers. At their instance, when Parliament had become completely seized of the question, he prorogued it on what were thought at the time factitious grounds, and relegated the inquiry to a Commission named by the Ministers themselves. He allowed letters written by himself to the Colonial Secretary, when the case was incomplete, to be laid before the House, for the purpose of influencing its judgment. It did not occur to him, nor does it occur to the constitutional writers who applaud him for continuing to give his confidence to his Ministers, that this case of confidence in Ministers, not a political question at all, but a State trial, with which he had no more business to interfere than he had to interfere with the course of justice in a court of law. It is true the tribunal in this case was equivocal and unsatisfactory, the question as to the retention of office by the Ministers being mixed up with the criminal indictment. There ought to be, though there is not at present, a regular process of impeachment, with a regular tribunal, and political corruption, whether in a Minister or any one else, ought to be made a distinct offence; it would seem to be as capable of definition as other breaches of trust, and it certainly is not less heinous. One of the convicted Ministers was afterwards made a knight. Nobody, it is right to say, suspected the Prime Minister on this or any other occasion of taking anything for himself. In that sense he certainly spoke the truth when, at the beginning of the affair, he declared to the Governor-General upon his honour as a Privy Councillor that he was innocent of the charge. The case of the Onderdonk contract, on the western portion of the same line, which was afterwards brought forward in Parliament, wore a very sinister aspect. But the Government had an overwhelming majority at its command.[1]

Strong evidences have unhappily been produced to show that by Government advertising and printing contracts, the system of corruption has been extended to the Press. What influences are behind the Press has become for all commonwealths alike one of the most serious questions of the day.

It is a comfort in speaking of these unsavoury matters to be able to reflect once more that Canadian society in general is sound, and that power in regard to the ordinary concerns of life is in the hands not of politicians but of the chiefs of commerce and industry, of judges and lawyers, of the clergy, and of the leaders of public opinion. Yet the character of the people cannot fail to be affected by familiarity with political corruption. Their political character, at all events, cannot escape the taint. A member of a local legislature is convicted, after investigation by a committee, of having on more than one occasion taken money corruptly. He nevertheless retains the support of his constituents. He is elected to the Dominion Parliament. The Prime Minister, whose henchman he is, makes him Chairman of the Finance Committee, and is prevented from making

1 An account of the case will be found in Mr. Collin's *Canada under the Administration of Lord Lorne*, p. 207 *et seq*. The section having been taken over by the C.P.R., that Company is now suing the Dominion for $6,000,000 on account of alleged defects or shortcomings in construction.

him Deputy Speaker only by the threat of an appeal to the record. The man is on the point, as is generally believed, of being made a Senator when another transaction comes to light, so foul in itself and in all its circumstances, that the Government is obliged with apparent reluctance to abandon its supporter to justice, and consent to the verdict of a committee pronouncing his conduct "discreditable, corrupt, and scandalous." Thereupon he resigns his seat, appeals to his constituents, pleading that he is no worse than the rest, and is re-elected. It has been asserted, on the strength it would seem of some highly official information, that in Canada scandals of corruption are almost unknown. If by this it is meant that few Canadian politicians take money for themselves, and that wealth amassed by corruption is rare among them, the statement is perfectly true, and it is equally true of the politicians in the United States, about whose illicit gains very exaggerated notions prevail. As a rule, politicians in both countries live and die poor; and, considering what they have to go through, it is wonderful that the attraction of politics should be so strong. But otherwise it is from the scandal, not from the corruption, that we are free. The pity is the greater because if ever a community was by its national character qualified for elective institutions it was that of the farmers of Canada. Political morality, and to some extent general morality with it, have been sacrificed to the exigencies of an artificial combination of provinces, and of an isolation of those provinces from their continent, which is equally artificial.

Nor are the sectional interests of Quebec and the other Provinces the only sectional interests, or the only interests of an anti-national character, with which the head of a Canadian Government has had to deal. He has had to propitiate with seats in the Cabinet and doles of patronage churches – above all the Roman Catholic Church – political combinations, such as Orangeism, and even a philanthropic combination like Prohibitionism, which at present has a seat in the Cabinet. The Roman Catholic vote is so well in hand that it is cast almost solid for one party in the Provincial elections of Ontario and at once transferred to the other in the Dominion elections, good consideration being received from both sides. The Premier of Ontario, though a zealous Presbyterian, finds himself compelled by the influence of the hierarchy not only to uphold the system of Separate Schools for Roman Catholics in the face of his own recorded protest against it, but to deny Roman Catholics the ballot in the election of School Trustees, which the more liberal of them demand, but to which the hierarchy object, because their control over the elections would thereby be impaired. The Irish vote is of course to a great extent identical with the Roman Catholic vote, yet as a political force it is distinct, and its power is inordinate. The lower are the political qualities of any body of men, and the less fit it is to guide the State, the more sure are its members politically to hold together, and the greater its influence will be. This is one of the banes of all elective government, and how it is we are to get rid of it or prevent it from growing, it is not easy to see. The abasement of American politicians and the American Press before the Irish vote is one of the most ignominious and disheartening passages in the history of free institutions. It reached its extreme point when, in miserable fear of the Irish groggeries of New York, the Senate of the United States refused to do honour to the memory of the great Englishman whose voice of power, in the darkest day of their fortunes, had triumphantly pleaded their cause before his country and the world. The motive for the resolutions passed by American Legislatures of sympathy with disunionism in Ireland, as well as the breach of international propriety which they involve, is freely admitted by American politicians. Similar resolutions from the same motive were passed by Canadian Legislatures, both Federal and Provincial, the Conservative Premier of the Dominion, with the Grand Cross of the Bath upon his breast, leading the way. Let Englishmen, before they welcome as the sincere expression of Canadian opinion, such manifestoes as the Loyalty Resolution passed by the Dominion Parliament of last session on the motion of Mr. Mulock, call to mind the fact that the same Assembly had before passed what was virtually a resolution in favour of the dismemberment of the United Kingdom. When Mr. William O'Brien came over to Canada with the avowed purpose of insulting, and if possible expelling from the country, Her Majesty's representative, those who, like the present writer, took an active part in opposing his irruption had the opportunity of seeing what the real influence of loyalty was among Canadian politicians compared with that of the Irish vote. That colonies would allow themselves to be used by Irish disaffection as levers for the disruption of the mother country was hardly foreseen as an incident of the system of dependence either by the opponents of the system or by its defenders.

Unhappily, England herself is in no position to cast a stone either at Canada or at the United States, for subserviency to the Irish, nor has there been anything in the conduct of the lowest of Canadian or American vote-hunters to match with the conduct of British statesmen who have leagued with the foreign enemies of their country and accepted aid from the Clan-na-Gael for the subversion of the Union. That the Irish should thus have been able by acting on the balance of parties to put the heads of the Anglo-Saxon commonwealths under their feet is surely a tremendous comment on the system of universal suffrage with government by faction.

What has been said will serve to explain two things apparently enigmatic. One of these is the stability of the Canadian government, which, saving one interruption, has remained unchanged for more than twenty years, while in Australia the changes of government have been prodigiously rapid. There having been really no Dominion parties, none, at least, united by any great principle or important issue, the Opposition has hitherto had no ground of attack or battlecry, while the Government, resting on its patronage and its bribery-fund has been always becoming more strongly entrenched, and has been able to carry the elections, at which no great question was presented, by dangling before the eyes of constituencies the Federal purse. Its election fund has also been much better supplied than that of the Opposition, which has had no crops of protected manufacturers to which to appeal, and no senatorships to hold out as prizes to the aspiring millionaire. The adverse influences which now threaten it, Nationalism in Quebec, by which its chief pillar is shaken, and the movement in favour of a reform in the tariff, which is evidently gaining strength, are of recent growth, and have never before had a chance of showing their force in a general election. The other phenomenon to be explained is the singular division of the power, the Dominion government being in the hands of the Conservative party, while the governments of the Provinces, saving the two least important of them, are in the hands of the Liberals. This has been supposed to prove that the people of the Dominion, whatever may be their local leanings, are all united in favour of the fiscal system or "National policy," as it is called, of Sir John Macdonald. What it really proves is that the Dominion bribery-fund is used in Dominion, not in Provincial, elections, and used with the more effect because a great many of the people, especially in the newly annexed Provinces, are comparatively apathetic about the affairs of the Dominion, while they feel a lively interest in their own. The truth of this solution is clearly shown in the case of Manitoba. To that Province, which has no manufactures, the tariff is an unmixed evil; it is an evil of the most oppressive kind, and, could it be submitted to the votes of the people, there would be an overwhelming majority in favour of its repeal. Yet Manitoba, while in her local legislature out of thirty-eight members four only are Conservatives, sends to Ottawa a Conservative delegation which supports the tariff, and not only thc tariff but railway monopoly, against which the Province is a unit. When the election comes round, the government secures the seats by petty bribes and by promises. This, new settlements being for the most part needy, it is too easy to do, the more so as the principal settlers, who would be likely to be independent and patriotic, are too much occupied with their own affairs to go to Ottawa, while for a government to find "heelers" is never difficult.

We cannot help once more warning the Australians that Federation under the elective system involves not merely the union of the several States under a central government with powers superior to them all; but the creation of Federal parties with all the faction, demagogism, and corruption which party contests involve over a new field and on a vastly extended scale. It is surprising how little this obvious and momentous consideration appears to be present to the minds of statesmen when the question of Federation is discussed.

It is a strong comment on the Protection system that since its inauguration there has not only been no abatement, but apparently an increase of the exodus from Canada to the United States. It is reckoned that there are now on the south of the Line a million of emigrants from Canada and half a million of their children. A local journal finds that it has 300 subscribers in the United States, and believes that in fifteen years it must have lost a thousand in that way; and from another journal, issued in one of the choicest districts of Ontario, we learn that the population there has been almost at a standstill. In one week 300 persons went from St. John and 400 from Montreal. The Americans may say with truth that if they do not annex Canada, they are annexing the Canadians. They are annexing the very flower of the Canadian population, and in the way most costly to the country from which it is drawn, since the men whom that country has been at the expense of breeding leave it just as they arrive at manhood and begin to produce. The value of farm property has declined in Ontario, according to the current estimate, 30 per cent, and good authorities hold that this estimate is within the mark. It would be wrong to ascribe either the exodus or the decline in the value of land directly and wholly to the fiscal system. There is a natural flow of population to the great centres of employment in the United States, and there is no real barrier of a national or sentimental kind to check the current, the two communities being, in all save political arrangements, one. The depression of agriculture and the fall in the value of farms are common in a measure to the whole continent, and are consequent on the depreciation of farm produce, perhaps also, so far as the United States are concerned, on a change in the once frugal habits of the farmer. But if Canada had fair play, if she were within the commercial pale of the Continent, by admission to a free market, combined with freedom of importing machinery, her minerals and other resources could be turned to the best account, she would have more centres of employment in herself, and her farmers would have more mouths to feed. There is a shifting of the agricultural population in the United States as well as in Canada, and many farms have been deserted in Massachusetts and Vermont. But these people are not lost to their country: [illegible] who emigrate from Canada to the States are. The promise of the Protectionist legislator to the farmer that he would give him a rich home market has at all events been signally belied. Nor is the wisdom of the policy demonstrated by a great decline in the value of that kind of property for which a special benefit was designed and the produce of which is the staple of the community. If the M‘Kinley Act remains in force, the consequence will probably be an increase of the exodus. Especially, there is likely to be a largely increased exodus from Quebec, the agricultural products of which are not of a kind suitable for exportation to a distant market, so that, the near market being closed, the people will have to suffer or to depart.

Strange to say, the exodus has told in favour of the stability of government; not only because it forms a vent but because the emigrants, as a rule, are the most active-minded, and there are probably among them at least two Liberals for one Conservative.

Government by subsidies and grants cannot be economically

carried on. Nor is the Canadian form of government in itself simple or inexpensive. Eight Constitutional Monarchies with as many Parliaments, four of the Parliaments having two Chambers, and the members of all being paid, are a considerable burden for a population under five millions and by no means wealthy. It is commonly said in Canada that we are "too much governed." Political architects in framing their Constitutions should have some regard for the cost of working among people whose wealth is not boundless. The work done by the eight Parliaments in the way of real legislation, apart from mere faction-fighting, would, if summed up, cut a poor figure in comparison with the expense. The eight Constitutional Monarchies have cost fully four millions of dollars since Confederation without doing any work at all. Hence, while the American debt, to which everybody pointed as a bugbear at the time of Confederation, has, notwithstanding the enormous squandering of public money by the tariff men, been rapidly decreasing, the Canadian debt has been almost as rapidly increasing, and now amounts to two hundred and forty millions net, or $50 per head of the whole population. The gross debt is two hundred and eighty millions, while of the securities some are very doubtful. If the demand for subsidies continues, the Canadian question may be settled by finance.

The Dominion has been immensely extended in territory since Confederation by the accession of the North-West and British Columbia. This extension has necessarily brought with it an addition of population and wealth, irrespectively of any stimulus given by institutions or political relations, though as we have seen, the growth of population in Manitoba and the rest of that region has been slow compared with its growth in the new States of the Union. But in Old Canada the growth of population and wealth is far from having kept pace with their growth within the commercial pale of the continent. In the six years, 1880-86, the natural growth of population in Ontario would have been 250,000, the actual growth was only 128,000. There is no estimate of the aggregate wealth, nor any means of distinguishing the savings of the people from the large amount of capital borrowed from England; but the visitor who crosses from the American to the Canadian side of the Line and compares the cities and towns on one side with those on the other can feel no doubt as to the effect of exclusion from the commercial pale.

The Canadian people are industrious, energetic, and thrifty; their country is rich in resources. The political institutions or relations must be bad indeed which could altogether arrest their progress. But this does not prove that an ill-cemented Confederation is or can be well cemented, that figureheads are useful, that a Senate which does nothing is worth the expense, that a fiscal policy of the Dark Ages promotes industry and commerce, or that it is a good thing to be governed by corruption.

Nor is there any pessimism in saying that the qualities and energies which in spite of an evil policy have done what we see, would under improved conditions do more. When Jingoism conspires with the party of commercial monopoly in the United States to bring on a tariff war, Canada is exhorted to show her fortitude, and told that if she does she will survive. No doubt she will survive; but like her neighbour across the Line and England herself she wants not only to live but to live well.

Chapter 10

The Canadian question

Dependence / The sanction of the mother country necessary for any change of political relations / Canada considering the problem of her future / Distinction between a colony and a colonial dependency / Misleading use of the term "Empire" / Supposed influence of sentiment on emigration / The strength of England lies in herself, not in her dependencies / England's protection of Canada precarious / Canada's complaints against British diplomacy / Political tutelage no longer possible / Society in the New World unalterably democratic / British interests in Canada / Value of the filial sentiment and that of dependence compared

Independence / The "Canada First" movement / Its tendency to independence / That solution of the problem probable in itself / Obstacles to its adoption / The moral of the movement

Imperial Federation / Origin of the movement / Absence of any definite plan / The scheme without precedent in history / What would be the object of the Association? / A limit to the effects of steam and telegraph in annihilating distance / What would be the relation of the Federal government to the British monarchy? / What diplomatic policy would prevail? / Complexities and embarrassments of the proposed system / Difficulties of setting the negotiations on foot / Difficulty of finding trustworthy representatives of the colonies / A moral federation of the whole English-speaking race more feasible / The colonies will not part with self-government

Political Union / "Annexation" an improper term / Union of Canada with the American Republic might be on equal and honourable terms, like that of Scotland with England / Service which Canada, if admitted to the Councils of the Union, might render to England / By entering the Union Canada need not forfeit her peculiar character or her historical associations / The idea that the connection would be one of moral disparagement unfounded / The evils and dangers of both countries substantially the same / Objections on the ground of over-enlargement of territory and populations / No line of political cleavage on the continent / Americans ready to welcome Canada into the Union / No thought of conquest or violent annexation / Difficulty of gauging Canadian sentiment / The Canadian people certainly in favour of free trade with their continent / Respecting their feeling as to political union nothing can be certainly said / Difficulty of bringing such a union about on the American as well as on the Canadian side / The primary forces will in the end prevail

Commercial Union / Mr. Bayard on the subject / The name Commercial Union adopted in contradistinction to Political Union. Account of the movement / Her own continent the natural market of Canada / Reciprocity of trade or reciprocity of tariffs the motto of the Conservative leader / The continent an economical whole / Reciprocity the dictate of nature / Special strength of the case with regard to the minerals of Canada / The shipping interest of Canada needs the freedom of the coasting-trade / The Americans on their side ready for Reciprocity / Policy of Mr. Blaine / Answer to the assertion of Protectionists that there cannot be a profitable trade between Canada and the United States / Remarkable growth of the trade in eggs when free from duty / Prevalence of smuggling under the present system / Special hardships resulting from the tariff to Manitoba and the Maritime Provinces / Comparison of the British with the American market / Reasons why the near market is the best / Counter-proposal of an Imperial Zollverein / Fatal objections to that plan / Efforts of the Canadian Government to open up new markets / The natural interests of Canada all in favour of Reciprocity / Objections to Commercial Union between the United States and Canada similar to those made between England and Scotland / Appeal of Protectionists to Imperial sentiment / Answer to the allegation that Commercial Union would be annexation in disguise /

Practical difficulties of the scheme enhanced by the M'Kinley tariff / The policy of the M'Kinley Act not likely to endure / A new commercial era apparently dawning for the United States

SECTION I. – DEPENDENCE

No one can now take up a Canadian newspaper or listen to a group of Canadians talking about politics without being made aware that Canada has the problem of her future before her. It is idle to suppose that Canadians will be prevented from discussing that problem or from conferring freely with their neighbours across the Line on a subject of the highest practical interest to both communities. If it is lawful for an ex-Governor-General of Canada to write on the Canadian question in an American magazine, surely it is lawful for Canadians and Americans to interchange their thoughts in the way they find convenient. Nor will free discussion do any harm. Not a plough will be stopped on the farm, not a spindle will cease to turn in the factory, not a politician will pause in his hunt for a vote because this debate is going on. Statesmanship is not made more practical or in any way improved by blindness to the future. The fruits of Canadian industry are being lavished by scores of millions on political railways and other works, the object of which is to keep Canada for ever separate from her neighbour. If perpetual separation is impossible, justice to the people requires that this waste of their earnings shall cease.

To answer at once the cries of treason which, as soon as the main question is approached, are raised by the official world and by the Protected Manufacturers, let us say that no Canadian, and so far as we are aware no American, has ever proposed that Canada should change her political relations to the mother country without the mother country's assent. If the Crown and Parliament of Great Britain sanction a change, the treason thenceforth will be in resistance. There must have been talk of the union between England and Scotland before it took place, and there has been talk of a union of Portugal with Spain; but so long as all was open and without prejudice to national duty on either side there could be no treason.

Let him who deals with the Canadian question first of all clear his mind of the confusion between a colony and a dependency. The proposal to put the coping-stone on colonial independence is branded as anti-colonial. Carthage was a colony but not a dependency of Tyre. The communities of Greater Greece were colonies, not dependencies of the Greece which sent them forth. The States of America are colonies of England, though they are dependencies no longer, and had they been let go in peace they would still be bound to the mother country by the filial tie. None are greater advocates of colonisation or cherish the link between the mother country and the colony more than those who are most opposed to the protraction of dependence. "Mother of free nations" is by all deemed the proudest title that England can bear, and a dependency is not a nation. The notion, peculiar to the moderns, that a colony ought to remain a dependency has its root not in any ground of reason or policy, but in the feudal doctrine of personal allegiance as an indefeasible bond between the liegeman and the lord. The founders of New England believed themselves, as their manifesto shows, to be indefeasibly liegemen of King James. But this fallacy has long been dead, and by the recent naturalisation treaties it has been buried. That the colonies in the early stage of their existence needed the protection of the mother country against the rival powers of Europe was a more substantial but still only a temporary reason for the connection. A better way was at one time opened. It was agreed by the Treaty of Neutrality between Louis XIV and James II (1686) that the colonies of England and France in America should remain at peace when the nations were at war. The Treaty came to nothing, but it pointed true.

Another fallacy to be shunned, especially when the horoscope of Canada is being cast, is that of treating "the Empire" in the lump, assuming a vital connection between all its parts and taking it for granted that the destiny of all of them is the same. Mr. Freeman may be rather rigorous on the subject of political nomenclature, but he has done a service by showing that the term Empire has been greatly misapplied and that its misapplication leads to practical delusion. It applies only to India, the Crown Colonies, and the military stations, which alone are held by a tenure really imperial and governed with imperial sway. An Asiatic dominion extending over two hundred and fifty millions of Hindoos, a group of West Indian islands full of emancipated negro slaves, a Dutch settlement at the southern point of Africa, occupied to secure the old passage to India, a conquered colony of France in the Indian Ocean, a factory like Hong Kong, military or coaling stations like Gibraltar, Malta, and Aden – what have these in common, or why are they likely to be for all time bound up with groups of self-governing British colonies in North America or Australia? Why again should Canada and Australia be treated as if their cases were identical, so that what is done with one must be done with the other, when Canada lies along the edge of a vast confederacy of kindred states with which are all her natural relations, diplomatic and commercial, while Australia lies in an ocean by herself, and such external relations as she has are with China? The real tie among the members of the motley group is England's command of the sea, which in successive wars has enabled her to pick off the transmarine possessions of her enemies. But the loud cries of high Imperialists for an increase of naval defences show that superior as Great Britain may still be in naval force to her rivals no single power any longer commands the seas. On the other hand, to fancy that because one possession or dependency is resigned all must go is surely a mere illusion, produced by the vague use of a common name for things which have nothing in common. Is England to be bound for ever, without any regard to change of circumstances, on penalty of the loss of her greatness and at the risk of all her general interests, to hold every sugar island taken in the days of slave-grown sugar, every coign of vantage occupied in the struggle against the continental system of Napoleon? When the cession of the Ionian Islands to Greece was proposed, the cry was raised that this would be the signal for general dissolution. Yet no dissolution ensued, nor was there any sign among the nations of diminished respect for Great Britain. She found herself all the stronger for being rid of a possession which in case of war must either have been garrisoned at a ruinous sacrifice or abandoned with disgrace, and the shrieks of dissolution were suspended, not to be raised again till the announcement of the cession of Heligoland. Let the Canadian question then be considered by itself and with reference to the circumstances of Canada, not to those of Jamaica, Malta, South Africa, or Hong Kong.

What is gained by the present system of dependence or semi-dependence as applied to Canada? What would be lost if it were exchanged for the filial tie? That is a question which, as even Imperial Federationists proclaim, the course of events has practically raised. That the connection lays on Great Britain heavy responsibilities, both military and diplomatic, that it adds not a little to the burdens and perils of empire, is plain. Were England to withdraw politically from the American continent she would be quit not only of the diplomatic entanglements and disputes with the United States about boundaries and fisheries, but of the ill-feeling which her presence on the continent enables her enemies in the United States to keep up against her, and which is adding seriously to her embarrassments in dealing with the Irish question. Hardly could any fisher of Irish votes succeed in inflaming the American people against a nation in another hemisphere with which they would no longer be brought into contact. What are the compensating advantages? The exclusive command of colonial markets which formed at least a substantial ground for the old colonial system, England has no more. No longer can she in the interest of her manufactures forbid a colony to make a horseshoe or a nail. Instead of that the Dominion of Canada lays protective duties on her goods. The chief of that which calls itself the loyal party in Canada has asserted Canada's right to do this, whether Englishman, Scotchman, or Irishman likes it or not, in ringing and almost defiant tones. It is still held that the colony cannot in her tariff discriminate against the mother country's goods; this little more than sentimental privilege is all in the way of commercial advantage that England has now. It is said that trade follows the flag. It follows the flag at first to a new colony which has no manufactures of its own. But apart from this and from national tariffs commerce is no discerner of nationalities. If the trade of Canada with Great Britain has hitherto exceeded (though it no longer exceeds) her trade with the United States, it is not because the British market is maternal, but because it is free. Find the merchant who in making a purchase, even of the bunting for the flag itself, has asked on patriotic grounds where the goods were made, and you will have some ground for saying that trade follows the flag. Did not the trade of England with her American Colonies, instead of diminishing, increase from the time when the Union Jack was exchanged for the Stars and Stripes, evil as the day of separation had been? To take the book trade as an example. At the very time when, in consequence of the *Trent* affair, Canadian feeling was excited against the Americans, the vast bulk of that trade – prices then ruling low and copyrights of great popular works not having expired – was going to the United States. Patriotic or philanthropic movements in favour of particular markets have been often set on foot, and to what have they come?

As to Emigration, there went in the year 1888 of British emigrants to Canada 49,168, to the United States 293,099; while of those who went to Canada half at least passed on to the United

States. What the emigrant wants is bread. That an Englishman in quest of employment will meet with a warmer welcome in Canada than in the United States is, as has already been said, a natural impression, but not the fact. There is nothing to make an emigrant prefer the British dependency to the Anglo-Saxon Colonies as his new home except the anti-British tone of American politics and of the American press; and on this probably few intending emigrants bestow a thought. It suffices them to know that they are going where their friends have gone before them, and where they will be better off than they are at home. Besides, as we have seen, the emigration question has now entered on a new phase, and the people of whom the mother country wishes to be rid the colony is no longer inclined, or not so well inclined as it used to be, to receive. It looks as though England might have for the future to close her own ports against the influx of Polish Jews or foreigners of any race, and in this or other ways to set bounds to the growth of her own population and find means of feeding her offspring at home.

Of dominion over the Colony barely a rag remains to the mother country, and even that remnant is grudged, and is being constantly nibbled away. The appellate jurisdiction of the Privy Council has been narrowed by the interposition of the Canadian Supreme Court; there is a smouldering agitation for the transfer of the military command from a British to a Canadian officer, and with regard to commercial matters there is a gradual assertion of diplomatic independence. This we have seen. The appointment of a Governor-General is about all that remains; and it perhaps may not be long before the Colonies generally improve upon the example of Queensland, which asserted a veto, and, under some constitutional form of recommending a name to Her Majesty, take the appointment to themselves.

That England can derive no military strength from a dependency 3000 miles away, without any army or navy of its own, and with an open frontier of 4000 miles, will surely be admitted by all, and is in effect proclaimed by Imperialists when they strive to goad Canadians into setting up a standing army. She cannot even derive that false show of strength solemnly styled "prestige": the weakness is too patent and too confessed to deceive even an opponent capable of taking pasteboard for a stone wall. Enlist soldiers in Canada England may, if she chooses to pay much higher wages than she pays her soldiers now, and perhaps bounties into the bargain; so, as the enlistments during the Civil War showed, can the American Government. The soldiers would no doubt be good, though British officers might have some trouble with democratic recruits not brought up like the British peasant to obey a gentleman. But Canada will never contribute to Imperial armaments at her own expense. Even Australia, which is more British than Canada, and has no New France in the heart of it, seems not likely to send another regiment at her own expense to an Imperial war; and when it was faintly proposed in Canada to emulate Australia in devotion there was a chorus of dissent, Conservative organs showing special anxiety to relieve their Government of the suspicion. The Conservative leader in Canada has intimated that the Colony will help the mother country only in case of defensive war; and he evidently did not regard as defensive the war in Afghanistan or that in Egypt. The mercantile marine of Canada claims the fourth place among those of the world. It is often spoken of as a nursery for the British navy. The mercantile marine of Great Britain can of course draw from it freely in case of need, as does the mercantile marine of the United States – for of those American fishermen about whose rights diplomatists contend the majority are said to be Canadians. But the new warships require seamen specially trained for the service. Besides, while people are dilating upon the military and naval resources of Canada as aids in time of need to the mother country, French Canada is left out of sight. Let the War Office ask the Canadian High Commissioner whether he thinks that Quebec would, under any conceivable circumstance, send contingents or subsidies to British armaments, or allow the Dominion, which is controlled by the French vote, to send them. The most likely antagonist of England is France, and in a war between France and England the hearts of the French Canadians, if not their arms, would be on the wrong side. There was no difficulty in raising Papal Zouaves.

"There are," says Sir George Cornewall Lewis,[1] "supposed advantages flowing from the possession of dependencies which are expressed in terms so general and vague that they cannot be referred to any determinate head. Such, for example, is the glory which a country is supposed to derive from an extensive Colonial Empire. We

1 *Essay on the Government of Dependencies,* p. 239.

will merely remark upon this imagined advantage that a nation derives no true glory from any possession which produces no assignable advantage to itself or to other communities. If a country possesses a dependency from which it derives no public revenue, no military or naval strength, and no commercial advantages or facilities for emigration which it would not equally enjoy though the dependency were independent ... such a possession cannot justly be called glorious." These are the words of a Minister of the Crown and a colleague of Lord Palmerston.

Great Britain may need a coaling station on the Atlantic Coast of North America, not for the purposes of blockade, which could no longer have place when all danger of war was at an end, but for the general defence of her trade. Safe coaling stations and harbours of refuge, rather than territorial dependencies, are apparently what the great exporting country and the mistress of the carrying trade now wants. Newfoundland would be a safe and uninvidious possession, and it has coal, though bituminous and not yet worked. The Americans do not covet islands, for the defence of which they would have to keep up a navy. The island itself would be the gainer; there would be some chance of the development of its resources; with nothing but the fishery the condition of its people seems to be poor. Let England then keep Newfoundland. Cape Breton is rather too close to the coast, otherwise it has coal in itself, and Louisbourg might be restored.

The strength of England is and always has been in herself, not in her dependencies. Alone she fought and vanquished Louis XIV and Napoleon, as well as Philip II. Some sepoys sent to Egypt in the war with France, some sepoys brought to the Mediterranean fourteen years ago as a demonstration against Russia, the regiment raised by Australia for the campaign in the Soudan – these are about the total amount of military contribution ever drawn by the Imperial country from what is called the Empire. Black regiments were raised in the West Indies, and the 100th Regiment was originally raised in Canada, but at Imperial expense. On the other hand, one dependency at least has drawn heavily on Imperial resources in an hour of extreme peril. When Wellington faced Napoleon at Waterloo he must, as he looked on the raw levies of foreign auxiliaries around him, have thought with bitterness of his victorious veterans who were on the wrong side of the Atlantic, engaged in what, as the conquest of Canada was the

American aim, was really a Colonial war. Had Canada then been in the American Union her friendly vote might have turned the scale of its councils generally in favour of England. The British in the United States have hitherto to a great extent declined naturalisation, repelled perhaps by the political feeling against their native country. But they have now been persuaded to take the wiser course, and are being naturalised in great numbers. As soon as their vote makes itself felt, the influence of the Irish vote and of the enemies of England on politics will decrease. The Nova-Scotian vote is said to have told the other day in Massachusetts. No other kind of aid will it be in Canada's power to lend. If this assertion is questioned, let the Canadian Government be called upon, while yet it is time, to say plainly what assistance, military or naval, it is able to afford, and in what contingency the assistance will be afforded.

Sir Henry Taylor cannot be said to have forfeited his character as a patriotic Englishman when he wrote, as Under-Secretary for the Colonies, to Lord Grey: "I cannot but regard the North-American Provinces as a most dangerous possession for this country, whether as likely to breed a war with the United States or to make a war otherwise generated more grievous and disastrous. I do not suppose the Provinces to be useless to us at present, but I regard any present uses not obtainable from them as independent nations as no more than the dust in the balance compared with the evil contingencies." It may be said that this was written in 1852, and that since that time we have had new lights. Some persons may have had new lights; but those who have not are no more unpatriotic in saying that the possession and that its uses are as dust in the balance compared with its evil contingencies than was Sir Henry Taylor.

Now on the side of the Colony. The disadvantages of dependence stare us in the face. If to be a nation is strength, energy, and grandeur, to be less than a nation is to have less than a full measure of all these. Nor can any one who has lived in a dependency fail to see that the high spirit of independence is not there. It absence is marked by restless and uneasy self-assertion, by a misgiving which sometimes lurks under an outward boastfulness, by a constant craving for the notice of the Imperial country, coupled with a jealousy of her superiority and of the supposed pretensions of those who belong to her. To live not to yourself but to another man, said the philosopher of old, is moral slavery, and a dependency lives to the Imperial country, not to herself. The full pride of country cannot have place, nor can the full attachment to country. The social centre of the rich and eminent is in the Imperial capital, and in their social centre are their aspirations and their hearts. There is not found in Canada the same public munificence which there is in the United States; nor are there found, as in the United States, great citizens who, without going into public life, without coveting its prizes, recoiling perhaps from it altogether, as it is under the party system – still take an active interest in all questions which deeply concern the welfare of the community, head movements of reform, political as well as social, throw themselves even into the political conflict when the salvation of the State hangs in the balance, and in a measure neutralise the evil influence of faction and its retainers. The dependency shares, it may be replied, the greatness of the Imperial nation. It does; but only as a dependent; it bears the train, not wears the royal robe.

Military and naval protection Canada may be said to receive; but it is protection of a very precarious kind. It is not pretended that the arm of England would save Canada from invasion: the most that is alleged is, that when Canada had suffered all the evils of invasion she would be redeemed by the pressure which the English navy would put upon the seaboard cities of the enemy. What amount of naval force Great Britain would be able to spare for the defence of colonial trade in case of a war between her and any other maritime power is a question which must be answered by the Admiralty, whose utterances on the subject hitherto have not been comforting. But it could hardly be such as to prevent a rise in the rate of insurance such as, the market of the United States being half closed by the tariff, would ruinously reduce Canadian trade. The saving to Canada of military and naval expense is one of the great inducements always held out to her for adhering to the connection. The other is the saving of diplomatic expense, which, however, will not be complete if the proposal to have residents at seats of commerce, in addition to the High Commissioner at London, is carried out. Diplomatic expense is not found intolerable by Switzerland, Denmark, Belgium, or Sweden, although they are mixed up with European diplomacy, of which Canada would be clear.

In the balance against this claim to protection and this saving of expense must be laid the heavy weight of a constant liability to entanglements in the quarrels of England all over the world, with which Canada has nothing to do, and about which nothing is known by her people. Her commerce may any day be cut up, and want brought into her homes by a war about the frontier of Afghanistan, about the treatment of Armenia or Crete by the Turks, about the relations of the Danubian principalities to Russia, or about the balance of power in Europe. No one in Canada who forms his estimate of public sentiment through his senses and not through his fancy can doubt what the result would be.

That in all diplomatic questions with the United States the interest of Canada has been sacrificed to the Imperial exigency of keeping the peace with the Americans is the constant theme of Canadian complaint. "I do not think" – these are the words of a Canadian knight – "that we are under any deep debt of gratitude to English statesmen, that we owe them much, unless, perchance, it may be the duty as Christian men to forgive them for the atrocious blunders which have marked every treaty, transaction, or negotiation which they have ever had with the United States where the interests of Canada were concerned, from the days of Benjamin Franklin to this hour, not excepting their first or second treaty of Washington." By the Treaty of 1783, confirming the independence of the United States, England not only resigned the territory claimed by each State of the Union severally, but abandoned to the general government immense territories "unsettled, unexplored, and unknown." That this was done partly through ignorance appears from the fact that in the Treaty the north-western angle of demarcation was fixed at the north-west corner of the Lake of the Woods, from which point of departure it was to run due west to the sources of the Mississippi; whereas the sources of the Mississippi were afterwards found many hundred miles to the south, so that the line prescribed was impracticable.[1] This is the beginning of a long and uniform story, in the course of which not only great tracts of territory but geographical unity has been lost. To understand how deeply this iron has entered into the Canadian soul the Englishman must turn to his map and mark how much of geographical compactness, of military security, and of commercial convenience was lost when Great Britain

1 See article "How Treaty-making unmade Canada," by the late Lieut.-Colonel Coffin, Ottawa, in the *Canadian Monthly,* May, 1876.

gave up Maine. The British statesman would with truth reply that he had done all that diplomacy could do, that he had gone to the very verge of war with the United States, and that with the world-wide empire and world-wide enmities on his hands he could not afford to go beyond. The Canadian, if he were reasonable, would acquiesce, but he would feel that the sincerest wish to protect without the power was not protection. A large portion of Minnesota, Dakota, Montana, and Washington, Canada also thinks she has wrongfully lost. These are causes of discontent; discontent may one day breed disaffection; disaffection may lead to another calamitous rupture; and instead of going forth into the world when the hour of maturity has arrived with the parent's blessing, the child may turn in anger from the paternal door.

About the advantages of political tutelage hardly a word need be said. Practically the idea has been abandoned. How could a democracy in Europe regulate, to any good purpose, the progress of a democracy in America about the concerns of which it knows almost nothing, and which is superior to itself in average education and intelligence? British democracy has enough to do in regulating itself. In former days, when the British Government consisted of the chief men of the nation exercising real power the illusion of tutelage was possible; but who can believe that a colony is the better for being guided by the delegates of an English caucus? Even the best informed in England are still too uninstructed about Canada to interfere usefully in her affairs? If the days are gone by when the Admiralty could send out sentry-boxes for the troops, water-casks for a flotilla on Canadian lakes, and spars for the use of vessels in a land of pine, the writer has seen posted in England a proclamation of the Privy Council in which Ontario was called "that town," and he has heard a well-educated Englishman congratulate a Canadian on the removal by the settlement of the Alabama question of all causes of enmity between Canada and Great Britain. The House of Commons notoriously cannot be got to attend to colonial questions. In the debate on the Quebec Act it was near being counted out, and in the division which was to decide the constitution and laws of the dependency only seventy-two members took part. An Act relating to the South-African Confederation was passed in an all-night sitting held to beat obstruction. Nobody blames people for knowing or caring little about matters with which they have nothing to do.

Canadians care and know little about Australia or the Cape of Good Hope. But to talk of tutelage is absurd. If British monarchists have continued to cherish the hope of establishing through the agency of Canada hereditary monarchy and aristocracy on this Continent, and thus wresting from democracy a part of its dominion, let that hope be for ever laid aside. The structure and spirit of Canadian as well as American society, it must be repeated, are thoroughly democratic. The homage paid to titled visitors from the old country and the social worship of the Governor-General are indications merely of personal habit, not of any political return to the past. Americans and Canadians are in this respect the same. In the hereditary principle there is not on the American Continent a spark of life. The abdication of the Brazilian dynasty was the knell. That democracy on the American continent and elsewhere may some day pass through faction into anarchy, and that out of the anarchy a strong government may arise, is among those possibilities in the womb of the future which no external power can help to the birth; but on the soil of the New World hereditary monarchy and aristocracy can never grow.

Canada has received, it is true, large advances of British capital. Her debt to England has been reckoned at $650,000,000, though of the portion invested in the construction of Canadian railways most may be practically written off. How far facility of borrowing is really a blessing to any country is a question which need not be discussed. English capital is now pouring into the United States; it has poured into the Argentine Republic, Spain, Russia, Egypt, Turkey, Mexico, and every country in which it appeared that profitable investments could be found. Investment is as cosmopolitan as trade. Let Canada keep up her credit and the British investor will not curiously inquire whether the Governor-General is sent out from England or elected by the Canadians themselves.

Sentiment then, apparently, is the sole life of the present connection. Of sentiment no one wishes to speak irreverently. But to be sound, it must after all have its root in some kind of utility, and when the root is dead the days of the flower are numbered. Besides it is but the exchange of one sentiment for another which is more certain to endure. Why is the filial sentiment of less value than the sentiment of dependence? It is surely rather the nobler of the two. The Greek colony which kept the fire taken from the mother country's altar always burning on its sacred hearth and assigned to the representatives of the mother country places of honour, effectively preserved, in its classic fashion, the bond of the heart; and why should not the same thing be done in forms suited to our time by a Colony at the present day? Protracted dependence may imperil the filial tie if resentment is caused on either side by the failure to render services which can no longer be rendered, and perform duties which can no longer be performed.

SECTION II. – INDEPENDENCE

Confederation was followed by a movement in the direction of Independence, chiefly among the young men of Ontario, which was called "Canada First." The name was the title of a pamphlet written in 1871 by Mr. W. A. Foster, a barrister of Toronto, which fired a number of young hearts. To independence the movement manifestly tended, if this was not its avowed or definite aim. The authors of Confederation, to induce the people to accept their policy, had set before them glowing pictures of the resources of the country, and made strong appeals to patriotic pride, hope, and self-reliance. These produced their natural effect on ardent and sanguine souls. It happened that just at the same time the generation of immigrants from England which had occupied many of the leading places in the professions and commerce was passing off the scene and leaving the field clear for native ambition, while the withdrawal of the troops also brought socially to the front the young natives who had before been somewhat eclipsed in the eyes of ladies by the scarlet. "Canada First" was rather a circle than a party: it eschewed the name of party, and the Country above Party was its cry. Some of the group were merely nativists who desired that all power and all places should be filled by born Canadians, that the policy of Canada should be shaped by her own interest, and that she should be first in all Canadian hearts. With some a "national policy" for the protection of Canadian manufactures was probably a principal object. But that to which the leading spirits more or less consciously, more or less avowedly, looked forward was Independence. That they aimed at raising Canada above the condition of a mere dependency and investing her with the dignity of a nation they loudly proclaimed, and they would have found that this could not be done without putting off dependence. "Canada First" was violently denounced and assailed by the politicians of the two old parties, who betrayed in their treatment of the generous aspirations to which they had themselves appealed the real source of their policy and the spirit in which they had acted as the authors of Confederation. The Court of Ottawa also exerted its influence, including its influence over the masters of the Press, in the same direction. The movement found a leader, or thought that it had found a leader, in a native Canadian politician, who was the child of promise and the morning star at that time. But at the decisive moment party ties prevailed, the leader was lost, and the movement collapsed, not however without leaving strong traces of its existence, which are beginning to show themselves among the younger men at the present day.

In one respect, at all events, the men of "Canada First" were right. They saw or at least felt – even the least bold and the least clear-sighted of them felt – that a community in the New World must live its own life, face its own responsibilities, grow and mould itself in its own way; that Anglo-Saxon nations in North America could no more be tied for ever to the apron-strings of the mother country than England could have been tied for ever to the apron-strings of Friesland, or France to those of the mother country of the Franks.

There was nothing on the face of it impracticable in the aim of "Canada First." There is nothing in nature or in political circumstances to forbid the existence on this Continent of a nation independent of the United States. American aggression need not be feared. The violence and unscrupulousness bred of slavery having passed away, the Americans are a moral people. It would not be possible for Clay or any other demagogue now to excite them to an unprovoked attack upon another free nation or even to a manifest encroachment on its rights. If they had been filibusters they would have shown it when they had an immense army on foot, with a powerful navy, and when they were flushed with victory. The New England States, and the non-slavery element of the nation generally, were opposed to the War of 1812. An independent Canada, however inferior to them in force, might rest in perfect safety by their side. But when "Canada First" was born the North-West had only just been acquired. British Columbia was as yet hardly incorporated, and the absolute want of geographical compactness or even continuity was not so apparent as it is now. Enthusiasm was blind to the difficulty presented to the devotees of Canadian nationality by the separate nationality of Quebec, or if it was not blind, succeeded in cajoling itself by poetic talk about the value of French gifts and graces as ingredients for combination, without asking whether fusion was not the thing which the French most abhorred. There is no reason why Ontario should not be a nation if she were minded to be one. Her territory is compact. Her population is already as large as that of Denmark, and likely to be a good deal larger, probably as large as that of Switzerland; and it is sufficiently homogeneous if she can only repress French encroachment on her eastern border. She would have no access to the sea: no more has Switzerland, Hungary, or Servia. Already a great part of her trade goes through the United States in bond.

The same thing might have been said with regard to the Maritime Provinces – supposing them to have formed a legislative union – Quebec, British Columbia, or the North-West. In the North-West, rating its cultivable area at the lowest, there would be room for no mean nation. But the thread of each Province's destiny has now become so intertwined with the rest that the skein can hardly be disentangled. That the North-West, if it is not released from the strangling tariff, may take a course of its own is not unlikely; but it is unlikely that the course will be Independence.

SECTION III. – IMPERIAL FEDERATION

It was probably the sight of the tie visibly weakening and of the approach of Colonial independence that gave birth, by a recoil, to Imperial Federation. But the movement has been strangely reinforced from another source. Home rulers, who, under that specious name would surrender Ireland to Mr. Parnell, think to salve their own patriotism and reconcile the nation to their policy by saying that in breaking up the United Kingdom they are only providing raw materials for a far ampler and grander union. In the case of the late Mr. Forster, the only statesman who has seriously embraced the project, something might be due to the Nemesis of imagination in the breast of a Quaker.

The Imperial Federationists refuse to tell us their plan. They bid our bosoms dilate with trustful enthusiasm for arrangements which are yet to be revealed. They say it is not yet time for the disclosure. Nor yet time when the last strand of political connection is worn almost to the last thread, and when every day the sentiment opposed to centralisation is implanting itself more deeply in Colonial hearts! While we are bidden to wait patiently for the tide, the tide is running strongly the other way. Now Newfoundland claims the right of making her own commercial agreements with the United States independently of other Colonies. Disintegration, surely, is on the point of being complete.

At least we may be told of whom the Confederation is to consist. Are the negroes of the West Indies to be included? Is Quashee to vote on Imperial policy? But above all, what is to be done with India? Is it, as a Canadian Federationist of thorough-going democratic tendencies demanded the other day, to be taken into Federation and enfranchised? If it is, the Hindoo will outvote us by five to one, and what he will do with us only those who have fathomed the Oriental mystery can pretend to say. Is it to remain a dependency? Then to whom is it to belong? To a Federation of democratic communities scattered over the globe, some of which, like Canada, have no interest in it whatever? Its fate as an Empire would then be sealed, if it is not sealed already by the progress of democracy in Great Britain. Or is it to belong to England alone? In that case one member of the Confederacy will have an Empire apart five times as large as the rest of the Confederation, requiring separate armaments and a diplomacy of its own. How would the American Confederation work if one State held South America as an Empire? Some have suggested that Hindostan should be represented by the British residents in India alone. If it were, woe to the Hindoos.

Again, the object of the Association must surely be known. Every Association of a practical kind must have a definite object to hold it together. The objects which naturally suggest themselves are common armaments and a common tariff. But Canada, as we have seen, refuses to contribute to common armaments, and Australia, though she sent a regiment to the Soudan, now apparently repents of having done it. Great Britain is a war power; the Colonists, like the Americans, are essentially unmilitary, and here would be the beginning of troubles. As to the tariff, the Canadian Protectionists, who make use of Imperial Federation as a stalking-horse in their struggle against free trade with the United States, are always careful to say that they do not mean to resign their right of laying protective duties on British goods. Victoria also seems wedded to her

Protective system. What remains but improvement of postal communication and a Colonial Exhibition, neither of which surely calls for a political combination unprecedented in history.

Unprecedented in history the combination would be. The Roman Empire, the thought of which, and of its *Civis Romanus sum,* is always hovering before our minds, was vast, but it was all in a ring-fence. Moreover, it had its world to itself, no rival powers being interposed between Rome and her Provinces. It was an Empire in the proper sense of the term. Its members were all alike in strict subordination to its head. The head determined the policy without question, and danger to unity from divided counsels there was none. We confuse our minds, as was said before, by an improper use of the term Empire. The name applies to India, but to nothing else connected with Great Britain unless it be the fortresses and Crown Colônies. Our self-governed Colonies are not members of an Empire, but free communities virtually independent of the mother country, which for the purpose of Confederation would be called upon to resign a portion of their independence. Of the Spanish Empire it is needless to speak. Its name is an omen of disaster and a warning against the blind ambition which mistakes combination for union and colossal weakness for power. After all, the Roman Empire itself fell, and partly because the life was drawn from the members to the head.

The Achaean League, the Swiss Bund, the Union of the Netherlands, the American Union, all were perfectly natural combinations, not only suggested but commanded by a common peril. In three out of the four cases the communities which entered into the compact were kindred in all respects; in the case of the Swiss Bund they were equal. In the case of the Confederation now proposed, they would be neither kindred nor equal; and fasten the people of the British Islands, those of the self-governed Colonies, the Hindoo, the African, and the Kaffir together with what legislative clamps you will, you cannot produce the unity of political character and sentiment which is essential to community of councils, much more to national union.

Steam and telegraph, we are told, have annihilated distance. They have not annihilated the parish steeple. They have not carried the thoughts of the ordinary citizen beyond the circle of his own life and work. They have not qualified a common farmer, tradesman, ploughman, or artisan to direct the politics of a world-wide State. How much does an ordinary Canadian know or care about Australia, an ordinary Australian about Canada, or an ordinary Englishman, Scotchman, or Irishman about either? The feeling of all the Colonists towards the mother country, when you appeal to it, is thoroughly kind, as is that of the mother country towards the Colonies. But Canadian notions of British politics are hazy, and still more hazy are British notions of the politics of Canada. When John Sandfield Macdonald, the Prime Minister of Ontario, died, his death was chronicled by British journals as that of Sir John A. Macdonald, the Prime Minister of the Dominion.

About India Englishmen know more, because their interest in it is so great; but Canadians know nothing. The framers of these vast political schemes, having their own eyes fixed on the political firmament, forget that the eyes of men in general are fixed on the path they tread. The suffrage of the Federation ought to be limited to far-reaching and imaginative minds.

A grand idea may be at the same time practical. The idea of a United Continent of North America, securing free trade and intercourse over a vast area, with external safety and internal peace, is no less practical than it is grand. The benefits of such a union would be always present to the mind of the least instructed citizen. The sentiment connected with it would be a foundation on which the political architect could build. Imperial Federation, to the mass of the people comprised in it, would be a mere name conveying with it no definite sense of benefit, on which anything could be built.

To press this receding vision a little closer, what would be the relation of the Federal Government to the British monarchy? Would the same Queen be sovereign of both? Would she have two sets of advisers? Suppose they should advise her different ways! Would she appoint, as she does now, the heads of all the other members of the Federation? It would hardly do to let the President of the United States appoint all the State Governors. How would the Supreme Court be constituted? Such an authority would certainly be needed to interpret the Constitution, and the British monarchy would have to be a suitor before it. How would the decrees of the Federationists be enforced, say, in case of refusal to send the war contingent? How, again, would the representation in the Federal Parliament be apportioned? If by population, the representation of the British

Islands would so outnumber the rest that the rest would deem their representation practically a nullity, and jealousy and cabals would at once arise. The very number, too, would be a difficulty. If Great Britain had members in proportion to St. Helena and Fiji, the Parliament would have to meet on Salisbury Plain. These are not questions of detail, nor do they attach only to a particular scheme: they are fundamental, and attach to every scheme that can be conceived.

The Parliament of Great Britain must cease to be a Sovereign Power. The Imperial Congress itself would not be a Sovereign Power. Like the Congress of the United States, it would be subject to the Federal Constitution, and would have so much authority only as that Constitution assigned it. The Sovereign Power would be in the people of the Empire at large, and a curious Sovereign they would be.

The same person could not be the head at once of a Federation and of one of the communities included in it any more than the same person could be President of the United States and Governor of the State of New York. Her Majesty would have to choose between the British and the Pan-Britannic Crown.

Canada is a Confederation in herself. Movements are on foot for a Confederation of the Australian Colonies and of those of South Africa. A Confederation of the West India Islands has also been proposed. We should thus have a striking novelty in political architecture in the shape of a Confederation of Confederations. But it seems certain that New Zealand would not, and that some isolated Colonies could not, join any Federation, in which case the members of the Central Parliament would represent partly Federations, partly single communities. Strange apparently would be the complication of fealties, obligations, and sentiments which would hence arise.

This Union, so complex in its machinery, with its members scattered over the world, and distracted by interests as wide apart as the shores of its members, Home Rulers think they could maintain, while they bid us despair of maintaining the Parliamentary Union of Ireland with Great Britain.

Even to assemble the Centralised Convention would be no easy task. The governments, British and Colonial, are all party governments and all liable to constant change. The delegate trusted by one party would not have the confidence of the other, and before the

Convention would proceed to business somebody's credentials would be withdrawn. We have seen in the case of Canadian Confederation how Nova Scotia, New Brunswick, and Prince Edward Island flew off from the agreement at which their delegates had arrived. In truth there would probably be a general falling away as soon as payment for Imperial armaments came into view.

The Federation would be nothing if not diplomatic. But whose diplomacy is to prevail? That of Great Britain, an European Power and at the same time Mistress of India? That of Australia, with her Eastern relations and her Chinese question? Or that of Canada, bound up with the American Continent, indifferent to everything in Europe or Asia, and concerned only with her relation to the United States? If we may believe Sir Charles Dilke, Australia avows her intention of breaking away from England should British policy ever take a line adverse to her special interests in the East.

Achaia, Switzerland, the Netherlands, the United States, all federated under the pressure of necessity, which, stern and manifest as it was, had yet scarcely the power to overcome the centralised forces. To do the work of that necessity there ought at least to be an equally strong desire. But what proof have we of the existence of such a desire? Australia, far from being eager, seems to be adverse; in some of her cities the missionary of Imperial Federation can scarcely find an audience. From South Africa comes no audible response. In British Canada the movement has no apparent strength except what it derives from an alliance with Protectionism, which, as has already been said, repudiates a commercial union of the Empire and insists on maintaining its separate tariff. To the French nationalists of Quebec anything that would bind their country closer to Great Britain is odious, and they were disposed to receive the present Governor-General coldly because they suspected him of favouring such a policy. In Great Britain itself the movement shows no sign of strength. For several years, under Lord Beaconsfield, Imperialism had everything its own way, yet not a step was taken towards Federation. That was the grand opportunity; but Federationists failed to grasp it by the forelock. Not a step has been taken to this hour beyond holding a meeting of Colonists, absolutely without authority, which dined, wined, and talked about postal communications, all power of dealing with the great question having been expressly withheld. Lord Beaconsfield's successor in the Tory leadership has plainly declined to commit himself to the project. We seem to be a long way from a spontaneous and overwhelming vote, nothing short of which would suffice. The approach to centralisation at once sets all the centrifugal forces in action; it did this even in the case of American federation, so that the project narrowly escaped wreck; and miscarriage would beget, instead of closer union, discord, estrangement, and perhaps rupture. Let us bear the warning example of the rupture with the American Colonies in mind.

What is the real motive for encountering all the difficulties and perils of this more than gigantic undertaking, for running laboriously counter to the recent course of Colonial history, as well as to the natural tendencies of our race, and for taking the political heart and brain, as it were, out of each of those free communities and transferring them to London? We are told that the Federal Empire would impose peace upon the world. This assumes that dispersion is strength, and that Great Britain would be made more formidable in war by being bound up with unmilitary communities. But suppose it true, surely the appearance of a world-wide power, grasping all the waterways and all the points of maritime vantage, instead of propagating peace, would, like an alarm gun, call the nations to battle! The way to make peace on earth is to promote the coming not of an exclusive military league but of the Parliament of Man, the moral Parliament of Man at least, by enlarging the action of international law and repressing the ambitious passions to which, however philanthropic may be our professions, Imperialism really appeals. If no distinct object can be assigned, if no definite plan can be produced, if the projectors are conscious that there is no practical step on which they can venture, surely the project ought to be frankly laid aside and no longer allowed to darken counsel, hide from us the real facts of the situation, and prevent the Colonies from advancing on the true path.

There is a Federation which is feasible, and, to those who do not measure grandeur by physical force or extension, at least as grand as that of which the Imperialist dreams. It is the moral federation of the whole English-speaking race throughout the world, including all those millions of men speaking the English language in the United States, and parted from the rest only a century ago by a wretched quarrel, whom Imperial Federation would leave out of its pale. Nothing is needed to bring this about but the voluntary retirement of England as a political power from a shadowy dominion in a sphere which is not hers. There is no apparent reason why, among all the states of our race, there should not be community of citizenship, so that a citizen of any one of the nations might take up the rights of a citizen in any one of the others at once upon his change of domicile, and without the process of naturalisation. This would be political unity of no inconsiderable kind without diplomatic liabilities, or the strain, which surely no one can think free from peril, of political centralisation.

Unless all present appearances on the political horizon are delusive, the time is at hand when the upheaval of the labour world, and the social problems which are coming into view, will give the politicians more serious and substantial matter for thought than the airy fabric of Imperial Federation.

The old project of giving the Colonies representation in the Imperial Parliament appears to have been laid aside. The objections urged against it by Burke on the ground of distance have been to a great extent removed by steam, though it might even now be difficult to call together a world-wide Parliament in time of maritime war. But the objection still decisive is that the Colonies would not put their affairs into the hands of an Assembly in which their representation would be overwhelmingly outnumbered. Nor could they trust representatives domiciled in London who, under the influence of London society, would be apt to become more British than the British themselves. These new countries, which have such difficulty in finding suitable men for their own legislatures, would have difficulty in finding men to represent them at Westminster at all. They might have to fall back on expatriated millionaires, in whom not the slightest confidence as representatives of Colonial sentiment could be placed. Supposing that the members for the Colonies remained colonial, and tried to make up for their lack of numbers at Westminster by combining among themselves and log-rolling, they might become a serious addition to the distractions of the British Parliament, which assuredly need no increase.

Let it be taken as certain and irreversible that the Colonies will not part with any portion of their self-government. If a scheme can be devised by which they can be governed by an Assembly at Westminster without any loss to them of self-government it may, supposing it to be presented to them in an intelligible and practicable form, stand a chance of consideration at their hands.

SECTION IV. – POLITICAL UNION

Annexation is an ugly word; it seems to convey the idea of force or pressure applied to the smaller State, not of free, equal, and honourable union, like that between England and Scotland. Yet there is no reason why the union of the two sections of the English-speaking people on this Continent should not be as free, as equal, and as honourable as the union of England and Scotland. We should rather say their reunion than their union, for before their unhappy schism they were one people. Nothing but the historical accident of a civil war ending in secession, instead of amnesty, has made them two. When the Anglo-Saxons of England and those of Scotland were reunited they had been many centuries apart; those of the United States and Canada have been separated for one century only. The Anglo-Saxons of England and Scotland had the memory of many wars to estrange them: the Anglo-Saxons of Canada and the United States have the memory, since their separation, only of one war.

That a union of Canada with the American Commonwealth, like that into which Scotland entered with England, would in itself be attended with great advantages cannot be questioned, whatever may be the considerations on the other side or the reasons for delay. It would give to the inhabitants of the whole Continent as complete a security for peace and immunity from war taxation as is likely to be attained by any community or group of communities on this side of the Millenium. Canadians almost with one voice say that it would greatly raise the value of property in Canada; in other words, that it would bring with it a great increase of prosperity. The writer has seldom heard this seriously disputed, while he has heard it admitted in the plainest terms by men who were strongly opposed to Union on political or sentimental grounds, and who had spent their lives in the service of Separation. The case is the same as that of Scotland or Wales in relation to the rest of the island of which they are parts, and upon their union with which their commercial prosperity depends. The Americans, on the other hand, would gain in full proportion as England gains by her commercial union with Wales and Scotland. These inducements are always present to the minds of the Canadian people, and they are specially present when the trade of Canada, with the rest of her Continent, is barred by such legislation as the M'Kinley Act, when her security is threatened by the imminence of war in Europe, or when from internal causes she happens to be acutely feeling the commercial atrophy to which her isolation condemns her. Canadians who live on the border, and who from the shape of the country form a large proportion of the population, have always before their eyes the fields and cities of a kindred people, whose immense prosperity they are prevented from sharing only by a political line, while socially, and in every other respect, the identity and even the fusion is complete.

On the other hand, there is the affection of the Colonists for the mother country, which has always been kind to them in intention, even if she has not had the power to defend their rights and her interference has ceased to be useful. This might prevail if union with the rest of the race on this Continent, under the sanction of the mother country, would really be a breach of affection for her. But it would be none. It would be no more a breach of affection than the naturalisation, now fully recognised by British law, of multitudes both of Englishmen and of Canadians in the United States. Let us suppose that the calamitous rupture of the last century had never taken place, that the whole race on this Continent had remained united, and had parted, when the time came, from the mother country in peace; where would the outrage on love or loyalty have been? Admitted into the councils of their own Continent, and exercising their fair share of influence there, Canadians would render the mother country the best of all services, and the only service in their power, by neutralising the votes of her enemies. Unprovoked hostility on the part of the American Republic to Great Britain would then become impossible. It is now unlikely, but not impossible, since there is no wickedness which may not possibly be committed by demagogism pandering to Irish hatred.

Nor need Canada give up any of the distinctive character or historical associations which she has preserved through the continuance of her connection with the mother country. Scotland is still Scotch, and her idol Sir Walter Scott was the type at once of patriotic Britons and of Scotchmen. The Federal system admits wide local diversities, and if Ontario or Nova Scotia clings to the British statute-book, to the British statute-book it may cling. There is no reason even why Canadians, who like to show their spirit by military celebrations, should not celebrate Canadian victories as the Scotch celebrate Bannockburn. Americans would smile. Of the antipathy to Americans sedulously kept up within select circles and in certain interests, there is absolutely none among the Canadian people at large. It would be strange if there were any, considering that half of them have brothers, sons, or cousins on the American side of the Line. "Bombard New York!" said a Canadian to the writer when somebody was declaiming in that vein; "why, my four sons live there!" On the Pacific Coast of the United States a British shell could scarcely burst without striking a Canadian home. The masses do not read much history or cherish antiquarian feuds. If the President of the United States were to visit Canada, he would be received as cordially as he is in any part of his own Republic; more cordially, perhaps, since in Canada the people of both parties would unite in the ovation.

If the language held by Canadian Jingoes or "Paper Tigers," as they are called, about American character were the truth or anything like the truth, union with such people ought indeed to be declined at any sacrifice of military security or commercial profit. But even those who hold it hardly believe it. An Imperialist journal in London the other day ended an article on the influence of Americans in England by saying that they are too like the English in all essential respects to produce any possible change in English character. That, as regards the normal American, is the fact. The present writer has known the Americans not, like most of their critics, only in the cities, but in the country and the country town. As a lecturer and resident in an American University he has been brought into contact with American youth; he has friends among Americans of all vocations and professions; he has seen the people under the ordeal of civil war, seen their conduct in the field, their care of the wounded, and their treatment of their captured enemies; and to him the idea that Canadians would undergo moral disparagement by the Union seems of all reveries the most absurd. Sheer snobbishness, to tell the truth, has not a little to do with the affectation of contempt for Yankees. This is one of the ways in which vulgarity tries to make itself genteel. The good feeling of Canadians towards their mother country is strong, genuine, disinterested, and cannot be too highly prized. But there is a blatant loyalty which it is very easy to prize too highly. If a man makes a violent and offensive demonstration of it against those whom he accuses of American sympathies, you are apt presently to find him in the employment of some American company, peddling for an American house, or accepting a call to the other side of the Line. We have already, in our historical retrospect, had occasion to observe that when by untoward circumstances interest is divorced from sentiment, the loyalism which before had been the most fiery in its manifestations can suddenly grow cold. If England ever has occasion to call on her children in Canada for a real sacrifice, she may chance to repeat the experience of King Lear.

There are varieties too little noticed by critics of American character in different parts of the Union. These are black spots. In certain districts lawlessness and want of respect for human life remain as the traces of slavery, whose cause Canadian Jingoism ardently espoused. New York has its shoddy wealth which the better Americans despise, and which British aristocracy, though scornful of American democracy, sometimes takes to its arms. Rapid commercial development has bred gambling speculation, and with it unscrupulousness, of which Canada also has her proportionate share, though in both cases the amount of knavery is small compared with that of sound and honest trade. Party politics are the same on both sides of the Line, and on neither side, happily, are they the whole of life. The Canadian politician exactly resembles the American, and none the less when he has been knighted. Both countries would be in a bad way if the demagogue ruled society and trade. Political corruption is on a far larger scale in the wealthier country, but it is more shameless in the poorer country. About the American Press there is a good deal to be said, but not more than there is about the successive personal organs of a Prime Minister of Canada. Canada has the advantage of not having broken with her history or bearing on her political character, like the American, the trace of a revolution; but America is gradually renewing her historical associations, and since she has had herself to contend with rebellion and been threatened within by the Anarchists, the revolutionary sentiment has been losing force. In the wealthier country and that which had the start in civilisation is found a higher standard of living, with more of science and culture; in the other, more frugality and simplicity of life. Both communities are threatened by the same social dangers and disturbances, nor is there any conservative force in one which there is not in the other, the phantom of monarchy in Canada being, as has been shown, no conservative force at all, but rather serving to disguise the action of forces the reverse of conservative. There is continual harping on the laxity of the American divorce law, and Canada was told that if she traded more with the Americans Canadian wedlock would be in danger of the contagion. Illinois and Indiana, where the laxity prevails, are not the United States. However, scarcely had the warning been penned, when we had proof that, even as it is, no impassable gulf of sentiment divides us from Indiana and Illinois.

The fear that with the addition of Canada the Union would be too large and that its cohesion might give way, which is felt both by Canadians and Americans, though natural, seems not to be well-founded. Slavery being extinct there is no longer any visible line of cleavage. So long as the freedom of the system is preserved, there seems to be no limit to its possible extension, provided the territory, though vast, is within a ring fence. Nobody is likely to rebel against an arrangement which, without fettering local self-development, gives safety against attack from without, peace and freedom of intercourse within. People must be revolutionary indeed if they can take arms against mere immunity from evils. The tariff question does not form a line of cleavage, and is in a fair way to be settled by the ballot. If 300,000,000 Chinese can get on well together under a centralised Government, surely 100,000,000 of the higher race can get on together under a government much more elastic. The problem of races at the South no doubt is still serious, but there is no tendency to a renewal of secession, and the South is becoming daily smaller and less important in proportion to the Union. The growth there of manufacturing industries will both modify political character and bind the States to their Northern market. Socialistic revolution, such as would take a State out of the Republic, and the occupation of the Pacific Coast by the Chinese, are contingencies which might threaten the Union, but at present they are very remote, while to Chinese irruption Canada on the Pacific is more open than the United States.

Again, Canadians who heartily accept democracy wish that there should be two experiments in it on this Continent rather than one, and the wish is shared by thoughtful Americans not a few. But we have seen that in reality the two experiments are not being made. Universal suffrage and party government are the same, and their effects are the same in both Republics. Differences there are, such as that between the Presidential and the Cabinet system, of a subordinate kind, yet not unimportant, and such as might make it worth while to forego for a time at least the advantages of union, supposing that the dangers and economical evils of separation were not too great, and if the territorial division were not extravagantly at variance with the fiat of Nature. The experiments of political science must be tried with some reference to terrestrial convenience. Besides, those who scan the future without prejudice must see that the political fortunes of the Continent are embarked in the great Republic, and that Canada will best promote her own ultimate interests by contributing without unnecessary delay all that she has in the way of political character and force towards the saving of the main chance and the fulfilment of the common hope. The native American element in which the tradition of self-government resides is hard pressed by the foreign element untrained to self-government, and stands in need of the reinforcement which the entrance of Canada into the Union would bring it. Canadians feel all this without being distinctly conscious of it: they are taking less interest in British and more in American politics: in British politics they would take but little interest if their attention were not turned that way by the efforts of the Irish to drag everybody into their clan feud. A Presidential election now makes almost as much stir in Canada as it does in the United States. There is something to be said in favour of recognising destiny without delay. The reasoning of Lord Durham with regard to French Canada holds good in some measure with regard to Canada altogether in its relation to the Anglo-Saxon Continent. He thought it best to make the country at once that which after the lapse of no long time it must be. And this reminds us of another reason for not putting off the unification of the English-speaking race, since it is perfectly clear that the forces of Canada alone are not sufficient to assimilate the French element or even to prevent the indefinite consolidation and growth of a French nation. Either the conquest of Quebec was utterly fatuous or it is to be desired that the American Continent should belong to the English tongue and to Anglo-Saxon civilisation.

The Americans in general are not insensible, perhaps they are more sensible than they sometimes affect to be, of the advantages and the accession of greatness which would accrue to the Republic by the entrance of Canada into the Union. They expect that some day she will come to them, and are ready to welcome her when she does. But few of them much desire to hasten the event, and hardly any of them think of hastening it by coercion. The M'Kinley Act was not intended to coerce Canada into the Union. Its objects were to rivet Protection and catch the farmer's vote, though it was welcomed by the Tory Prime Minister of Canada and his following as a plausible ground for insulting demonstrations against the Americans, and this at the moment when Great Britain was carrying on difficult negotiations at Washington on Canada's behalf. Of conquest there is absolutely no thought. The Southern violence and the Western lawlessness which forced the Union into the War of 1812 are things of the past. The American people could not now be brought to invade the homes of an unoffending neighbour. They have no craving for more territory. They know that while a despot who annexes may govern through a viceroy with the strong hand, a republic which annexes must incorporate, and would only weaken itself by incorporating disaffection. The special reason for wishing to bring Canada at once into the Union, that she might help to counterbalance the Slave Power, has with the Slave Power departed. So far as the Americans are concerned, Canada is absolute mistress of her own destiny, while she is welcome to cast in her lot with the Republic. Such is the impression made upon the writer by his intercourse with Americans of all classes during twenty years.

Of Canadian opinion the one thing that can be said with certainty is that the great mass of the people, and especially those who dwell along the border of Ontario, in the Maritime Provinces, in Manitoba or other districts of the North-West, and those who are engaged or wish to be engaged in the mining, lumbering, or shipping trade, strongly desire freedom of commercial intercourse with their own Continent. Such appears to be the wish of the people and of the politicians in Quebec also, as well indeed it may be, since the American market is the only market which Quebec has. The tendency of the priesthood is isolation, as the safeguard of their dominion and of their tithe; but their position is in all respects somewhat altered by the exodus, and it is doubtful whether they would dare to oppose themselves directly to the material welfare of the masses. Nothing apparently can save the restrictive policy of the present Government and its confederate, the protected manufacturer, except the use of the same engines which have so long sustained a similar policy in the United States. On the question of political union apart from commercial union there are no means of gauging popular sentiment, the question never having been brought definitely before the people and expression not being free. But the English inquirer had better be cautious in receiving the confident reports of official persons, or listening to public professions of any kind. The very anxiety shown to gag opinion by incessant cries of disloyalty and treason shows that there is an opinion which needs to be gagged. People were taken by surprise when in 1849, under the pressure of commercial distress, a manifesto in favour of annexation appeared with the signatures of a number of the leading men of the country. In these democracies, where everybody from his cradle is thinking of votes, and to be in a minority is perdition, political courage, whether in action or speech, is not a common virtue. Politicians especially tremble at the very thought of a premature declaration of any kind. But the notion that a man who at a meeting of ordinary Canadians should avow his belief in an ultimate reunion of the two sections of his race would be "stoned" or even hissed, may be proved from experience to be a mistake. A bold man had avowed annexationist opinions in official company at Ottawa. One of the company, horrified at his profanities, told him that he should feel it his duty to denounce them if he were not restrained by social confidence. "Come down," was the reply, "into the street, collect the biggest crowd, you can, and I will soon relieve you of the restraint of social confidence." The other day an ex-Governor-General undertook to assure the world that the slightest suspicion of annexationism would be absolutely fatal to a candidate in an election. Almost on the very day on which his ex-Excellency's paper reached Canada an avowed annexationist was elected by a large majority for a county in Ontario. Annexation is not the platform of either party, and as a rule, nobody can get himself elected without a party nomination. But supposing a candidate had the party nomination and were locally strong the suspicion of annexationism would do him very little harm. Of this, indeed, we have already had practical proofs, besides the example just cited. Since the passing of the Jesuits' Estates Act and the revelation in connection with it of priestly influence and designs, the saying of Lord Durham's Report that the day might come when English Canadians to remain English would have to cease to be British, or something like it, has been heard on many sides.

There is a conflict of forces, and we must judge each for himself which are the primary forces and likely to prevail. Prevail the primary forces will in the end, however long their action may be suspended by a number of secondary forces arrayed against them. In the case of German and in that of Italian unity the number and strength of the secondary forces arrayed against the event were such, and the action of the great forces was so long suspended by them, that it seemed even to sagacious observers as if the event would never come. It came, irresistible and irreversible, and we see now that Bismarck and Cavour were the ministers of destiny.

In the present case there are, on one side, geography, commerce, identity of race, language, and institutions, which with the mingling of population and constant intercourse of every kind, acting in ever-increasing intensity, have brought about a general fusion, leaving no barriers standing but the political and fiscal lines. On the other side, there is British and Imperial sentiment, which, however, is confined to the British, excluding the French and Irish and other nationalities, and even among the British is livelier as a rule among the cultivated and those whose minds are steeped in history than among those who are working for their bread; while to set against it there is the idea, which can hardly fail to make way, of a great continent with an almost unlimited range of production forming the home of a united people, shutting out war and presenting the field as it would seem for a new and happier development of humanity. Again, there are bodies of men, official, political, and commercial, whose interests are bound up with the present state of things, whose feelings naturally go with those interests, who in many cases suffer little from the economical consequences of isolation, and who, gathered in the capital or in the great cities, exercise an influence out of proportion to their numbers on public opinion and its organs. Great public undertakings involving a large expenditure, produce fortunes to which titles are sometimes added, and which form strong supports of the existing system, though they are no indications of general prosperity, and the interests of their possessors is as far as possible from being identical with that of the farmer, who meantime is paying ruinous duties on his farm implements and on some of the necessaries of life. Repulsion is also created by the scandals of American politics, by the corruption which has reigned of late, by the turmoil of Presidential elections, and by such enormities as the Pension List, while political scandals and evils at home, being familiar, are less noted. Men of British blood, moreover, even when they are friendly to closer relations with the United States, are disgusted by the anti-British language of the American Press and of some of the American politicians. Above all there is the difficulty of getting any community, but especially a democracy in which there is no strong initiative, to quit the groove in which it has long been running. On the American side there is, to countervail the promptings of high policy and natural ambition, the partisan's fear of disturbing the adjustment of parties. There is the comparative indifference of the Southern States of the Union to an acquisition in the North. There is, moreover, a want of diplomatic power to negotiate a Union. The southern politicians were statesmen after their kind, secure in their seats and devoted to public life. They governed the country as a nation, though with ends of their own. Their successors, besides being by no means safe in their seats, are to a great extent delegates of local interests, each of which, like the members of a Polish diet, has and exercises a veto in the councils of the nation. Upon successive attempts to pursue a definite policy towards Canada the veto has been put by one local interest or another. If negotiations for a Union were set on foot, the party out of power would of course do its best to make them miscarry, and a patriotic Press would not fail to lend its aid. Every sort of susceptibility and jealousy on such occasions is wide awake. The great English statesmen, trained in the highest school of diplomacy, who negotiated the Union with Scotland found their task hard though they operated under far easier conditions. However, if the primary forces are working towards an event, sooner or later the crisis arrives; the man appears, and the bidding of Destiny is done.

SECTION V. – COMMERCIAL UNION[1]

"I am confident," said Mr. Bayard, the American Secretary of State, to Sir Charles Tupper, "that we both seek to attain a just and

1 For all that relates to the question of Commercial Union, and the whole subject of Canadian commerce and industry in connection with that movement, see the *"Handbook of Commercial Union:* a collection of papers read before the Commercial Union Club, Toronto, with speeches, letters, and other documents in favour of Unrestricted Reciprocity with the United States." Toronto: Hunter, Rose & Co. [294 pp. Crown 8vo, 25 cents = 1s. stg.] 1888.

permanent settlement – and there is but one way to procure it, and that is by a straightforward treatment on a liberal and statesman-like plan of the entire commercial relations of the two countries. I say commercial, because I do not propose to include, however indirectly or by any intendment, however partial and oblique, the political relations of Canada and the United States, nor to affect the legislative independence of either country." The object of the movement now on foot under the name of "Commercial Union" is to bring Canada within the commercial pale of her own continent, and thereby put an end to the commercial atrophy which her isolation entails. A reciprocal benefit would of course be afforded to the United States in an increase of commercial area and opportunities of opening up new sources of wealth. The name Commercial Union, which has been challenged as suggestive of political union, was adopted in contradistinction to it, and in exact accordance with the intention of Mr. Bayard. The measure would be necessarily accompanied by an assimilation of the excise and of the seaboard tariff, without which there would be smuggling of liquors across the line, and of goods through the ports of one country into the other. Whether there should be a pooling of the seaboard duties is a separate question. Community of Fisheries, the Coasting Trade, and Water-ways is included in Commercial Union.

The movement in Canada originated with a Farmers' Convention in Toronto, and was taken up by the Farmers' Institutes of the Province. On the farmer's mind had dawned the fact that he was the sheep, and the protected manufacturer was the shearer. The special organ of the movement has been the Commercial Union Club, an association independent of political party. The policy of Reciprocity, however, has been embraced by the Liberal Party now in Oppostition: it forms the main plank in the platform of that party; and will, in all probability, be the issue at the coming elections. On the American side a resolution in Congress authorising the President to treat for Commercial Union with the Canadian Government has been brought forward by Mr. Hitt, of Illinois, and has been passed unanimously by the House of Representatives, while in the Senate it has failed of unanimous consent only by one vote. Another resolution pointing the same way was brought forward by Mr. Butterworth, the member for Cincinnati, one of the foremost men in the Republican party, and like Mr. Hitt thoroughly friendly both to

Canada and to Great Britain. Life has been given to the movement by the public spirit and energy of Mr. Erastus Wiman, a Canadian who has won his way to a high place in American commerce without ceasing to be a Canadian, and has done more than any other man to keep up attachment both to Canada and England and to sustain the honour of the British flag at New York, so that he is well placed for dealing with any question in the interest of all three countries. A word of justice is due to him, since he has not been fairly treated by certain journals in England whose confidence is abused by their correspondents in Canada on this and on other Canadian questions.

That the market of her own continent is the natural market of Canada, both as a seller and a buyer, even so strong an Imperialist as Sir Charles Dilke admits, and no one but a protected manufacturer or a fanatical Tory would attempt to deny. The Conservative leader, Sir John Macdonald, has always professed to be doing his utmost to bring about reciprocity. His motto has been Reciprocity of Trade or Reciprocity of Tariffs, meaning that if he had recourse to reciprocity of tariffs it was only because he could not get reciprocity of trade, and in order to enforce it. His Protectionist Tariff Act contained a standing offer of reciprocity in natural products. This, as has been said before, was illusory, inasmuch as the Americans evidently could not, in common justice to their own interests, allow their manufactures to be excluded while they admitted the natural products of Canada; but it was at all events the homage paid by political strategy to commercial wisdom. If the offer has now been cancelled, this, it may safely be said, is not because conviction has changed on the commercial question, but because the irritation bred by the M'Kinley Act presents an opportunity for an appeal to that feeling against American connection which is the life of the existing system. M. Chapleau, one of Sir John Macdonald's French colleagues, still declares for Reciprocity in the teeth of the declaration of Mr. Colby, another member of the Government, against it, as well as of the general action of the Administration, showing thereby apparently his sense of the fact that Reciprocity is a prime necessity in the French Province. Let any one scan the economical map of the North American continent with its adjacent waters, mark its northern zone abounding in minerals, in bituminous coal, in lumber, in fish, as well as in special farm products, brought in the north to hardier perfection, all of which the southern people have need: then let him look to its southern regions, the natural products of which as well as the manufactures produced in its wealthy centres of industry are needed by the people of the northern zone: he will see that the continent is an economic whole, and that to run a Customs line athwart it and try to sever its members from each other is to wage a desperate war against nature. Each several Province of the Dominion is by nature wedded to a commercial partner on the south, though a perverse policy struggles to divorce them. The Maritime Provinces want to send their lumber, their bituminous coal, and their fish to the markets of New England; Ontario and Quebec want to send their barley, eggs, and other farm products, their horses, their cattle and their lumber to New York and other neighbouring States; Manitoba and the North-West want to send their superior wheat, their barley, their wool, and the fish of their great lakes to St. Paul and Minneapolis; British Columbia wants to send her bituminous coal, her salmon, and the timber of which she is the mighty mother, to California and Oregon. All of them want to get American manufactures as well as the products of a more southern climate in return. It must be long before Canada can produce a first-rate printing press. Even when an article is made in the Dominion, the freight from one of the scattered Provinces to another may be ruinous. British Columbia was paying for nails a price for transit exceeding their first cost at Montreal.[1] Canada is not one market but four, widely separated from each other, and each of them sparse in itself.

It is in regard to minerals, perhaps, that the case of Canada is the hardest. She has all the economic minerals except tin. She has vast stores of magnetic and hematatic iron, such as would make the best of iron and steel. In some districts she is rich in copper and nickel. She has valuable veins of silver and gold-bearing quartz, the former in the Lake Superior district, the latter in Nova Scotia and British Columbia. She has abundance of coal, both in British Columbia and in Nova Scotia. Chemical minerals she has also in abundance, and stores of mineral manure. Yet the total value of her mineral exports for 1888, was under $5,000,000, of which nearly a half was for bituminous coal, while she imported hard coal to nearly the same value. What she wants is a free market, free inflow of American

1 See *Handbook of Commercial Union*, p. 56.

capital, free purchase of mining machinery.[1] On the American shore of Lake Superior mining is rife, and its yield is immense; on the Canadian shore, which is not less rich in minerals, it sleeps. Continual appeals are made to the Government by Protectionist patriotism to "open up" the mines, as though a Government could open up production of any kind otherwise than by giving it fair play. With free trade Port Arthur, in the centre of an immensely rich mining district, instead of being, as it now is, a mere village, might be a mining city. Let the mines be opened and there would be a mining population such as would give the Canadian farmer a home market for which he would not have to pay. For the home market which Protectionism gives him he pays both in the price and quality of the goods. An interest or a country trying to make itself prosperous by such means is, as has been truly said, like a man trying to lift himself up by his boot-straps.

The shipping interest of Canada again pines for the freedom of the coasting trade. Canadian vessels are not allowed to trade between American ports, and have often to return without a cargo. The consequence is that the Canadian marine is fast disappearing from the Lakes. Of the vast trade in ore and grain on the Upper Lakes less than 10 per cent is now carried in Canadian bottoms. The Canadian tonnage passing through the Sault Ste. Marie Canal has fallen to 4 per cent, the rest being American. The new Canadian-built tonnage in the past five years is not over 5 per cent of that launched from Lake shipyards. There is little use in constructing at immense expense a special lock for Canada alongside of the American lock at the "Soo," while Canadian shipping is being made the victim of a policy of extermination. The Dominion *Statistical Abstract,* for 1889, admits a decrease of the amount even of the seagoing trade of the country carried in Canadian bottoms compared with that carried in foreign bottoms. There has also, according to the same authority, been a steady decline in the number and tonnage of the vessels built in the Dominion during the last ten or twelve years, that is since the inauguration of the Protectionist policy of Sir John Macdonald. Protectionists who profess that it is an object of their system by multiplying industries to diversify national character, should

1 See *Handbook of Commercial Union,* pp. 73 *et seq.*

consider whether a variety of it will not perish with the mariner.

The Americans, on their side, want to buy things which Canada has to sell; they want an extended market for the products of a more southern climate, such as fruits; they want an extended market for their manufactures. They can manufacture as a rule better and more cheaply, because they do it on a larger scale and can specialise; whereas the manufacturer with a small market is obliged to produce several kinds of goods to keep his hands employed. All this is most strongly felt at Detroit, Buffalo, and other commercial cities along the frontier which find themselves cribbed and confined by the Customs line. It has been objected by some American Protectionists that America would be giving a market of 65,000,000 in exchange for one of 5,000,000, as though markets when thrown together were exchanged and not enjoyed in common. According to this reasoning the 60,000,000 of Americans outside the State of New York would be better off without the 6,000,000 of that State. But American capital also wants free access to the natural resources of Canada, her mineral resources especially, which await only the touch of capital, together with the opening of the market, in order to turn them into wealth for the benefit of all the people of the continent. Mr. Blaine, the political leader of the Protectionist party in the United States, has shown himself alive to the need of new markets by declaring in favour of Reciprocity, and he will not be long in finding that the only American community reciprocal trade with which would be of much value is the Dominion of Canada. The half-civilised masses of South America want little except gaudy cottons, with which they are supplied to their satisfaction by England.

It is alleged by Protectionists that there cannot be a profitable trade between Canada and the United States, because the products of the two countries are the same. The products of the two countries, even their natural products, leaving out of sight special manufactures, are not the same. In the United States are included regions and productions almost tropical. Canada, on the other hand, has bituminous coal, for which there are markets in the United States, and plenty of nickel, of which the United States have but little. Canada has lumber to export, and the United States want all they can get. Both countries produce barley, but the Canadian barley is the best for making beer, and its exclusion by the M'Kinley Act brought out a heavy vote at Buffalo against the party of Mr. M'Kinley. This is the first answer. The second and the most decisive is that, in spite of the tariff, Canada has actually been trading with the United States more than with England or any other country in the world, and nearly as much as with all the other countries in the world put together. In 1889 her exports to Great Britain were $38,105,126; her imports from Great Britain were $42,249,555. Her exports to the United States were $48,522,404; her imports from the United States were $56,368,990. Of the total trade of Canada, in the same year, 41.35 per cent was with Great Britain; 49.65 was with the United States; while only 9 per cent was with the rest of the world. To take even the case of farm products, of 18,799 horses which Canada sold in one year, the United States bought 18,225. Of 443,000 sheep, they bought 363,000. Of 116,000 head of cattle, they bought 45,000. Of $107,000 worth of poultry, they bought $99,000 worth. Of $1,825,000 worth of eggs, they bought all. Of $593,000 worth of hides, they bought $413,000 worth. Of 1,416,000 pounds of wool, they bought 1,300,000 pounds. Of $9,456,000 worth barley, they bought all. Of $743,000 worth of hay, they bought $670,000 worth. Of $439,000 worth of potatoes, they bought $338,000 worth. Of $83,000 worth of vegetables, they bought $75,000 worth. Of $254,000 worth of miscellaneous agricultural products, they bought $249,000 worth. Manitoba and the North-West believe that, were the tariff wall out of the way, the United States would be their best customer for a great deal of high-class wheat. In spite of the fisheries disputes and taxes, out of $7,000,000 worth of fish, the United States take annually about $3,000,000 worth.[1]

The case is specially strong with regard to some of the smaller Provinces. Prince Edward Island exported in 1889 only $800 worth of agricultural products to Great Britain, while she exported to the United States $466,000 worth. The total export of her own produce to all countries in that year amounted to $974,000, of which $686,000 worth went to the United States. The exports of British Columbia for 1889 amounted to $4,284,000, of which $2,782,000 in value went to the United States, and only $870,000 went to Great Britain. To these Provinces the tariff war is ruinous, and they have some reason for demanding compensation in subsidies from the Dominion.

1 See speech in the Dominion House of Commons of Sir Richard Cartwright, ex-Minister of Finance, March 14, 1888.

High as the tariff wall between Canada and the United States is, trade, we see, has climbed over it. Wherever an opening is made in the wall, trade at once rushes through. Before the removal of the duty on eggs, the trade in them was nominal: it rose, when the duty was removed, to over $2,000,000 in 1889. The M'Kinley tariff sends it down again.

Smuggling, as might be expected, is rife along the whole Line, with the usual consequences to popular morality and honest trade. When a border township in which the potato crop is short cannot go to the adjoining township for potatoes, a severe appeal is made to the hamlet's respect for law.

To Manitoba and the North-West, which neither have manufactures, nor, as farm products are their staple, are likely to have them, the tariff is a curse, without even a shadow of compensation. It is difficult to believe that in that region it will be possible for ever to maintain the Custom line, the frontier being merely an imaginary boundary drawn across the prairie for 800 miles, with identically the same population on each side of it, so that a village, even a house, may be placed astride the line, and the housewife with a new kettle may be liable to duty in passing from one room to the other; while the Ottawa Government, for the benefit of which the duties are imposed, is remote and, with too good reason, unbeloved. But the case of Manitoba is hardly worse than that of Nova Scotia and New Brunswick, which get absolutely nothing to make up for their exclusion from their natural market in New England, the attempt to force Ontario, by violent legislative pressure, to buy her coal of Nova Scotia instead of buying it of Pennsylvania having utterly failed.

The assertion that the British market is better for Canada than the American market has already been met by the figures. If for a time the English market was better than the American the reason was that the British market was open, whereas the American market was half closed by the tariff. Remove the Customs line between Canada and the United States and there can be no doubt about the value of the American compared with that of the British market. No people are individually so rich as the Americans, or so ready to pay freely for everything they want or fancy. The American market is always increasing with the rapid growth of population. It is also secure, whereas that of England, or any transmarine country, would become very insecure if England were at war with a maritime power.

Canada would then be without any free market at all. But it is needless to discuss this question, because when the American market was opened to Canada that of England would not be closed. Canada would enjoy them both.

The near market must as a rule be the best, not only on account of the difference in freights, but in many cases on account of the perishableness of goods. It must be best for fruits, fish, vegetables, and even for poultry and eggs. It is the best for horses, the breeding of which is a great Canadian industry, and might be a greater. The American comes to Canada and buys the horses on the spot, whereas if the horses are sent to England, unless they at once take the fancy of the market, they may eat up a great part of their value before they are sold. Not till the American market is opened can its full value be understood. Commercial Union between Scotland and England gave a value to black cattle and kelp which could hardly have been foreseen. Production would adapt itself to the new demands, and new roads to wealth would be found. Besides, Canada wants to buy as well as to sell, and the near market, even irrespectively of freights, is preferable as the most convenient and the most likely to produce exactly the kind of goods required. This will be acknowledged by the buyers of farm machines and implements in the North-West.

It has been proposed that rather than succumb to the force of nature, and allow Canada to secure her destined measure of prosperity by trading with her own continent, England should put back the shadow on the dial of economical history, institute an Imperial Zollverein, and restore to the Colonies their former protection against the foreigner in her market It is hardly necessary to discuss a policy in which Great Britain would have to take the initiative, and which no British statesman has shown the slightest disposition to embrace. The trade, both of imports and exports, of England with the Colonies was, in 1889, £187,000,000; her total trade in the same year with foreign countries was £554,000,000. Is it likely that she will sacrifice a trade of £554,000,000 sterling to a trade of £187,000,000 sterling? The framers of an Imperial Zollverein, moreover, would have some lively work in reconciling the tendencies of strong Protectionist Colonies, such as Victoria and Canada, with the free trade tendencies of Great Britain and New South Wales. The Conservative Prime Minister of England, if he has been correctly reported, holds that the adoption of Protection, on which the Imperialists of Canada insist as a condition of any arrangement, would in England kindle a civil war.

The Canadian Government shows its sense of the situation and of the real effect of its policy by trying to open up new markets in distant countries, in the West Indies, in Brazil, in the Argentine Republic, in France, in Spain, in Australia – in the Moon. It thus hopes to stay the craving of Canadian commerce and industry for their natural market. It has been compared to the father who told his boy that he could not be taken to the circus, but that if he was good he should be taken to see his grandmother's tomb. If the Canadian manufacturer, as the Protectionists aver, is unable to compete in his own market with the American, how can he compete with him in the markets of other countries?

It may safely be said that all the natural interests in Canada, the farming interest – which is much the greatest of all – the lumber interest, the mining interest, and the shipping interest, would vote for a measure which would admit them freely to the American market. On the other side are only the protected manufacturers. But the protected manufacturers are strongly organised, whereas the other interests, notably the farmers', are comparatively unorganised; so that, as was often said in the case of the United States, the fight between Protection and Free Trade is a fight between an army and a mob. The Protectionists have a firm hold upon the present Government, the existence of which is completely bound up with their system, and which looks to them largely for its election fund. It has, however, been already said that they are the hot-house industries which are alarmed. Of the Canadian manufacturers who feel that their business is natural and has a sound basis not a few avow themselves ready for an open market. They would have in some cases to put their production on a new footing, making fewer articles and on a larger scale, but, this being done, they do not fear the competition. They would still have the advantage of somewhat cheaper labour. Sir George Stephen, than whom there can be no higher authority, in a circular addressed in 1875 to the heads of the woollen trade, with which he was then connected, said that if Canada could have free interchange with the United States of all products, whether natural or manufactured, she "would become the Lancashire of the continent and increase in wealth and population to a degree that could hardly be imagined." That some of the weaker houses might suffer is acknowledged, and is to be lamented. All possible consideration is due to those whom Parliament has encouraged to invest. But the whole community cannot be allowed to suffer, nor can commerce and industry be kept for ever on an unsound basis, for the sake of a few. Besides, it will be mercy to shut the door of unsound investment. But this is the bane of the Protectionist policy: when its unwisdom appears, you can hardly draw back from it without doing injury to artificial industries which it has created, and those engaged in them. Not that the artisans will suffer.[1] For them the expansion of natural industries would furnish fresh employment, if not in Canada in the United States, to which they pass with little hesitation when the labour market invites.

Canadians are told, to scare them from Commercial Union, that if the tariff wall were out of the way they would become "hewers of wood and drawers of water for the Yankees." Hewers of wood for the Yankees they are already to their own great profit. It is not obvious why the producer of raw materials should be deemed so much beneath the factory hand; perhaps looking to the effect of manufactures on national character in England we might think that a nation would be wise in contenting itself with so much of factory life as nature had allotted it. Whatever yields most wealth will raise highest the condition of the people, their standard of living, and their general civilisation. Another bugbear is the fear that Canadian cities will be swallowed up by New York, though the cities of the State of New York itself, Buffalo, Rochester, Syracuse, Oswego, and even Albany, which is within four hours' run of New York, are growing all the time.[2] These vague alarms remind us of those raised on commercial grounds by the opponents of the union between England and Scotland. The English were told that their wealth would be devoured by the hungry Scots, the Scotch were told that they would become commercial slaves to the wealthy English, and "with their grain spoiling on their hands, stand cursing the day of their birth, dreading the expense of their burial." The able and eloquent Lord Belhaven formally paused in the middle of his speech that he might shed a tear over the approaching ruin of his country which he foresaw in a vision of woe. Lord Marchmont in reply said

1 See *Handbook of Commercial Union,* pp. 122 *et seq.* Mr. Jury.
2 See *Handbook of Commercial Union,* pp. 86 *et seq.* Mr. Janes.

that he thought a short answer would suffice. "Behold, he dreamed; but, lo, when he awoke, behold, it was a dream." The reality was what the Duke of Argyll in his work on Scotland calls "The Burst of Industry." It was the works and warehouses of Glasgow, the shipbuilding yards of the Clyde, and the farms of the Lothians.

To make up for the dearth of economical arguments against Reciprocity its opponents appeal to Loyalty and the Old Flag. "Discriminate against the Mother Country! Never!" So with uplifted hands and eyes cry Protectionists who are running to Ottawa to get higher duties laid on British goods, and would not be sorry to shut the gate, if they could, against British importation altogether. Canada does already discriminate against Great Britain, if not on any specific article, on the aggregate trade. It has been shown that she collects about four per cent more in the aggregate on British than on American goods, and admits more American than British products free.[1] When the privileges enjoyed by the Colonies in the British market were withdrawn and the commercial unity of the Empire was broken up, notice was in effect given to each member of the Empire to do the best that it could for itself under its own circumstances. The circumstances of Canada are those of a country commercially bound up with another country much larger than itself and with a high tariff. It is surely too much to expect that all Canada shall remain in a state of commercial atrophy for the sake of a few exporting houses in Great Britain. The British people themselves would never be brought to make such a sacrifice. The discrimination would not, like the duties imposed by Canadian Protectionists on British goods, be directed against British commerce; it would be merely, like the equalisation of excise, a necessity incidental to an arrangement for the benefit of Canada with the United States; so that no breach of good feeling would be involved. Not a penny would be taken from the British Crown. Nor would England be really a loser; she would gain by the enhanced value of her Canadian investments more than she would lose by the reduction of her exports.

It is further alleged that Commercial Union would be Annexation in disguise. When railways were introduced it was thought that a gauge uniform with the American would be annexation in disguise

1 See *Handbook of Commercial Union*, pp. 175 *et seq.* Mr. Dryden.

and a difference of gauge was insisted on accordingly. Is there a natural tendency on the part of Canada to political union? If there is, increased intercourse of any kind, whatever locomotive or commercial, will no doubt help it; but nothing can help it more than the fusion of population by the exodus which the separatist policy keeps up. The enemies of Reciprocity forget that they are themselves the most active of annexationists, if not in regard to the Canadian territory, in regard to the Canadian people. Canada would be as much as ever mistress of her own political destinies, nor could any step towards political union be taken without the free vote of her citizens. If her nationality is sound what does she require more? That would be a weak nationality indeed which should depend on a Customs line. The German Zollverein, which is pointed out as a warning example, would never have unified Germany or tended much to her unification had not she already been a nation, though in a state of political disruption. Zollvereins are now, it seems, being proposed between other communities of Central Europe without any idea of altering political relations. If the reciprocity in natural products enjoyed under the Elgin treaty did not impair Canada's independence, why should reciprocity in manufactures destroy it? Not only did the Elgin treaty not impair independence but it put an end to the movement in favour of annexation, which commercial distress had generated, and which had led to the Annexationist manifesto of 1849. In entering into any contract, the parties, whether nations or men, must give up their independence to the extent for which they covenant: in no other sense would a commercial treaty, however extensive, if freely made on both sides, be on either side a surrender of independence. Dependent on the Americans for her winter ports Canada already is, and large branches of her railway system are on their soil and in their power. Americans who desire immediate Annexation are always against Commercial Union.

Commercial Union would include mutual participation in the fisheries, in the coasting trade, and in the use of the canals and water-ways. In this it is distinguished from Unrestricted Reciprocity, which would equally involve the complete removal of the Customs line. In regard to the fisheries it would give effect to the policy of British statesmen who desired, as Shelburne and Pitt seem to have desired, that England and her American colonies should not become foreign nations to each other, but divide amicably between them the family heritage. In no other way is the dispute about the fisheries likely to be ended. Even supposing a treaty satisfactory to diplomacy to be made, fishermen are not diplomatists; they are naturally tenacious of the trade by which they live; they will always be prone to deny their rivals the facilities and hospitalities incident to treaty rights, and thus quarrels will be apt to arise.

The main objection to Commercial Union is the difficulty of framing, in concert with the Americans, a uniform seaboard tariff. This difficulty, however, as matters stood before the passing of the M'Kinley Act, was by no means insuperable, the principle of the American and Canadian tariffs being the same, and the difference of rates not very great. The smaller interest in case of disagreement might, as in ordinary bargains, without loss of honour, yield a point. An arrangement would probably have been brought about easily enough by a conference of commercial men, free from the malign influences of party, and unaffected by the appeals to national pride and jealousy which, if the negotiation were in the hands of a party government, the opposite party, in its anxiety to discredit its rivals would be sure to make. Nor need there be any fears of subsequent disturbance of the agreement, from any source, at least, but a quarrel between Great Britain and the United States, such as that by which the Reciprocity Treaty was overturned. Commerce after a little experience would be too sensible of the benefit to renounce it or allow the politicians, whom, by a resolute effort, she can even in the United States control, to wrest it from her. The line of Custom houses built across a continent which nature has forbidden to be divided, once pulled down, will never be built up again. Fresh obstacles and of a serious kind might have been created by the M'Kinley Act. Commercial Unionists did not feel themselves called upon to raise the general questions between Protection and Free Trade, so far as the seaboard tariff was concerned. They confined their aim to the removal of the Customs line across their own continent, which on any rational hypothesis is an evil, unless it would be a good thing to have a Customs line between Pennsylvania and New York, or between York and Lancashire. But there must be limits to the compromise of principle, even for the sake of an immediate advantage so great as Commercial Union will bring. Canada cannot commit treason against civilisation. However, the manifest faults of the measure, combined with the enormous waste of public money incurred in baling out surplus revenue to avert a reform of the tariff, have proved too much for the superstition or the sufferance of the American people. Symptoms of a change of opinion had even before appeared. At the last Presidential election, Mr. Cleveland was defeated more by party than by protection, and more by the manufacturers' money than either, and there was a marked increase of the mechanics' vote in favour of a reduction of the tariff, showing that the fallacious belief in protection as a mode of raising wages was losing its hold. Moreover, protection was being nullified by the extension of its own area, which exposed the protectionist to increased competition, national it might be, but not more welcome to him, in spite of his patriotic professions, than that of the foreigner. New England is now praying for free admission of raw materials. The Republican party in the United States is the war party kept on foot for the sake of maintaining the war tariff in the interest of the protected manufacturers. It has made a desperate effort to retain power and to rivet its policy on the nation by means which have estranged from it the best of its supporters; but in the late elections it has received a signal, and probably decisive, overthrow. What all the preachings of economic science were powerless to effect has been brought about at last by the reduction of the public debt and of the necessity for duties as revenue. A new commercial era has apparently dawned for the United States, and the lead of the United States will be followed in time by the rest of the world.

By the abandonment of the Customs duties on American goods, the Canadian government would lose revenue perhaps to the amount of $7,000,000. This loss might be made up partly by new taxes of such a character as not to press on industry or shackle trade – to begin with, an increase of the excise – partly by economy in subsidies to Provinces, public works undertaken for political purposes, and needless expenditure on legislation and government. To say that such economy is impracticable, would be to admit that a confederation, united by no natural bond of geography, race, language, or commercial interest, can be held together only by corruption.

While these pages are going through the press, Canada is the scene of a general election. Seeing that the tide in favour of free trade with the continent was rising, and, before the constitutional time for the next election came round, might rise to an overwhelming height, the Protectionist Government of Sir John Macdonald has sprung a dissolution on the country, the Governor-General passively lending the prerogative for that purpose. There is not a shadow of constitutional ground for the step, and the reason alleged – that the Government contemplates making overtures on the trade question to the Americans, and cannot do this without a fresh Parliament at its back – was evidently hollow. The Government at first sought to head off the current of opinion and dish the Opposition by declaring for Restricted against Unrestricted Reciprocity. But this strategy has failed of effect, and the appeal on the part of the Government is now to "The Old Flag," with which are coupled "The Old Leader," and "The Old Policy," against American connection. On the issue thus raised the deliverance of the country will be made. The verdict will be greatly confused, not only by local questions, such as that of a Submarine Tunnel for Prince Edward Island, which seems uppermost in the Islander's mind, but by the Equal Right movement against Jesuit and priestly aggression, which is still strong, and cuts across the lines of political and commercial party. The Protected Manufacturers will do their best, and the Government will ply all the engines which it has long had at its command. To ply those engines in Nova Scotia the Canadian High Commissioner has been brought over from England. Nor have party names and shibboleths lost their extraordinary power. Tories, though in favour of Reciprocity, will still vote Tory. To stimulate the enthusiasm of loyalty "Annexation plots" are being discovered, and the discoveries are paraded with all the resources of emotional eloquence and sensation type. What will come out of this chaos is, at the time of our writing, uncertain. But already tidings reach us from the rural districts which seem to show that the farmer, however much he may care for the Old Flag, cares also for his bread. Should the Government be beaten or even hard pressed in a pitched battle of its own seeking on the question of relation with the United States, the result will be full of meaning.